T0301684

Productivity in Asia

Productivity in Asia

Economic Growth and Competitiveness

Edited by

Dale Jorgenson

Samuel W. Morris University Professor, Harvard University, USA

Masahiro Kuroda

President, Economic and Social Research Institute, Cabinet Office of the Japanese Government, Japan

Kazuyuki Motohashi

Professor, University of Tokyo and Faculty Fellow, Research Institute of Economy, Trade and Industry, Japan

Edward Elgar
Cheltenham, UK • Northampton, MA, USA

Published by
Edward Elgar Publishing Limited
Glensanda House
Montpellier Parade
Cheltenham
Glos GL50 1UA
UK

Edward Elgar Publishing, Inc.
William Pratt House
9 Dewey Court
Northampton
Massachusetts 01060
USA

A catalogue record for this book
is available from the British Library

Library of Congress Cataloguing in Publication Data

Productivity in Asia : economic growth and competitiveness / edited by Dale Jorgenson, Masahiro Kuroda, Kazuyuki Motohashi.
     p. cm.
   Includes bibliographical references and index.
   1. Industrial productivity—Asia. 2. Asia—Economic conditions. 3. Competition—Asia. 4. Industrial productivity—United States. I. Jorgenson, Dale Weldeau, 1933– II. Kuroda, Masahiro, 1941– III. Motohashi, Kazuyuki.

   HC415.I52P747   2007
   338.6095—dc22
                                                                    2007017138

ISBN 978 1 84720 399 1

Printed and bound in Great Britain by MPG Books Ltd, Bodmin, Cornwall

Contents

Contributors

Bongchan Ha, Associate Research Fellow, Korea Institute for Industrial Economics and Trade, Korea.

Mun S. Ho, Fellow, John F. Kennedy School of Government, Program on Technology and Economic Policy, Harvard University/Visiting Scholar, Resources for the Future, USA.

Dale Jorgenson, Samuel W. Morris University Professor, Harvard University, USA.

Masahiro Kuroda, President, Economic and Social Research Institute, Cabinet Office of the Japanese Government, Japan.

Chi-Yuan Liang, Research Fellow, Institute of Economics, Academia Sinica, Taiwan.

Kazuyuki Motohashi, Professor, University of Tokyo/Faculty Fellow, Research Institute of Economy, Trade and Industry (RIETI), Japan.

Hak K. Pyo, Professor, Division of Economics, Seoul National University, Korea.

Ruoen Ren, Professor in Economics and Statistics, Beihang University/ Director, Center for Competitiveness and Risk Analysis/Senior Consultant, SEEC Beijing, PRC.

Keun-Hee Rhee, Senior Researcher, Korea Productivity Center, Korea.

Kazushige Shimpo, Professor, Faculty of Business and Commerce, Keio University/Former Faculty Fellow, Research Institute of Economy, Trade and Industry (RIETI), Japan.

Kevin J. Stiroh, Vice President and Head of Banking Studies Function, Federal Reserve Bank of New York, USA.

Lin lin Sun, PhD Candidate, Economics and Statistics, Beihang University.

Marcel P. Timmer, Assistant Professor, Groningen Growth and Development Centre, University of Groningen, the Netherlands.

Gerard Ypma, Database Manager and Junior Researcher, Groningen Growth and Development Centre, University of Groningen, the Netherlands.

Figures

Tables

Introduction to RIETI

The Research Institute of Economy, Trade and Industry (RIETI), an incorporated administrative agency, was established on 1 April, 2001 to conduct wide-ranging policy research and formulate policy recommendations. RIETI capitalizes on its location in Tokyo's Kasumigaseki district, the political and economic nerve center of Japan, to take full advantage of the synergy between policy-makers, researchers, industry leaders and other stakeholders. RIETI promotes policy formulation backed by theoretical and analytical research from a global perspective, not restricted to traditional approaches, with the ultimate goal of building a mature and dynamic Japanese society. To this end, RIETI has established research domains that respond to Japan's economic and industrial policy needs, within which individual research projects interact organically. To disseminate research results and promote policy recommendations effectively, RIETI makes aggressive use of its website, printed publications and a variety of other tools. RIETI pledges to continue to influence policy debate and policy-making through continually active delivery of policy recommendations. For more information, please visit http://www.rieti.go.jp/en/index.html.

1. Introduction

**Dale Jorgenson, Masahiro Kuroda and
Kazuyuki Motohashi**

The outstanding economic performance of East Asian countries has been investigated by numerous studies. Common factors behind high economic growth rates include stable macroeconomic conditions and active investment in human capital (World Bank, 1993). There are some studies touching upon the question of whether a high economic growth rate comes from factor inputs or total factor productivity growth. In general, growth accounting results at a macroeconomic level show that the Asian economic miracle has been achieved by factor accumulation rather than by productivity growth (Young, 1995; Kim and Lau, 1994; Bosworth and Collins, 1999). The factor accumulation theory is consistent with the human capital explanation of the economic growth of Asian countries, if labor quality upgrading is correctly measured.

However, all of these studies are conducted at a macro level, or fairly aggregated level, and the role of structural factors is ignored in the process of economic development. In the process of economic development, significant changes in industrial structure from agriculture to manufacturing can be found in Japan, Korea, China and other countries. Comparable industry-level data is needed to analyze such trends. In addition, the importance of export in economic development is sometimes stressed in literature (Motohashi, 2003). In this respect, industry-level productivity analysis is useful to assess the impact of exporting sectors on the aggregated economic growth of East Asian countries.

RIETI (Research Institute of Economy, Trade and Industry) has launched a research project for international comparison of productivity among Asian Countries at industry level to undertake a broad examination of the sources of economic growth and competitiveness through large-scale, internationally comparable databases. This project is called ICPA (International Comparison of Productivity among Asian Countries), consisting of a team of researchers from China, Korea, Japan, Taiwan and the United States. This book contains the results of this project, that is, the industry-level productivity comparison of these five countries.

1

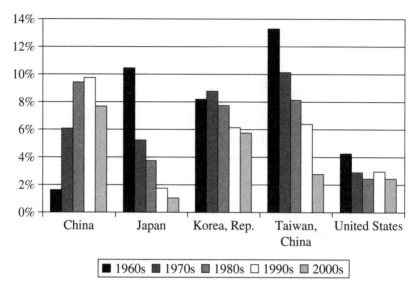

Figure 1.1   GDP growth rate by decade

The major objective of this project is to construct comparable datasets
of productivity analysis, such as input–output tables, as well as labor and
capital input data. This dataset is sometimes called 'KLEM' data, that is,
industry-level data on capital (K), labor (L), energy (E) and material (M),
as well as gross output, to come up with TFP (Total Factor Productivity)
growth. An international productivity comparison based on this KLEM
approach can be found in a previous Japan–US comparison (Jorgenson
and Kuroda, 1995), and recently in an EU-wide research project called
EU-KLEMS, initiated by an international consortium headed by the
University of Groningen. However, the ICPA project is the first attempt to
construct a comparable productivity dataset involving national statistical
offices as well as productivity experts among Asian countries.

The period of coverage of this study is from 1980 to 2000. Due to data
constraints, particularly in China, it is impossible to construct high quality
comparable industry accounts before 1980. Therefore, the period of observation is relatively short. On the other hand, this study covers the data after
the Asian crisis, which is not covered by most other productivity studies in
Asian countries. As is shown in Figure 1.1, we can see a recent divergence of
economic performance in the five countries. In Japan, a sharp slowdown of
economic growth rate is found after the 1990s, while the growth rate in each
decade is quite stable in the United States. Slowdown of growth rate can be
seen in both Korea and Taiwan, but it is faster for Taiwan. Compared to

these countries, the economic growth rate becomes faster after the 1970s in China. Finding whether these trends come from factor inputs or TFP sheds a new light on the different economic performances of these countries.

The methodology is based on the growth accounting framework, with internationally comparable measurements of the service flow of labor, capital and other intermediate inputs, gross output, and productivity economy-wide and at industry levels. This framework is consistently related to the national accounts statistics and the input–output tables of each country. The analytical framework on international comparison of TFP growth and level is provided in Kuroda et al. (1996). Empirical works on this framework include Kuroda and Nomura (1999), Jorgenson et al. (2002) and Keio University (1996).

It is important to come up with a common industrial classification as well as classifications of types of capital and labor input. Proper aggregation of labor and capital inputs based on detailed data by type allows us to make a distinction between quantity and quality improvement for each factor input. In the case of capital inputs, the divisia index of capital service (K^{PK}) is derived as follows:

$$\ln\left(\frac{K_t^{PK}}{K_{t-1}^{PK}}\right) = \sum_i \bar{v}_{i,t} \ln\left(\frac{K_{i,t}}{K_{i,t-1}}\right)$$

where $\bar{v}_{i,t} = \frac{1}{2}(v_{i,t-1} + v_{i,t})$ and $v_{i,t} = \dfrac{P_{k,i,t}K_{i,t}}{\sum\limits_i P_{k,i,t}K_{i,t}}$

This capital service index is a weighted average of capital stock (K_i) for each type 'i' by the share of rental services from this type of capital stock ($P_{k,i,t}K_{i,t}/\Sigma P_{k,i}K_i$). Capital service price ($P_{k,i}$) is based on the rental service price with asset price data, rate of depreciation, rate of return on asset and proper tax treatment in rental service equation. The growth rate of the rental service index can be decomposed into the following two parts: quantity growth and quality growth.

$$\ln\left(\frac{K_t^{PK}}{K_{t-1}^{PK}}\right) = \underbrace{\ln\left(\frac{\sum K_{i,t}}{\sum K_{i,t-1}}\right)}_{\text{quantity growth}} + \underbrace{\left(\sum_i \bar{v}_{i,t}\ln\left(\frac{K_{i,t}}{K_{i,t-1}}\right) - \ln\left(\frac{\sum K_{i,t}}{\sum K_{i,t-1}}\right)\right)}_{\text{quality growth}}$$

Labor input and intermediate input (energy, material and service) can be estimated in the same framework. Labor input is estimated as a weighted

average of hours worked by hourly wage by type of labor, and the divisia
index of energy and material inputs can be derived from input–output
tables. Finally, growth accounting decomposition of output (Y) can be conducted as follows:

$$\ln\left(\frac{Y_t}{Y_{t-1}}\right) = s_k\ln\left(\frac{K_t^{PK}}{K_{t-1}^{PK}}\right) + s_l\ln\left(\frac{L_t}{L_{t-1}}\right) + s_e\ln\left(\frac{E_t}{E_{t-1}}\right)$$

$$+ s_m\ln\left(\frac{M_t}{M_{t-1}}\right) + \ln\left(\frac{TFP_t}{TFP_{t-1}}\right)$$

where S^* is an average share of each factor input '*' in a period '$t-1$' and 't'.

In the ICPA project, the productivity *level* is compared as well as the productivity *growth* of each industry, because this framework can be applied
to the level comparison across countries as well. Growth accounting
decomposition of output Y in country 'j' as compared to country 'i' can be
described as follows:

$$\ln\left(\frac{Y_j/P_{j/i}^y}{Y_i}\right) = s_k\ln\left(\frac{K_j^{PK}/P_{j/i}^k}{K_i^{PK}}\right) + s_l\ln\left(\frac{L_j/P_{j/i}^l}{L_i}\right) + s_e\ln\left(\frac{E_j/P_{j/i}^e}{E_i}\right)$$

$$+ s_m\ln\left(\frac{M_j/P_{j/i}^m}{M_i}\right) + \ln\left(\frac{TFP_j}{TFP_i}\right)$$

where $P_{j/i}^*$ is relative price of '*' in country 'j' as compared to country 'i'.

The framework of international productivity level comparison under the
KLEM dataset is presented in Kuroda et al. (1996), and empirical works
of this framework include Jorgenson and Kuroda (1990), Kuroda and
Nomura (1999), Jorgenson et al. (2002) and Keio University (1996).

This book consists of eight chapters including this introduction. From
Chapter 2 to Chapter 6, a description of the data and TFP growth results for
Japan, the US, China, Korea and Taiwan are each presented respectively. In
Chapter 2, Masahiro Kuroda, Kazuyuki Motohashi and Kazushige Shimpo
provide datasets for Japan, based on the Keio Economic Observatory (KEO)
database, and also discuss the role of structural changes on productivity
growth in the Japanese economy. The slowdown of total factor productivity
growth in the 1990s is investigated from an industry-level growth accounting
database, and it is shown that the aggregated productivity slowdown comes
from non-ICT sectors. In Chapter 3, Dale Jorgenson, Mun Ho and Kevin
Stiroh present the United States' results. In the United States, productivity

resurgence can be seen in the 1990s, in contrast to Japan. It is found that the wholesale/retail sector as well as financial services contributed to this trend.

In Chapter 4, Ruoen Ren and Lin lin Sun provide the results for China. Due to the change from MPS to SNA for China's national account statistics in the mid-1980s, it was a major task for the Chinese team to construct time series input–output tables from 1981 to 2000. In China, the productivity growth rate becomes slower in the 1990s, and high economic growth has been achieved by factor accumulation, particularly by capital inputs. In Chapter 5, Hak K. Pyo, Keun-Hee Rhee and Bongchan Ha show the TFP trend of the Korean economy from 1984 to 2002. In this period, the Korean economy grew at 7.95%, but they found that TFP contribution was only 0.57%. In Chapter 6, the results for Taiwan are presented by Chi-Yuan Liang. He argues that the factor accumulation theory used by Krugman (1994), Kim and Lau (1994) and Young (1995) is invalidated because TFP growth rate in Taiwan in the 1980s and 1990s is higher than that of Japan or the United States. However, it is also found that a significant contribution to economic growth in Taiwan is, again, coming from capital inputs.

In Chapter 7 and Chapter 8, productivity levels among the five countries are compared. Chapter 7, by Marcel P. Timmer and Gerard Ypma, reports on relative producer price estimates for the five countries. Relative producer price is a key input to estimate international productivity level. Finally, Chapter 8, written by Kazuyuki Motohashi, shows the results of the comparison of the relative productivity of China, Korea, Taiwan and the United States to Japan. Japan is in second place among these countries, and due to the slow pace of TFP growth in the 1990s, the gap with other Asian countries has narrowed, while that with the United States has become wider.

REFERENCES

Ark, van B. and M. Timmer (2002), 'Measuring productivity levels – A reader', OECD Working Party on Industrial Statistics, Paris: OECD.

Ark, van B. and M. Timmer (2003), 'Asia's productivity performance and potential: The contribution of sectors and structural change', GGDC, University of Groningen, www.eco.rug.nl/~ark/pdf/Asia%20paper 4.pdf.

Bosworth, B. and S. Collins (1999), 'Capital flows to developing economies: Implications for saving and investment', *Brookings Papers on Economic Activity*, **1**, 143–69.

Jorgenson, D.W. and M. Kuroda (1990), 'Productivity and international competitiveness in Japan and the United States, 1960–1985', in C.R. Hulten (ed.) *Productivity Growth in Japan and the United States, Studies in Income and Wealth*, vol. 53, Chicago: University of Chicago Press, pp. 29–55.

Jorgenson, D.W. and M. Kuroda (1995), 'Productivity and international competitiveness in Japan and the United States, 1960–1985', Chapter 9 in D.W.

Jorgenson, *International Comparisons of Economic Growth*, Cambridge, MA: The MIT Press.

Jorgenson, D.W. and K. Motohashi (2005), 'Information technology and Japanese economy', *Journal of Japanese and International Economics*, **19**(4), 460–81.

Jorgenson, D.W., K. Stiroh and M. Ho (2002), 'Growth of US industries and investments in information technology and higher education', presented at the *Conference on Research in Income and Wealth*, Washington, DC, April.

Keio University (1996), KEO database, Keio University Observatory Monograph series No. 8 (in Japanese).

Kim, J.I. and L.J. Lau (1994), 'The sources of economic growth in the East Asian newly industrialized countries', *Journal of the Japanese and International Economies*, **8**, 235–71.

Krugman, P. (1994), 'The myth of the Asian miracle', *Foreign Affairs*, **73**(6) November/December, 62–89.

Kuroda, M. and K. Nomura (1999), 'Productivity comparison and international competitiveness', *Journal of Applied Input Output Analysis*, **5**, 1–37.

Kuroda, M., K. Motohashi and K. Shimpo (1996), 'Issues on the international comparison of productivity: Theory and measurement', in *Industry Productivity: International Comparison and Measurement Issues*, Paris: OECD, pp. 49–95.

Motohashi, K. (2003), 'Japan's long-term recession in the 1990s: Fall of industrial competitiveness', Institute of Innovation Research Working Paper No. 04-08, Hitotsubashi University.

OECD (1996), *Industry Productivity: International Comparison and Measurement Issues*, Paris: OECD.

Timmer, P. and G. Ypma (2004), 'Purchasing power parities for international comparison of output and productivity in Japan, South Korea, Taiwan and the US', Final Report for the ICPA project, March 2004, GGDC University of Groningen.

Young, A. (1995), 'The tyranny of numbers: Confronting the statistical realities of the East Asian growth experiences', *Quarterly Journal of Economics*, **110**, 641–80.

World Bank (1993), *The East Asian Miracle: Economic Growth and Public Policy*, Washington, DC: The World Bank.

2. Investigating productivity slowdown in the 1990s by using the KLEM database in Japan

Masahiro Kuroda, Kazuyuki Motohashi and Kazushige Shimpo

1. INTRODUCTION

The Japanese economy has been experiencing a long term economic down-turn since the early 1990s. Hayashi and Prescott (2002) argue that the stagnation in economic growth can be explained by the productivity slowdown since the 1990s. They show that an increasing capital–output ratio and low rate of return on capital can be observed at the same time as a productivity slowdown through their economic model. A slowdown of aggregated total factor growth rate can also be observed elsewhere in the literature (Jorgenson and Motohashi, 2005; Fukao et al., 2006).

While there is a consensus that productivity slowdown partly explains the stagnant economic growth rate of Japan in the 1990s, an investigation of the factors behind such a productivity trend has not been completed and is still underway. Nishimura and Shirai (2003) found that only modest productivity growth can be found in IT-using sectors, and underinvestment in IT may explain this. Jorgenson and Nomura (2005) confirm this finding by using comparative data between Japan and the United States on industry-level growth accounting. Shimpo (2005) focuses on inter-industry effects of productivity growth in Japan, finding that weakened linkage among sectors in the 1990s reduced the strength of inter-industry effects of productivity growth.

In this chapter, the slowdown of total factor productivity growth in the 1990s is revisited by using the KLEM database of the Japanese economy, which has been compiled for the ICPA (International Comparison of Productivity among Asian Countries) Project. This introduction is followed by a section on the framework of the KLEM database and underlying data sources. Then, analytical results are provided. In this chapter, the total factor productivity (TFP) growth rate is compared between the 1980s and 1990s. In addition, the Japanese data is compared to that of the US in

8

Productivity in Asia

the 1990s. Finally, this chapter concludes with a summary of its observations and next steps for research.

2.   FRAMEWORK OF KLEM DATABASE

Suppose that an industry with a state of technology, $T(t)$, at the time period 't' is described by a linear homogeneous production function with n inputs,

$$Zj = fj(Xj1, Xj2...., Xjn, T(t)) \qquad (2.1)$$

where the function is twice-differentiable, concave and monotonic. Under competitive market conditions, the producer's behavior is alternatively described by a price possibility frontier dual to (2.1):

$$qj = gj(pj1, pj2, ..., pjn, T(t)) \qquad (2.2)$$

where qj and Zj stand for the vector of prices and quantities of outputs of the j-th sector and pji and Xji represent the prices and quantities of inputs of the j-th sector, respectively.

Assumption of the producer's behavior in the competitive market is a sort of working hypothesis in our analysis. Changes in the relative factor prices had a serious impact on the shifts of resources among factors and the allocations of those among sectors. From equations (2.1) and (2.2), the growth rate in technical efficiency in the production function, and the growth rate of output price reduction derived from technical change, are defined respectively as follows:

$$\frac{\partial \ln Z^j}{\partial T} \frac{dT}{dt} = \frac{d \ln Z^j}{dt} - \sum_{i=1}^{n} \left(\frac{\partial \ln Z^j}{\partial \ln X_i^j} \right) \cdot \left(\frac{d \ln X_i^j}{dt} \right), \qquad (2.3)$$

and

$$-\frac{\partial \ln q^j}{\partial T} \frac{dT}{dt} = -\frac{d \ln q^j}{dt} + \sum_{i=1}^{n} \left(\frac{\partial \ln q^j}{\partial \ln p_i^j} \right) \cdot \left(\frac{d \ln q_i^j}{dt} \right). \qquad (2.4)$$

Using the Konus–Byushgen lemma under the condition of producers' equilibrium in a competitive market, we obtain:

$$\frac{\partial \ln Z^j}{\partial \ln X_i^j} = \frac{(\partial Z^j / \partial X_i^j) X_i^j}{\sum_{i=1}^{n} (\partial Z_i^j / \partial X_i^j) X_i^j}$$

$$= \frac{p_i^j X_i^j}{\sum_{i=1}^{n} p_i^j X_i^j} = v_i^j. \tag{2.5}$$

Symmetrically applying Shephard's lemma to the dual price possibility frontier function, we obtain:

$$\frac{\partial \ln q^j}{\partial \ln p_i^j} = \frac{p_i^j X_i^j}{\sum_{i=1}^{n} p_i^j X_i^j} = v_i^j. \tag{2.6}$$

Inserting (2.5) and (2.6) into (2.3) and (2.4) respectively we obtain:

$$\frac{\psi^j}{\psi} = \frac{\partial \ln Z^j}{\partial T} \frac{dT}{dt}$$

$$= -\frac{\partial \ln q^j}{\partial T} \frac{dT}{dt}. \tag{2.7}$$

On the other hand, as a definition of the accounting balance in the *j*-th sector, the following equation can be introduced:

$$qjZj = PjXj, \tag{2.8}$$

where *Pj* and *Xj* stand for the vectors of prices and quantities of inputs. Differentiating by time,

$$\frac{\dot{q}^j}{q^j} + \frac{\dot{Z}^j}{Z^j} = \frac{\dot{p}^j}{p^j} + \frac{\dot{X}^j}{X^j} \tag{2.9}$$

we can deduce the TFP growth rate of the *j*-th sector from equation (2.9) as follows:

$$\frac{\psi^j}{\psi^j} = \frac{\dot{Z}^j}{Z^j} - \frac{\dot{X}^j}{X^j} = \frac{\dot{p}^j}{p^j} - \frac{\dot{q}^j}{q^j} \tag{2.10}$$

where ψj is Zj/Xj, that is, an index of TFP. Equation (2.10) implies that the TFP growth rate as an integrated measure of the efficiency of production can be defined as the difference of the growth rates between output and inputs. Under the condition of producer's equilibrium in a competitive market, it completely corresponds to the formulation of the rate of technical change of (2.7).

The necessary conditions for producer equilibrium are combined with growth rates of inputs and output in each sector to provide the index of sectoral technical change that depends only on prices and quantities of the sector's inputs and output. Considering data for the j-th industrial sector at any two discrete points in time, the average rate of TFP change in that sector can be expressed as the difference between successive logarithms of output less a weighted average of the differences between successive logarithms of capital (K), labor (L), energy (E) and intermediate inputs (M):

$$\ln Zj(t) - \ln Zj(t-1) = vjK[\ln Kj(t) - \ln Kj(t-1)]$$
$$+ vjL\,[\ln Lj(t) - \ln Lj(t-1)]$$
$$+ vjE\,[\ln Ej(t) - \ln Ej(t-1)]$$
$$+ vjM[Mj(t) - \ln Mj(t-1)]$$
$$+ vjT, \quad (j = 1, ...J). \tag{2.11}$$

The weights are given by the average shares of capital, labor, energy, intermediate and service inputs in the value of output:

$$vjK = 1/2\,[vjK(t) + vjK(t-1)],$$
$$vjL = 1/2[vjL(t) + vjL(t-1)],$$
$$vjE = 1/2[vjE(t) + vjE(t-1)],$$
$$vjM = 1/2[vjM(t) + vjM(t-1)],$$

and:

$$vjT = 1/2[vjT(t) + vjT(t-1)], \quad (j = 1, ...J).$$

Two components of this index taking account of technical change – the translog quantity indices of change in sectoral labor input and in sectoral capital input – will be discussed in detail later. Indices are based on translog aggregator functions, defining sectoral labor input and capital input over each input's individual components. Likewise, the translog specification for the aggregator function of intermediate input can be written as:

$$X^j = \exp\left[\sum_i^J \alpha_i^j \ln X_i^j + 1/2 \sum_i^J \sum_h^J \beta_{ih}^j \ln X_i^j \ln X_h^j\right] \tag{2.12}$$

Considering data for the j-th sector at any two discrete points in time, the quantity index of change in sectoral intermediate and energy inputs can be written as the weighted average of the differences in logarithms of individual inputs:

$$\ln E^j(t) - \ln E^j(t-1) = \sum_i v^j_{Ei}[\ln E^j_i(t) - \ln E^j_i(t-1)],$$

$$\ln M^j(t) - \ln M^j(t-1) = \sum_i v^j_{Mi}[\ln M^j_i(t) - \ln M^j_i(t-1)]. \quad (2.13)$$

where the weights are given by the average value shares of the *j*-th industry's total intermediate input outlay accruing to respective types of intermediate material ($X=M$) and energy ($X=E$) inputs:

$$vjXi = 1/2[vjXi(t) + vjXi(t-1)],$$

and where the value shares of each intermediate input is:

$$v^j_{Xi} = \frac{p^j_{Xi}X^j_i}{\sum_{i=1}^{n}p^j_{Xi}X^j_i}$$

In the KLEM framework, we should prepare for the U-table (commodity × industry input–output table), not for the A-table (commodity × commodity input–output table) in time-series. This is because of the consistency of the data concept between the intermediate input including material input (M) and energy input (E) and the factor inputs (K and L). Material and energy input are derived from time series U-tables by using equation (2.13). In Japan, the Economic and Social Research Institute (ESRI) published SNA input–output tables. Both U-tables and V-tables (industry × commodity table) are published by SNA, and here time series input–output tables are based on this data.

In terms of labor input data, denoted by p^j_{Ll}, the price of the *l*-th component of the *j*-th sector's labor input, the value share v^j_{Ll} of that component in the total labor compensation of the sector is:

$$v^j_{Ll} = \frac{p^j_{Ll}L^j_l}{\sum_{l=1}^{n}p^j_{Ll}L^j_l} \quad (2.14)$$

Considering labor input data for the *j*-th sector at any two discrete points in time, the translog quantity index of change in sectoral labor input can be written as the weighted average of the growth rates of man-hours worked by different types of labor Lj,

$$\ln L^j(t) - \ln L^j(t-1) = \sum_l v_{Ll}^j [\ln L_l^j(t) - \ln L_l^j(t-1)]. \qquad (2.15)$$

where the weights are given by the average value shares of the *j*-th industry's total labor compensation accruing to respective types of labor services:

$$vLli = 1/2[vjLl(t) + vjLl(t-1)]$$

An alternative formulation of this quantity index facilitates the allocation of the change in real labor input to three sources: (1) changes in employment, (2) changes in average hours worked, and (3) changes in quality of labor force. We note that man-hours worked by the *l*-th type of labor in an industry *Ljl* can be expressed as the product of three terms: (1) the total number of persons employed per period of time in the *j*-th industry *Mj*, (2) the average hours worked per person per period of time in the *j*-th industry *Hj*, and (3) the proportion of man-hours worked by the *l*-th type of labor in the *j*-th industry *djl*:

$$Ljl(t) = djl(t)Mj(t)Hj(t), \quad (j=1,...,J; l=1,...,N) \qquad (2.16)$$

The quantity index of change in sectoral labor input can then be expressed as follows:

$$\ln Lj(t) - \ln Lj(t-1)$$

$$= [\ln Mj(t) - \ln Mj(t-1)] + [\ln Hj(t) - \ln Hj(t-1)]$$

$$+ \sum_l v_{Ll}^j [\ln d_l^j(t) - \ln d_l^j(t-1)] \qquad (2.17)$$

The first two terms, the change in employment and the change in average hours worked, account for the change in the quantity of total labor input in the *j*-th sector. The last term is the weighted average of the change in the man-hour proportions worked by different types of labor, and reflects the change in the structure of the sectoral labor force. The weights are income shares which, under the assumption of producer equilibrium, are identified with output elasticity of the respective types of labor. Thus, the last term measures the effect of structural change in the *j*-th sector's labor force upon its output as labor shifts from one type to another, and it can be interpreted to account for the change in quality of labor input per man-hour worked. We refer to this expression as the translog index of change in labor quality.

It is useful to review here, however, some of the theoretical foundations upon which the analysis of the present study is constructed. Recall that our analytical framework is based on the economic theory of production, and that within this framework we have treated sectoral labor input as an *aggregate* over its different components. Each component of labor, $Ljl(t)$ ($l=1,..,N$) represents man-hour worked input for the different categories of labor. Then, we conceived of labor as an aggregate:

$$Lj(t)=Lj[Lj1(t), Lj2(t), ..., Ljn(t), ..., LjN(t)], \quad (j=1,...,J) \quad (2.18)$$

Weak separability over its components with respect to all other inputs is assumed. Given the existence of this aggregate Lj, we further assumed the linear homogeneity of the aggregate over its components and the producer equilibrium condition that all labor is paid according to its marginal product. This implies that if there are differences in the marginal productivity between any different categories of labor, we define the quality of these labors as different. In other words, we assume that any specific category of labor $Ljl(t)$ ($l=1,...,N$) corresponds to a certain homogeneous quality of labor. In the aggregates in (2.18), we can deduce the growth rate of a divisia aggregate index of labor input as follows:

$$\frac{\dot{L}^j(t)}{L^j(t)} = \sum_l v_l^j(t)\frac{\dot{L}_l^j(t)}{L_l^j(t)},$$

where

$$v_{Ll}^j = \frac{p_{Ll}^j L_l^j}{\sum_{l=1}^{n} p_{Ll}^j L_l^j}$$

Labor input data is derived from various labor-related statistics. In Japan, there is a decennial population census, with a mid-term simplified survey every five years. In addition, the survey of wage structure gives detailed data for wages by different category of employees. Finally, monthly employer surveys and labor force surveys give an annual trend of labor input as well as hours worked data.

As is the case for labor input, our analytical framework requires the flow of productive services provided by capital assets to be separated between quantity of the flow of services and the service (rental) price per unit of flow. If we could observe the amount of capital service time utilized, say machine hours, and the rental rate per machine hour, then the measurement of sectoral capital input would be a relatively straightforward task.

The markets for capital inputs, however, are asymmetric to labor markets on the demand side (the users of capital services) and the supply side. Evidence suggests that most capital inputs are owner-utilized. For those markets where the distinction between the owners of capital assets and the users of capital services can be made, data on market service prices and quantity flows are only sparsely available. The lack of explicit capital service price and quantity in the market requires a methodological framework that enables us to impute these flow variables. We can infer the level of capital input from the level of capital stock. We can also infer capital service price – based on the asset price to service price correspondence – implicitly in the equality of the value of an asset to its discounted flow of future services. Service prices of capital assets are then seen to depend on such parameters as the tax structure faced by respective industries. The inter-industry flow of rented capital assets can be assumed to be insignificant for Japan during the period under study, so that the property income from the ownership of capital assets coincides with the income from the utilization of those assets.

We begin with the measurement of sectoral capital input by estimating the stock levels of various capital assets including both depreciable and non-depreciable assets in each sector. We should begin with the definition of gross capital formation in System of National Accounts (SNA). In the 1968 UN recommendation, the concept of gross capital formation is composed of inventory increases and gross domestic capital formation, which are defined as the productive expenditures – excluding intermediate goods – by private and government enterprises, general government, private non-profit institutions serving households, and non-corporate firms. The productive expenditure as capital formation is distinguished from the intermediate goods by the properties of the commodities in which they contribute to the benefit, not as the intermediate inputs in the current production process, but as capital inputs in the future production process. In particular, gross domestic capital formation is categorized by capital goods (including land reform) and fixed capital formation (including machinery) and other new durable goods, except used goods and scrap. They include (1) durable goods including housing for production, structure and machinery, (2) large scale repair of fixed assets, (3) land reform, including extension and development, and (4) margin and cost for transaction and transfer of land, mineral deposit and forestry. In the Japanese data, we are able to connect a fixed capital formation matrix in the input–output table (IO-FCFM) as a benchmark with SNA statistics. Unlike the definition in SNA, capital formation in IO-FCFM includes scrap and transaction trade margin in used capital goods. The other main parts of the concepts are, however, consistent with those in SNA.

3. RESULTS

Table 2.1 shows the growth decomposition results for the whole period, 1980–2000. The gross output growth rate varies from −9.75% to 7.67%. There are nine sectors with negative gross output growth, while a positive growth rate can be found in 23 sectors. Negative growth sectors include the coal mining sector (which almost stopped its activities in the late

Table 2.1   Gross decomposition results, 1980–2000

	Gross Output	Energy	Material	Labor	Capital	TFP
Agriculture	−0.12%	−0.04%	−0.18%	−0.98%	0.11%	0.80%
Coal mining	−9.75%	−1.09%	−3.33%	−4.65%	−1.22%	−2.79%
Metal	−2.15%	−0.50%	−0.38%	−0.62%	0.01%	−1.03%
Oil extraction	–	–	–	–	–	–
Construction	1.41%	0.07%	0.78%	0.34%	0.83%	0.18%
Food	0.99%	0.06%	1.19%	0.26%	0.58%	0.09%
Textile mill	−3.26%	−0.11%	−2.73%	−1.79%	−0.23%	−1.14%
Apparel	−1.70%	0.02%	−0.43%	−0.86%	0.03%	−0.88%
Lumber	−1.44%	−0.01%	−1.49%	−0.54%	−0.01%	−0.88%
Furniture	−1.02%	−0.01%	−0.31%	−0.45%	0.19%	−0.76%
Paper	0.73%	−0.03%	−0.22%	−0.05%	0.41%	0.39%
Printing	2.67%	0.04%	1.41%	0.55%	0.56%	1.51%
Chemicals	2.26%	−0.07%	0.59%	0.11%	0.74%	1.47%
Petroleum	1.29%	−0.07%	−0.91%	−0.06%	0.53%	0.89%
Leather	−2.23%	0.02%	−1.67%	−0.54%	0.12%	−1.83%
Stone	0.06%	−0.22%	−0.12%	−0.20%	0.25%	0.23%
Primary metal	−0.73%	−0.25%	−0.81%	−0.16%	0.36%	−0.69%
Fabricated metal	1.72%	0.02%	1.14%	−0.09%	0.33%	1.46%
Machinery	2.38%	0.01%	1.26%	0.36%	0.78%	1.23%
Electrical mach.	7.67%	0.07%	3.75%	0.39%	1.39%	5.83%
Motor vehicles	2.94%	0.02%	2.17%	−0.03%	0.39%	2.57%
Transport mach.	0.71%	0.02%	0.43%	−0.58%	−0.17%	1.44%
Instruments	1.44%	0.00%	0.46%	−0.36%	0.58%	1.23%
Rubber	0.99%	0.01%	0.74%	−0.40%	0.65%	0.74%
Misc. manuf.	2.93%	0.05%	1.81%	0.14%	0.42%	2.32%
Transportation	1.68%	0.17%	1.00%	0.30%	0.00%	1.21%
Communications	7.45%	0.05%	2.09%	0.71%	1.54%	5.16%
Electrical utilities	13.37%	−0.34%	0.43%	0.06%	2.41%	1.24%
Gas utilities	3.23%	0.15%	0.82%	0.22%	1.69%	1.16%
Trade	1.93%	0.03%	0.62%	0.15%	0.56%	1.19%
FIRE	4.57%	0.03%	1.27%	0.25%	1.95%	2.34%
Other services	3.50%	0.12%	1.97%	0.89%	0.89%	1.59%
Government	2.59%	0.11%	1.76%	−0.13%	0.09%	2.51%

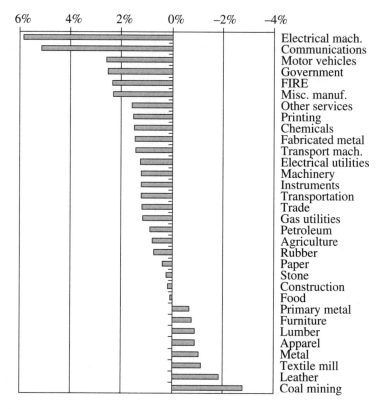

Figure 2.1   Average TFP growth (1980–2000)

1990s), agriculture, metals, as well as some manufacturing sectors such as textile and apparel. In contrast, strong performance can be found in non-manufacturing sectors, such as communications services, utilities and FIRE (finance, insurance and real estate). Within manufacturing sectors, electrical machinery shows a large positive growth rate, reflecting the sharp decline of the constant quality price index.

In terms of inputs, energy and material inputs generally move in the same direction as gross output. As for labor input, a negative growth rate can be found in 18 out of 32 sectors, while capital input grows in most sectors. During the period from 1980 to 2000, factor substitution from labor to capital can be found in most industries. For example, in the agriculture sector, while gross output decreases, capital deepening with a sharp decline of labor inputs leads to positive TFP growth.

In Figure 2.1, the average TFP growth rate from 1980 to 2000 is presented. Electrical machinery and communications services are in first and

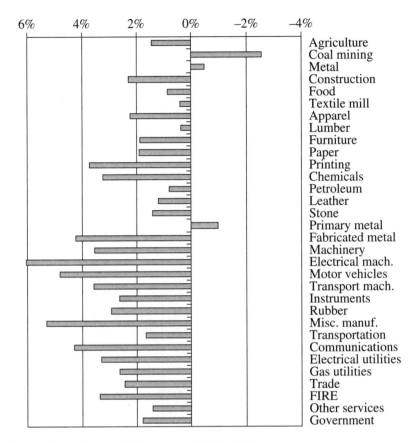

Figure 2.2   Average TFP growth (1980–1990)

second position respectively. Rapid technological development in ICT sectors may contribute to the productivity performance of these sectors. Then motor vehicles, government and FIRE follow. In contrast, 8 out of 32 sectors show a negative TFP growth rate. In those sectors, factor input adjustment does not occur flexibly, corresponding to declining gross output.

Figures 2.2 and 2.3 compare TFP growth rate between the 1980s and 1990s. In the 1980s, a negative TFP growth rate can be seen in only three sectors. However, in a substantial number of sectors, the TFP growth rate turns negative in the 1990s. In the 1990s, only electrical machinery and communications services show strong TFP growth, reflecting the IT revolution. We have confirmed that the slowdown of the GDP growth rate in the 1990s comes from TFP deceleration. Here, it should be noted that

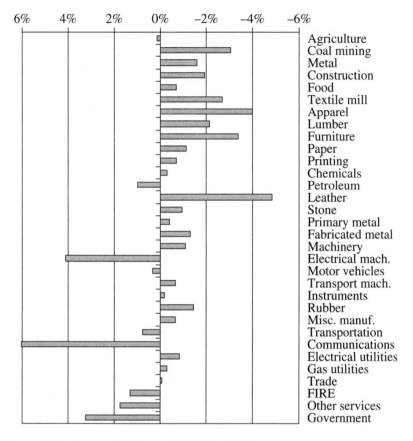

Figure 2.3   Average TFP growth (1990–2000)

TFP slowdown is not only found in a small number of sectors, but in many sectors. Therefore, productivity slowdown in the 1990s is not some sector-specific phenomenon, but is related to macro-level economic factors.

In order to see the sectoral contribution of productivity slowdown, we have aggregated sectoral TFP growth rate by using Domer weights (Jorgenson et al., 1987). The aggregated TFP growth rate in the 1980s is estimated to be 2.57%, while that in the 1990s is 0.77%. Figure 2.4 shows the sectoral contributions to this decline of aggregated TFP growth rate. Construction, trade and FIRE are the top three sectors displaying aggregated productivity slowdown. These three sectors are responsible for about half of the 1.80% decline at the macro level. Three

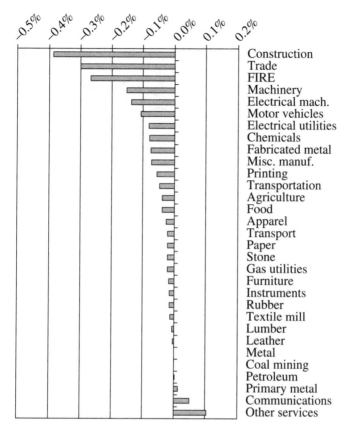

Figure 2.4   TFP slowdown from the 1980s to 1990s (Domer weight contribution)

machinery sectors, general machinery, electrical machinery and motor vehicles, follow. It is found that not only the non-manufacturing sector, but also the manufacturing sector contributes to productivity decline in the 1990s.

Finally, we compare sectoral TFP performance in Japan with that in the United States. In contrast to Japan, US productivity rebounded in the early 1990s and a productivity resurgence can be seen (Figure 2.5). Here, US data compiled for the ICPA project (Jorgenson et al., 2007) is used for comparison. An aggregated TFP growth rate by Domer weight is 1.08% and 1.77% in the 1980s and 1990s, respectively. Figure 2.6 shows the sectoral contribution of TFP growth difference between the two countries in the 1990s. General machinery, construction and trade are the top three sectors, and

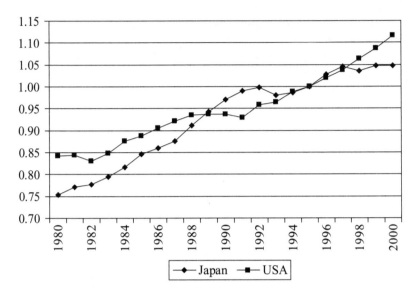

Figure 2.5   Aggregated TFP index: Japan and USA

these sectors are responsible for over 0.60% of the TFP difference, about 60% of 1% difference at the macro level.

4. CONCLUSION

In this chapter, the KLEM database as an input to the ICPA project is used for the analysis of productivity slowdown of the Japanese economy in the 1990s. It is confirmed that the total factor productivity growth rate declines significantly after the 1990s. It is also found that the decline is not confined to a few specific sectors, but is found in most sectors. However, it should be noted that there are some sectors showing productivity acceleration, such as communications services. In addition, in electrical machinery, strong productivity performance can be found even in the 1990s. Therefore, productivity slowdown is found particularly in other sectors, that is non-ICT sectors.

In this chapter, sectoral productivity performance in Japan is also compared to that of the United States. The greatest difference in productivity between the two countries in the 1990s can be observed in three sectors: general machinery, construction and trade.

An obvious next step for this research is to investigate the factors behind productivity slowdown. For example, the role of information technology in

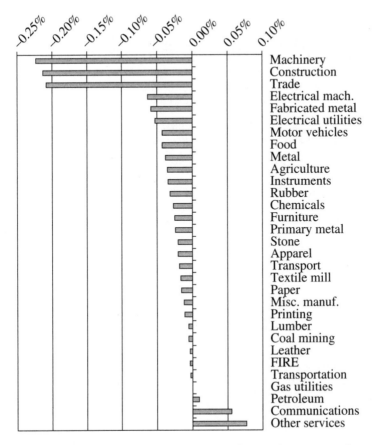

Figure 2.6   TFP differences between Japan and USA (Domer weight contribution)

productivity growth could be one such factor. In order to go forward down this avenue, it is necessary to estimate IT capital input separately from machinery capital in the ICPA project. Jorgenson and Nomura (2005) have compiled such a database, and found that IT's contribution to economic growth is smaller in Japan than in the United States.

Another avenue for further study is the relationship between innovation and productivity. Due to the sluggish economy, private investments in R&D fell in the early 1990s, while active R&D investment can be seen in the United States (Motohashi, 2005). As an additional component in the ICPA KLEM database, sectoral R&D investment data is a good candidate for future exploration.

REFERENCES

Fukao, K., H. Kwon, T. Miyagawa, T. Inui, J. Hamagata, K. Orii, J. Tokui, T. Makino and Y. Yakahashi (2006), *JIP Database 2006*, Tokyo: RIETI.
Hayashi, F. and E.C. Prescott (2002), 'The 1990s in Japan: A lost decade', *Review of Economic Dynamics*, **5** (1), 206–35.
Jorgenson, D.W., M.S. Ho and K.J. Stiroh (2007), 'The sources of growth of US industries', Chapter 3 in this volume.
Jorgenson, D.W. and K. Motohashi (2005), 'Information technology and the Japanese economy', *Journal of the Japanese and International Economies*, **19**, 460–81.
Jorgenson, D.W. and K. Nomura (2005), 'The industry origins of Japanese economic growth', *Journal of the Japanese and International Economies*, **19**, 482–542.
Jorgenson, D.W., F.M. Gollop and B.M. Fraumeni (1987), *Productivity and US Economic Growth*, Cambridge, MA: Harvard University Press.
Kuroda, M., K. Shimpo, K. Nomura and N. Kobayashi (1996), 'Keio Economic Observatory database: measurement of output, labor and capital inputs', in *Keio Economic Observatory Monograph Series*, **8**, Keio Economic Observatory (in Japanese).
Motohashi, K. (2005), 'Is Japan's industrial competitiveness falling?', investigation by Productivity Statistics, Research Center for Advanced Science and Technology, University of Tokyo, December (in Japanese).
Nishimura, K. and M. Shirai (2003), 'Can information and communication technology solve Japan's productivity slowdown?', *Asian Economic Papers*, **2** (1), 85–136.
Nomura, K. (2004), *Measurement Capital and Productivity* (in Japanese), Tokyo: Keio University Press.
Shimpo, K. (2005), 'Interindustry effects of productivity growth in Japan: 1960–2000', *Journal of the Japanese and International Economies*, **19**, 568–85.

3. The sources of growth of US industries*

Dale Jorgenson, Mun S. Ho and Kevin J. Stiroh

I. INTRODUCTION

The American economy has undergone a remarkable revival since the mid-1990s, with accelerating growth in output, labor productivity and total factor productivity. The acceleration of GDP growth from 2.8% per year during 1973–95 to 3.6% during 1995–2004 has attracted much comment and research. Many observers have put the development of information technology at the center of this resurgence, for example, Fernald and Ramnath (2004), Jorgenson et al. (2004), Baily (2002) and Oliner and Sichel (2002). However, these studies have focused on the economy as a whole, missing the great heterogeneity in the performance of individual industries. As shown in Jorgenson et al. (2005), TFP growth in the Computer and Office Equipment industry was rising at 17% per year during the 1995–2000 boom, while Insurance, Health Services and Construction had negative TFP growth.

In this chapter we provide a breakdown of growth for the 33 industries in the International Comparison of Productivity (ICPA) project, calculating the contributions to output growth of capital input, labor input, energy input, non-energy inputs and total factor productivity. We give this growth accounting for the 1980–2000 period and also for sub-periods in order to show the dramatic and widespread resurgence after 1995. The 33 industries include Machinery, which covers computers and office equipment, and Electrical Machinery, which covers telecommunications equipment and electronic components. The Services industry includes computer services (software); however, this is only 9% of total Services.

Productivity growth in the two main IT manufacturing industries has steadily risen in importance, generating a relentless decline in the prices of information technology equipment. This decline in IT prices is rooted in developments in technology that are widely understood by technologists and economists, particularly the continuous improvement in the performance of semiconductors captured by Moore's Law (Jorgenson, 2001). Information technology has reduced the cost and improved the performance of products and services embraced by US businesses, households, and government. The enhanced role of investment in information technology is a conspicuous feature of the recent US economy and a growth revival is under way in many important IT-using industries.

The mechanisms for diffusion of advances in information technology are twofold. First, advances in semiconductors generate continuing price reductions for a given level of performance. These price reductions drive demands for intermediate inputs in semiconductor-using industries such as Machinery, Electrical Machinery, and a host of others. Second, the industries that use semiconductors as inputs generate price declines that drive investments in information technology equipment like computers and telecommunications equipment. Advances in equipment production augment the downward pressure on prices, steadily redirecting the rising IT investment flow toward its most productive uses.[1]

On the labor side, college-educated workers are often identified as 'knowledge workers' who make use of information technology equipment and software, so we have constructed labor input indices that track the rising ratio of college to non-college workers. Obviously, not every knowledge worker is a college graduate, nor is every college graduate a knowledge worker. On average, the gap in marginal productivities of these two groups, as reflected in their wage rates, is large, and has risen substantially between 1980 and 2000.[2]

Energy inputs played an important role in US productivity growth during the first three decades of the postwar period, when manufacturing was a larger share of total output. Jorgenson et al. (1987) showed how the rise in energy prices in the 1970s is correlated with the sharp fall in TFP growth in many industries. The manufacturing share of GDP has fallen continuously, however, from 23% in 1980 to 18% in 2000, and energy prices have played a smaller role in the 1980–2000 period. This period was marked by the second oil shock at the beginning, followed by a steady decline in oil prices, leading to an upward trend in the contribution of energy inputs.

Our growth accounts are reported for the entire 1980–2000 period, as well as the sub-periods 1980–1990, 1990–1995, and 1995–2000. While these time periods are conventional, we should make a few observations about the choice of the periods. The first sub-period is dominated by the 1980 oil shock and recovery from the 1981 recession. The IBM 8086 personal computer was a novelty item in 1984. The year 1991 is the end of the last recession in the period we cover and the year 1995 corresponds to a surge in economic growth, as well as a jump in the rate of decline of IT prices.

There are few other studies of productivity growth at the detailed industry level for the US using the gross output measure. The Bureau of Labor Statistics has a multifactor productivity program concentrating on the manufacturing industries and selected others as described in Gullickson (1995). Triplett and Bosworth (2002) estimated the productivity change in detailed service industries. Bartelsman and Beaulieu (2004) is one study that covers all industries and most closely resembles ours.

This chapter concentrates on the 33 ICPA industries. To give a quick sense of the overall economy we now summarize the aggregate results in Jorgenson et al. (2005). Aggregate real value added growth was 2.93% per year during 1977–90, 2.35% during 1990–95 and 4.20% during 1995–2000. The growth rate during the 1995–2000 boom was a remarkable 1.85 percentage points higher than that during 1990–95. Capital input contributed 1.02 percentage points of this 1.85; a little more than half of this is due to the surge in IT investment, and the rest due to more rapid accumulation of non-IT assets. Labor input contributed 0.44 percentage points, with college-educated workers contributing 0.34 and non-college workers 0.10 to the growth resurgence. Faster growth in total factor productivity contributes the remaining 0.40 percentage points.

In other words, capital continued to be the most important source of US economic growth, as in the earlier postwar decades documented in Jorgenson et al. (1987). The contribution of IT capital input rose from 0.55 percentage points during 1990–95 to 1.11 during 1995–2000 in response to the sharp price declines. Non-IT capital, however, still predominates in the contribution of capital input, and remains the most important source of US economic growth throughout the period 1980–2000.

The contribution of labor input is next in importance as a source of US economic growth and plays a vital role in the resurgence after 1995. The contribution of college-educated workers dominates the growth of labor input during the period 1980–2000, even though these workers are less numerous than non-college workers. This reflects the higher marginal product of college-educated workers and their faster growth compared to growth of non-college workers. Both college and non-college workers, however, contributed to the growth revival after 1995. As the unemployment rate fell in the late 1990s, all types of workers found employment.

Finally, growth in total factor productivity (TFP) has been the least important of the three proximate sources of US economic growth. TFP growth essentially disappeared during 1980–90. During the past decade productivity growth revived modestly during the sub-period 1990–95 and accelerated considerably after 1995.

Jorgenson et al. (2005) also divided the contribution of capital input between the contributions of capital stock and capital quality (quality is defined in Section III below). The growth of capital quality reflects the rise in the relative importance of IT equipment and other forms of capital with higher rental prices. Of the 1.02 percentage points rise in capital input contribution between 1990–95 and 1995–2000, capital quality contributed 0.61 while capital stock contributed 0.41. Similarly, the growth of labor quality captures the rise in the relative importance of college-educated workers and other workers with higher compensation per hour. While labor quality was rising throughout this period, the growth rate fell during the boom period due to the rapid rise in less educated workers. Of the 0.44 percentage points rise between 1990–95 and 1995–2000, labor quality contributed −0.06, and hours contributed 0.51.

We also decompose growth in labor input into growth of hours worked and growth of labor productivity. For the period 1977–2000, hours worked predominate, rising at 1.68% per year, while ALP grew at 1.39% per year. ALP growth depends on capital deepening, labor quality growth, and the growth of TFP. Jorgenson et al. (2005) attribute the slow growth of labor productivity in the 1970s and 1980s to a slump in capital deepening. The boom of 1995–2000 saw ALP growth accelerating by 0.93 percentage points. Capital deepening contributed 0.60 percentage points and increased TFP growth 0.40 percentage points. The decline in the growth rate of labor quality contributed −0.07 points.

The remainder of the chapter is organized as follows. Section II presents our methodology for measuring output and intermediate inputs. In Section III we outline our methods for measuring capital input, while Section IV is for labor input. In Section V we present an analysis of the sources of US economic growth at the industry level.

II. MEASURING OUTPUT AND INTERMEDIATE INPUT

This methodology for measuring industry outputs, intermediate inputs and value added is similar to the general procedure in the ICPA project using a time series of input–output (I/O) tables. In this section we summarize the special features of the US data and data sources. A detailed description is given in Jorgenson, Ho and Stiroh (2005), hereafter abbreviated JHS (2005).

(a) Methodology

Using P_{Y_j} to denote the price of output to producer in industry j, and Y_j the quantity of output, we have the value of output equal to the value of all inputs:

$$P_{Y,j}Y_j = P_{K,j}K_j + P_{L,j}L_j + \sum_i P_i^X X_{i,j}. \tag{3.1}$$

K and L denote capital and labor input, $X_{i,j}$ is the quantity of input i into industry j and the P's are the corresponding prices. We assume that the price of intermediate input i, P_i^X, is the same for all purchasing sectors.

We define the *quantity of energy intermediate input* as a translog index of the five components (coal mining, oil and gas mining, petroleum refining, electric utilities, gas utilities[3]):

$$\Delta\ln E_j = \sum_{i \in E} \bar{v}_{i,j}\Delta\ln X_{i,j} \tag{3.2}$$

where the weights are the average shares of the components in the value of energy input:

$$\bar{v}_{i,j} = \frac{1}{2}\left(\frac{P_{i,t}^X X_{i,j,t}}{\sum_{i \in E} P_{i,t}^X X_{j,t}} + \frac{P_{i,t-1}^X X_{i,j,t-1}}{\sum_{i \in E} P_{i,t-1}^X X_{i,j,t-1}} \right). \tag{3.3}$$

The price index of energy input $P_{E,j}$ is equal to the value of total energy input, divided by the quantity index E_j. Note that this price is specific to industry j, even if the prices of the component inputs are the same for all industries, since the shares of the components differ among industries.[4]

A similar pair of indices, M_j and $P_{M,j}$, is defined for non-energy intermediate input, aggregating over the remaining 28 commodities.

We derive both outputs and intermediate inputs from a time series of inter-industry transactions tables. These tables consist of a Use Table that allocates the use of each commodity among intermediate inputs and final demand categories, and a Make Table that allocates the output of each commodity among the industries that produce it. The output of a given commodity by all industries and the input of this commodity by all industries must be equal; our system of industry accounts satisfies this accounting identity.

In nominal terms, the sum of the elements in column j of the Use Table is the value of industry j's output. In the US accounts, unlike those in some other countries, this is equal to the producer receipts, plus taxes paid on this industry output, T_j:

$$P_{YT,j}Y_j = P_{Y,j}Y_j + T_j \tag{3.4}$$

where the price paid by the purchaser is $P_{YT,j}$.

An industry may produce several commodities,[5] and a commodity may be produced by several industries. In the Make Table, $M_{j,i}$ denotes the value of commodity i produced by j, at purchaser's price. The value of the output of industry j is equal to the value of all the commodities it produces:

$$P_{YT,j}Y_j = \sum_i M_{j,i} \qquad (3.5)$$

The total value of domestically produced commodity i is given by summing over all industries:

$$VC_i = P_{YC,i}YC_i = \sum_j M_{j,i} \qquad (3.6)$$

where YC_i denotes the quantity and $P_{YC,i}$, the price.

We assume that each commodity is an aggregate of the quantities produced in various industries and the price of the ith commodity $P_{YC,i}$ is given by:

$$\ln P_{YC,i} = \sum_j \frac{M_{j,i}}{VC_i}\ln P_{YT,j} \qquad (3.7)$$

The Use Table also includes sales to final demand – consumption, government, investment, exports and imports, denoted c_i, i_i, g_i, x_i and m_i respectively. Total supply of commodity i is the sum of the domestic and imported varieties. The supply–demand balance for commodity i in value terms is thus:

$$P_{YC,i}YC_i + P_{m,i}m_i = \sum P_i^X X_i + P_i^X(c_i + i_i + g_i + x_i). \qquad (3.8)$$

We assume that all buyers purchase the same basket of commodity i, that is, the same share of the imported variety. The quantity of the total supply of commodity i, YS_i, is assumed to be a translog index of the two varieties, and the price is defined to make the value identity hold:

$$\Delta \ln YS_i = \bar{v}_C \Delta \ln YC_i + \bar{v}_m \Delta \ln m_i$$

$$P_i^X YS_i = P_{YC,i}YC_i + P_{m,i}m_i \qquad (3.9)$$

Note that this price P_i^X is the price paid by producers for their input in Equation (3.2). This completes our inter-industry accounting system.

(b) Data

The starting point for constructing our system of inter-industry accounts is the official benchmark US Inter-Industry Transactions tables produced by the Bureau of Economic Analysis (BEA). These are available for the years 1977, 1982, 1987 and 1992.[6] The Office of Occupational Statistics and Employment Projections of the Bureau of Labor Statistics (BLS) uses these benchmark tables to generate a time series of inter-industry transactions tables for 1983–2000.[7] These data are combined with the time series of industry outputs, from the same BLS Office, giving us both values and prices. The major difference between the BEA 1992 benchmark table and the BLS input–output tables is the treatment of software; BLS includes an explicit estimate of software for each sector.

We consolidate and reorganize the BLS inter-industry transactions tables from 192 industries to the 33 industries covered here.[8] The major differences are the following: (a) we treat owner-occupied housing as a direct purchase of capital input by households, rather than a purchase of housing services from the real estate industry; (b) we consolidate privately owned electric utilities with publicly owned utilities in Industry 28, and consolidate the remaining government enterprises (mostly Postal Service) with Communications; (c) we treat non-profit producers symmetrically with the other producers; (d) we have adjusted the tables for 1998–2000 to match the GDP given in the *Survey of Current Business* August 2001; the BLS series are based on a previous revision of the NIPA.

For the period 1977–82, prior to the beginning of the current BLS time series of inter-industry transactions tables, we use a previous version of these BLS tables for 1977–95, based on the 1987 benchmark tables. We consolidate the earlier tables in the same way and link them to the current tables for 1983–2000. To make them comparable, we adjust the 1977–82 tables to the new values of industry output produced by the BLS, using the method of iterative proportional fitting ('RAS') discussed by Jorgenson et al. (1987, pp. 72–5). Our final set of matrices for 1977–2000 is thus consistent with the latest estimates of industry output from BLS and the annual update of GDP published by the BEA in 2001.

The total of all entries in each column of these Use Tables is consistent with another BLS time series, *Industry Output and Employment*.[9] This dataset provides the value of output, the price of output, and employment for the same 192 industries for the period 1977–2000. We aggregate the 192 prices to obtain output prices for each of our 33 industries. The exceptions to this are Communications Equipment (BLS industry 53) and Computer and Data Processing Services (BLS industry 147), where we replace the BLS prices with BEA prices that are adjusted for quality change.[10] The prices received by producers are obtained by subtracting output taxes from the purchasers' prices, as in Equation (3.4).

The BLS input–output dataset also includes the final demand categories – c,i,g,x,m – in both current and constant prices. Using information on imports by commodities, we derive the price for imports $P_{m,i}$. We calculate a price index for the total supply of commodity i using Equation (3.9). Finally, we derive the prices and quantities of intermediate inputs. The value of input i into industry j is given by the Use matrix. The price P_i^X has been calculated, as described above, so that we can derive the quantities of inter-industry transactions $X_{i,j}$. From Equations (3.2) and (3.3) we calculate the quantity of energy and non-energy intermediate inputs for each industry.

The BLS time series only provides total value added unlike the benchmark BEA tables. To divide this among capital compensation, labor compensation and indirect business taxes, we employ GDP by Industry data produced by BEA. These annual data give, for each industry, the components of Gross Product – compensation of employees, proprietors' income, corporate profits, indirect business taxes, and so on.[11] The value of labor input described in section IV below is the sum of compensation of employees and our estimated value of self-employed labor compensation. The estimation of the value of capital input is described in Section III below and includes property compensation, less the imputed value of self-employed labor compensation, plus certain property taxes. The remainder of GDP after subtracting the value of capital and labor compensation is equal to sales taxes, net of subsidies, T_j.[12]

(c)   Results

Table 3.1 gives the results for value of output, value added and number of workers for the 33 industries. The biggest industry by value added in 2000 is Other Private Services, contributing 23% of total GDP, followed by Finance, Insurance and Real Estate (FIRE), and Public Services. The Trade industry has the second largest number of workers after Other Private Services. The biggest manufacturing industries are Electrical Machinery, Machinery and Chemicals; these together only contributed 6.0% to GDP.

The growth rate of output for the 1980–2000 period is given in Table 3.2 for each industry, and Figure 3.1 ranks them from fastest to slowest. The two IT producers dominated this period; Electrical Machinery grew at 9.2% per year, while Machinery grew at 7.3%. The unusual role of these industries is illustrated by the fact that the next fastest industry, Motor Vehicles, only grew at 4.9%. Recall that in this period US GDP was growing at only 3.1% per year. The big sectors that grew at above average rates are

Table 3.1   Industry output, valued added and employment, 2000

Code	Industry name	Output	Value-added	Employment	SIC (1987)
1	Agriculture	388,995	195,781	3,622	01–02, 07–09
2	Coal Mining	23,081	14,175	80	11–12
3	Metal and Non-metallic Mining	1,018,360	433,375	8,692	10, 14
4	Oil and Gas Extraction	136,651	72,669	322	13
5	Construction	995,279	419,200	8,612	15–17
6	Food & Kindred Products	523,440	166,235	1,755	20
7	Textile Mill Products	61,629	21,811	412	22
8	Apparel and Textiles	84,273	32,899	799	23
9	Lumber and Wood	115,974	43,305	923	24
10	Furniture and Fixtures	87,965	39,619	583	25
11	Paper & Allied	175,955	72,942	658	26
12	Printing and Publishing	233,523	137,723	1,661	27
13	Chemical Products	422,654	183,438	1,043	28
14	Petroleum Refining	235,145	26,422	126	29
15	Leather Products	10,616	4,028	76	31
16	Stone, Clay and Glass	111,040	53,522	601	32
17	Primary Metals	190,627	59,691	704	33
18	Fabricated Metals	279,540	125,540	1,562	34
19	Machinery, non-electrical	472,251	193,646	2,153	35
20	Electrical Machinery	433,257	195,913	1,728	36
21	Motor Vehicles	427,709	83,072	1,024	371
22	Other Transportation Equipment	186,241	87,121	843	372–379
23	Instruments	183,293	104,351	851	38

Table 3.1   (continued)

Code	Industry name	Output	Value-added	Employment	SIC (1987)
24	Rubber and Misc. Plastic	170,270	77,459	1,021	30
25	Miscellaneous Manufacturing	52,715	21,889	450	39
26	Transport and Warehouse	553,535	263,335	4,963	40–47
27	Communications	686,598	398,749	3,413	48, Govt. Enterp.
28	Electric Utilities	245,950	166,618	558	491, part of 493
29	Gas Utilities	81,196	26,421	156	492, part of 493, 496
30	Trade	1,965,715	1,187,179	32,727	50–59
31	FIRE	2,009,430	1,240,039	8,458	60–67
32	Other Private Services	3,455,269	2,197,343	45,600	70–87, 494–495
33	Public Services	1,194,161	1,194,161	21,151	Government

Note: Millions of current dollars and workers.

those that one associates with the 'new economy' – Other Private Services (4.1% per year), FIRE (4.0%) and Trade (3.5%). These three industries are intensive users of information technology as described in JHS (2005). At the other end, mining and those low-skilled industries most exposed to international competition saw little growth – Oil and Gas Extraction shrank at 0.9% per year, Leather shrank at 1.9%, while Apparel and Primary Metals grew at less than 0.5%. The slowest growing industry was Gas Utilities, with a negative growth rate of −2.72%; this may be due in part to an imprecise allocation of activity between joint electric and gas utilities.

Table 3.2 also gives growth rates of output for the sub-periods 1980–90, 1990–95, and 1995–2000. The dominance of the two IT-producing sectors is even more pronounced during the 1990s, when they grew at double-digit rates, far exceeding the next fastest, Furniture, at 7.6%. In the boom period 1995–2000 the other rapid growth industries were Motor Vehicles (6.1%), Other Transportation Equipment (6.0%), FIRE (5.3%) and Communications (5.3%). An acceleration of growth rates occurred in almost all industries; only nine industries had slower growth during 1995–2000, compared to the 1980–90 period. Figure 3.2 ranks the industries

Table 3.2   Growth of industry output by sub-period

	1980–2000	1980–90	1990–95	1995–2000
Agriculture	2.56	2.52	1.87	3.33
Coal Mining	1.30	2.19	−0.01	0.80
Metal and Non-metallic Mining	1.93	1.71	−0.07	4.38
Oil and Gas Extraction	−0.93	−1.84	−1.13	1.10
Construction	1.96	1.71	−0.07	4.48
Food & Kindred Products	1.68	1.55	2.05	1.57
Textile Mill Products	1.32	1.07	2.68	0.47
Apparel and Textiles	0.39	0.50	3.13	−2.57
Lumber and Wood	1.53	2.28	0.97	0.58
Furniture and Fixtures	3.81	2.43	2.79	7.59
Paper & Allied	1.67	2.14	1.62	0.79
Printing and Publishing	1.97	2.97	−0.05	1.97
Chemical Products	2.04	2.30	1.36	2.20
Petroleum Refining	0.48	−0.05	0.53	1.50
Leather Products	−1.95	−3.75	−3.09	2.79
Stone, Clay and Glass	2.10	0.80	1.19	5.60
Primary Metals	0.48	−1.80	2.49	3.04
Fabricated Metals	2.34	0.31	3.18	5.58
Machinery, non-electrical	7.30	3.99	8.94	12.26
Electrical Machinery	9.15	4.39	11.87	15.94
Motor Vehicles	4.87	3.67	6.08	6.07
Other Transportation Equipment	1.21	2.14	−5.43	5.99
Instruments	3.21	3.31	1.46	4.78
Rubber and Misc. Plastic	4.61	4.86	5.28	3.45
Miscellaneous Manufacturing	2.12	1.73	2.71	2.29
Transport and Warehouse	2.92	2.67	3.55	2.81
Communications	3.17	2.09	3.24	5.26
Electric Utilities	1.97	1.91	1.19	2.87
Gas Utilities	−2.72	−4.00	−2.24	−0.65
Trade	3.50	3.46	2.92	4.17
FIRE	4.04	3.84	3.14	5.33
Other Private Services	4.06	4.17	3.01	4.88
Public Services	1.62	2.04	1.10	1.29

Note: All figures are average annual growth rates.

by the size of the growth acceleration between 1980–95 and 1995–2000. The declining industries are those identified above – mining and low-skilled industries.

Table 3.3 gives growth rates of total intermediate input, energy input and non-energy intermediate input. The three industries with the fastest

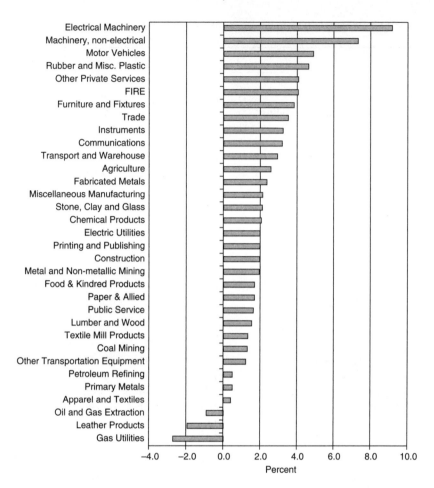

Figure 3.1   Output growth, 1980–2000

output growth had the most rapid intermediate input growth –
Machinery, Electrical Machinery and Motor Vehicles. Those with negative output growth also saw falling intermediate input. However, there
is no tight link between output and intermediate input; 20 of the 33
industries have output growth exceeding intermediate input growth,
while 13 have more rapid intermediate input growth. In the industry
making semiconductors and communications equipment, intermediate
input growth was 6.0% per year versus 9.1% for gross output. At the
other extreme, the intermediate growth in Construction was 3.08% versus
1.96% for output.

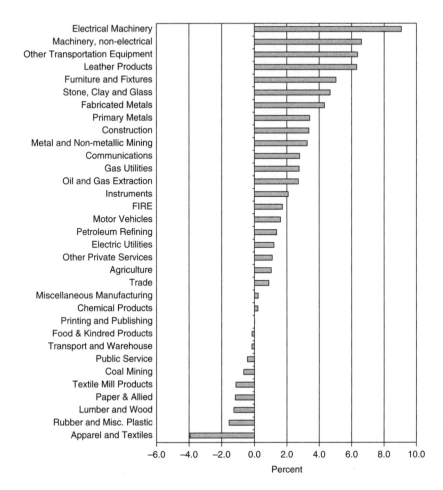

Figure 3.2   Change in output growth, 1995–2000 less 1980–1995

When we divide total intermediate inputs between energy and non-energy we find that they behave differently; 12 industries experienced such great energy conservation that energy inputs fell in spite of substantial growth in output. These include Primary Metals, Apparel, Textiles, and Coal Mining. On the other hand, only one industry with positive output growth had falling non-energy input – Petroleum Refining. The greatest gap between output growth and energy input growth is in Electrical Machinery (9.2%−1.6%=7.6%), followed by Machinery (6.7%), Coal Mining (3.1%), and Agriculture (3.1%). Within the energy industries, Oil & Gas Extraction had a gap of 2.7%, Electric Utilities 0.6%, Gas Utilities

Table 3.3   Growth of output and intermediate inputs, 1980–2000
(% per year)

	Output	Intermediate inputs		
		Total	Energy	Materials
Agriculture	2.56	0.50	−0.51	0.57
Coal Mining	1.30	−0.48	−1.79	0.16
Metal and Non-metallic Mining	1.93	3.00	0.53	3.11
Oil and Gas Extraction	−0.93	−1.75	−3.68	0.85
Construction	1.96	3.08	1.31	3.16
Food & Kindred Products	1.68	1.34	−0.35	1.38
Textile Mill Products	1.32	0.20	−0.90	0.26
Apparel and Textiles	0.39	0.37	−1.36	0.42
Lumber and Wood	1.53	1.26	−0.17	1.34
Furniture and Fixtures	3.81	4.23	2.56	4.29
Paper & Allied	1.67	1.37	−0.15	1.51
Printing and Publishing	1.97	2.29	1.49	2.33
Chemical Products	2.04	1.86	0.38	2.06
Petroleum Refining	0.48	0.13	0.71	−2.49
Leather Products	−1.95	−1.51	−1.43	−1.51
Stone, Clay and Glass	2.10	1.91	0.11	2.20
Primary Metals	0.48	−0.06	−2.19	0.17
Fabricated Metals	2.34	2.51	0.85	2.57
Machinery, non-electrical	7.30	5.53	0.55	5.64
Electrical Machinery	9.15	6.00	1.59	6.12
Motor Vehicles	4.87	5.66	1.96	5.71
Other Transportation Equipment	1.21	2.10	0.49	2.14
Instruments	3.21	4.20	0.20	4.31
Rubber and Misc. Plastic	4.61	3.63	1.93	3.73
Miscellaneous Manufacturing	2.12	1.80	−0.18	1.86
Transport and Warehouse	2.92	2.61	1.93	2.92
Communications	3.17	3.82	2.47	3.95
Electric Utilities	1.97	1.70	1.35	2.23
Gas Utilities	−2.72	−2.29	−2.79	1.10
Trade	3.50	2.71	1.10	2.87
FIRE	4.04	4.54	3.50	4.56
Other Private Services	4.06	4.64	2.47	4.76
Public Services	1.62	0.00	0.00	0.00

Note: All figures are average annual growth rates.

0.1%, while Petroleum Refining had negative 0.2% as mentioned. Recall that oil prices were high at the beginning of this period after the second oil shock, and fell gradually over time.

Unlike the widespread energy conservation, non-energy intermediate input growth exceeded output growth in 18 of the 33 industries, with material saving only in the remaining 15 industries. Electrical Machinery saw the biggest material savings, the gap between output and non-energy inputs was 3.0% (9.1% minus 6.1%), followed by Petroleum Refining (with a 3.0% gap), Agriculture (2.0% gap) and Machinery (1.7% gap). At the other extreme the industry with the biggest increase in materials relative to output growth is Gas Utilities, followed by Oil & Gas Extraction, Food Manufacturing and Metal & Non-metal Mining. The large input of semiconductors into the manufacture of computers and office equipment can be seen by the 5.64% growth rate of materials in Machinery compared to the output growth of 7.30%.

The change in intermediate input growth over the various sub-periods will be discussed in Section V when we give the sources of growth decomposition.

III. MEASURING CAPITAL INPUT

We measure capital input for each industry following the well-known methodology that accounts for substitution among assets with different marginal products. This method is used in the ICPA project and conforms to the international standards recommended by Blades (2001) and Schreyer (2001) of the OECD. Our procedures are described in detail in JHS (2005) and we summarize them here, describing the special features of the US data. We use asset-specific revaluation terms in the service price equation and assume that capital service flows from new investments become available in the middle of the year, rather than at the end of the year as in our earlier work.

a) Methodology for Estimating Capital Service Flows

For each industry, we begin with data on the quantity of investment in asset k in industry j, $I_{k,j}$. This is derived from a price index for each asset which is assumed to transform nominal investment in different time periods into identical 'efficiency units' over time, so that investments of different vintages are perfect substitutes in production. Improvements in the performance of capital input are incorporated into the price index that transforms the current vintage of investment into an equivalent number of efficiency units of earlier vintages.

We transform investment into capital stocks through the perpetual inventory method, which is consistent with the assumption of perfect substitutability across vintages, and defines the *capital stock* for each industry and asset as:

$$Z_{k,j,t} = Z_{k,j,t-1}(1 - \delta_k) + I_{j,k,t} = \sum_{\tau=0}^{\infty}(1 - \delta_k)^{\tau} I_{j,k,t-\tau}. \qquad (3.10)$$

The efficiency of an asset is assumed to decline geometrically with age at the rate δ_k. We assume that these rates are constant over time and identical for all industries. Since all capital is measured in base-year efficiency units, the appropriate price for valuing the capital stock is the investment price deflator $P_{I,k}$.

The stock of capital $Z_{k,j}$ represents the accumulation of past investments, but we are interested in the flow of capital services from that stock during period t, $K_{k,j}$. For individual assets we assume that new investment becomes available for production at the mid-point of the year so the *flow of capital services* for each industry and each asset is proportional to the arithmetic average of the current and lagged capital stock:

$$K_{k,j,t} = \tfrac{1}{2} q_{k,j}(Z_{j,k,t} + Z_{j,k,t-1}) \qquad (3.11)$$

where $q_{k,j}$ denotes the proportionality coefficient, which we assume is constant through time and normalize to one.

Using $P_{K,k,j,t}$ to denote the rental price, we employ the well-known cost-of-capital formula that takes into account the essential elements of the US tax code:

$$P_{K,k,j,t} = \frac{1 - ITC_{k,t} - \tau_t z_{k,t}}{1 - \tau_t}[r_{k,j,t} P_{I,k,j,t-1} + \delta_k P_{I,k,j,t}] + \tau_{p,t} P_{I,k,j,t-1}, \qquad (3.12)$$

where $ITC_{k,t}$ is the investment tax credit, τ_t is the statutory tax rate, $z_{k,t}$ is the present value of capital consumption allowances for tax purposes, $\tau_{p,t}$ is a property tax rate.

For the corporate sector, the rate of return, $r_{k,j,t}$ is calculated as:

$$r_{k,j,t} = \beta_j[(1 - \tau_t)i_t - \pi_{k,j,t}] + (1 - \beta_j)\left[\frac{\rho_{j,t} - \pi_{k,j,t}(1 - t_q^g)}{(1 - t_q^e)\alpha_j + (1 - t_q^g)(1 - \alpha_j)}\right], \qquad (3.13)$$

where β is the debt/capital ratio, i_t the interest cost of debt, $\rho_{j,t}$ the rate of return on equity, $\alpha_{j,t}$ is the dividend payout ratio, and t_q^g and t_q^e are the tax rates on capital gains and dividends, respectively. The asset-specific inflation rate for asset k, $\pi_{k,j,t} = (P_{I,k,j,t} - P_{I,k,j,t-1})/P_{I,k,j,t-1}$ allows the rate of return $r_{k,j,t}$ to vary across assets.[13]

We assume the after-tax rate of return to all assets in each industry is the same and estimate $\rho_{j,t}$ as the return that exhausts the payments to capital across all assets in the corporate sector of each industry. That is, we estimate the rate of return and the capital service prices jointly in order to satisfy the following restrictions:

$$\sum_k P_{K,k,j,t} K_{k,j,t} = VA_{j,t} - P_{L,j,t} L_{j,t}$$

$$P_{K,k,j,t} = \frac{1 - ITC_{k,t} - \tau_t Z_{k,t}}{1 - \tau_t}[r_{k,j,t} P_{I,k,j,t-1} + \delta_k P_{I,k,j,t}] + \tau_p P_{I,k,j,t-1} \quad (3.14)$$

where $r_{k,j,t}$ is defined as in Equation (3.13), $VA_{j,t}$ is nominal industry value added and $P_{L,j,t} L_{j,t}$ is the value of labor input.[14]

Equations (3.10) to (3.14) describe our estimation procedure for the capital service flow and capital service price, $K_{k,j,t}$ and $P_{K,k,j,t}$, respectively, for each asset, industry and time period. We combine capital services for all assets within an industry by means of a translog index; the quantity index of *capital input* for industry j is:

$$\Delta \ln K_j = \sum_k \bar{v}_{k,j} \Delta \ln K_{k,j} \quad (3.15)$$

where weights are the two-period average of nominal shares of capital income:

$$\bar{v}_{k,j,t} = \frac{1}{2}\left(\frac{P_{K,k,j,t} K_{k,j,t}}{\sum_k P_{K,k,j,t} K_{k,j,t}} + \frac{P_{K,k,j,t-1} K_{k,j,t-1}}{\sum_k P_{K,k,j,t-1} K_{k,j,t-1}} \right). \quad (3.16)$$

The corresponding *price index of capital inputs* $P_{K,j}$ is defined implicitly to make the value identity hold:

$$P_{K,j} K_j = \sum_k P_{K,k,j} K_{k,j} \quad (3.17)$$

Similarly, the *quantity of industry capital stock* is defined by:

$$\Delta \ln Z_j = \sum_k \bar{w}_{k,j} \Delta \ln K_{k,j} \quad (3.18)$$

where the weights are the two-period average nominal shares of capital stock:

$$\bar{w}_{k,j,t} = \frac{1}{2}\left(\frac{P_{I,k,j,t}K_{k,j,t}}{\sum_k P_{I,k,j,t}K_{k,j,t}} + \frac{P_{I,k,j,t-1}K_{k,j,t-1}}{\sum_k P_{I,k,j,t-1}K_{k,j,t-1}} \right). \qquad (3.19)$$

The corresponding *price index for capital stock* $P_{Z,j,t}$ is defined implicitly from the identity:

$$P_{Z,j,t}Z_{j,t} = \sum_k P_{I,k,j,t}K_{k,j,t}. \qquad (3.20)$$

Finally, we define *capital quality* $Q_{K,j}$, for industry j as the ratio of capital input to capital stock:

$$Q_{K,j} = \frac{K_j}{Z_j}. \qquad (3.21)$$

It follows that the growth rate of capital quality is defined as the difference between the growth rates of capital input and capital stock:

$$\Delta\ln Q_{K,j,t} = \Delta\ln K_{j,t} - \Delta\ln Z_{j,t}. \qquad (3.22)$$

Note that quantity indexes of capital inputs and capital stocks aggregate the same asset quantities $K_{k,j}$ by means of a translog index; the difference is the use of service prices versus asset prices as weights. This implies that growth in capital quality reflects substitution towards assets with relatively high service prices, that is assets with large depreciation rates and rapid downward revaluations such as computers have their weights in an index of capital *services* greatly exceeding their weights in an index of capital *stock*. Substitution toward computers as computer prices fall implies that capital input grows faster than capital stock, that is, a rising index of capital quality. Second, our measure of industry capital stock is implicitly a two-period average, since it aggregates two-period averages of capital stocks using current asset prices.

b) Data

Our primary data source for capital input is the Tangible Wealth Survey produced by the Bureau of Economic Analysis (BEA), and described in

Herman (2000a, 2000b). These data include detailed investment by industry and asset class and contain historical cost investment and chain-type quantity indexes for 61 types of non-residential assets from 1901 to 2000, 48 types of residential assets from 1901 to 2000, and 13 different types of consumers' durables from 1925 to 2000. Non-residential investment is available for 62 industries, which we collapse into 33 industries, plus private households and governments.

We have made several adjustments to the BEA data. First, we reclassify the data on 61 non-residential assets into 52 non-residential assets. The residential assets and 13 consumers' durable assets are allocated to the real estate and household industries. Second, we combine investment in residential equipment with other equipment in the non-residential category. Third, we control the total value of investment in major categories – equipment and software, non-residential structures, residential structures, and total consumer durables – to match the totals in the US National Income and Product Accounts (NIPA). These adjustments lead to a complete time series of 57 assets in both current and chained 1996 dollars for each of the 33 industries. The investment and capital data are then allocated across three ownership categories – corporate, non-corporate, and households – based on shares provided by BEA. There is no ownership breakdown for household and government industry data. Finally, we use prices for each asset from the NIPA.

Geometric depreciation rates for the perpetual inventory calculations are based on Fraumeni (1997) with the exceptions of computers and automobiles. BEA (1999) reports that depreciation is non-geometric and varies over time for most computer components and peripherals, based on the work of Oliner (1993, 1994). We estimated a best-geometric approximation to the latest depreciation profile for different types of computer assets; this generates an average geometric depreciation rate of 0.315, which we have used for computer investment, software investment, and consumer durable purchases of computers, peripherals and software. For automobiles, BEA derives a depreciation profile from new and used car prices. We estimated a best geometric approximation to the depreciation profile for autos, obtaining an estimate of 0.272.

We have collected data on inventories and land to complete our capital estimates. Inventory data come primarily from the NIPA in the form of farm and non-farm inventories, allocated across industries. These are measured in current dollars with a corresponding price index. Inventories are assumed to have a depreciation rate of zero and do not qualify as investment tax credit or capital consumption allowances for tax purposes, so the capital rental price formula is a simplified version of Equation (3.12).

Data on land are more problematic. Through 1995 the Federal Reserve Board (1995, 1997) published detailed data on land values and quantities in its 'Balance sheets for the US Economy', but the underlying data became unreliable and are no longer published. We use the limited land data available in the 'Flow of funds accounts of the United States' and historical data described in Jorgenson (1995) to estimate a price and a quantity of private land. As a practical matter, this quantity series varies very little, so its major impact is to slow the growth of capital stock and capital input. Like inventories, the depreciation, investment tax credit, and capital consumption allowance for land is zero.

Finally, we obtain industry-level value added from the 'Gross product originating' database maintained by the BEA and described in Lum and Moyer (2000) and from the BLS, as described in Section II. The BEA data include the value of output, value added and intermediate inputs for 62 industries from 1947 to 2000. We have aggregated these industries to match the ICPA industries. For the estimation of capital service prices, we begin with value added in the corporate sector and subtract corporate labor income to estimate the amount of income available to corporate capital. Similarly, we subtract non-corporate labor income from value added, as described in the following section, to obtain the value of non-corporate capital income.

c) Issues

Implementation of the perpetual inventory methodology requires the resolution of several issues. This subsection discusses these issues and describes our solutions to them.

i) Negative service prices

The procedures require that the value of capital service flows exhaust capital income; however, there is very little capital income for some industries in some years, leading to negative estimates of service prices. This happens when asset inflation rates are high relative to the interest rate. Berndt and Fuss (1986) discuss this issue in more detail. Negative service prices make aggregation difficult and we make adjustments for several assets, notably inventories, land, and structures in the 1970s, when inflation was high. Our first adjustment was to use a smoothed inflation rate from the surrounding years rather than the current inflation in the cost of capital calculation. Land showed large capital gains throughout and has no depreciation, and so we used the economy-wide rate of asset inflation for all years. When these adjustments were not sufficient, we imputed additional income, adding to both capital income and the value of output. This is a small issue empirically.

ii) Deflators

The Tangible Wealth Survey assumes that all industries pay the same price for a particular type of asset. However, there are rounding errors in the quantity data and we ensure that the national deflator is used. Jorgenson and Stiroh (2000) also point out that the deflators here do not fully account for quality change in software and communications equipment. We do not address this issue here, but simply observe that this may understate the growth of IT capital.

iii) Depreciation rates

Oliner (1993, 1994) and Whelan (2002) have pointed out that if the quantity of investment is constructed with a constant-quality deflator, the depreciation rate should be obtained from constant-quality price data by age of asset. The BEA depreciation rates currently incorporate Oliner's (1993, 1994) estimates for all computer components except personal computers. According to Herman (2000a), the personal computer depreciation profile is based on a study by Lane (1999). Our geometric approximation to the BEA depreciation rates, however, employs the earlier BEA profile based on the work of Oliner (1993, 1994).

iv) Corporate and non-corporate capital services

The allocation of capital between the corporate and non-corporate sectors is important because of the differential taxation of corporate income. BEA data permit us to split the capital stock, but we have no direct information on the capital income to allocate to each sector. We allocate income to the non-corporate sector by assuming that labor compensation per hour is equal for employees and self-employed and unpaid family workers for each type of labor in each sector.[15] We then estimate capital income in the non-corporate sector as a residual (observed non-corporate value added less imputed labor income). While this leads to fluctuations in the rate of return for some sectors, the relatively small size of the non-corporate sector in most industries mitigates this effect.

d) Results

Table 3.4 gives the growth rate of capital input for the period 1980–2000. The growth of capital input is greatest for Instruments at 7.9% per year, followed by Trade (6.6%), Other Private Services (6.5%), and Electrical Machinery (6.0%). We can see that the industries with the fastest growth in output are not those with the fastest growth in capital input; for example, Machinery, which includes the computer-making business, managed a 7.3% output growth rate with only a 4.7% growth in capital input.

Table 3.4   Growth of capital input, stock and quality, 1980–2000

	Capital input	Capital stock	Capital quality
Agriculture	0.31	−0.09	0.40
Coal Mining	−0.33	0.58	−0.91
Metal and Non-metallic Mining	1.77	1.49	0.28
Oil and Gas Extraction	1.51	1.55	−0.04
Construction	1.97	1.48	0.48
Food & Kindred Products	2.08	1.94	0.14
Textile Mill Products	1.50	0.18	1.32
Apparel and Textiles	2.08	1.46	0.62
Lumber and Wood	0.31	0.31	0.00
Furniture and Fixtures	2.92	2.18	0.73
Paper & Allied	2.68	2.02	0.66
Printing and Publishing	5.08	3.16	1.93
Chemical Products	2.56	2.30	0.26
Petroleum Refining	0.97	0.30	0.66
Leather Products	−0.73	−1.20	0.47
Stone, Clay and Glass	1.03	0.76	0.27
Primary Metals	−0.12	−0.88	0.76
Fabricated Metals	1.70	1.18	0.52
Machinery, non-electrical	4.69	2.82	1.87
Electrical Machinery	6.01	4.72	1.29
Motor Vehicles	2.34	1.84	0.50
Other Transportation Equipment	4.94	1.92	3.02
Instruments	7.92	4.06	3.86
Rubber and Misc. Plastic	4.05	3.19	0.86
Miscellaneous Manufacturing	1.88	1.44	0.44
Transport and Warehouse	1.73	0.46	1.28
Communications	4.91	4.51	0.40
Electric Utilities	1.97	1.62	0.35
Gas Utilities	2.34	1.51	0.84
Trade	6.56	4.12	2.44
FIRE	4.52	2.42	2.10
Other Private Services	6.53	4.49	2.04
Public Services	2.95	1.95	1.00

Note: All figures are average annual growth rates.

Altogether, fourteen industries had capital input growth smaller than output growth. Some industries even saw a fall in capital input despite rising output – Coal Mining and Primary Metals. The industry which shrank the most, Leather, had the largest fall in capital input. At the other end, capital input in Gas Utilities rose at 2.34% despite output falling at 2.72%, in Trade capital rose at 6.56% compared with output at 3.50%, and in Printing & Publishing capital rose at 5.08% compared with output at 1.97%.[16]

The ratio of capital input to stock is capital quality, and the growth rates of all three series are given in Table 3.4 for the 1980–2000 period. The instruments industry had the fastest growth of capital quality at 3.86% per year, followed by Other Transportation Equipment (3.0%), Trade (2.4%), Finance, Insurance & Real Estate (2.1%), and Other Private Services (2.0%). This rapid growth of quality in the Trade sector is part of the much publicized use of information technology by retailers such as Wal-Mart; their massive investment in IT assets led to a sharp rise in the ratio of short-lived IT assets to long-lived structures. The IT transformation of the finance sector is also well-known and reflected in this fast growth of capital quality. For the two IT producers, Machinery also had a good growth rate of capital quality of 1.87%, while Electrical Machinery had the fastest growth rate of capital stock among the 33 industries but only a more modest 1.29% growth in capital quality.

Apparel is one of the low-skilled industries that saw little output growth and had a modest 0.6% rise in capital quality. The Textiles industry, on the other hand, is more technology-intensive, and had higher output growth; its capital quality rose at 1.3% per year. At the other end of industry experience, two mining industries had a fall in quality, and Lumber had zero growth. Every other sector saw a positive growth in quality during this period. Motor Vehicles, which had a relatively high growth rate of output, had a slow growth of capital quality of 0.5% per year, Communications was an IT-intensive industry even at the beginning of the period, and thus saw a slow 0.4% growth in capital quality with the large investments in the long-lived assets such as cable infrastructure.

The most important overall conclusion from these results is that the pervasive rise in capital quality reflects the rapid investment growth in IT assets which have short service lives and high cost of capital. All industries, IT-producing and IT-using, have invested substantially in all types of capital assets, and the rise in quality indicates that they all invested relatively more in IT capital. Investment in IT is very widespread, encompassing manufacturing, services, utilities, and mining industries.

IV. MEASURING LABOR INPUT

The methodology for deriving labor input takes into account the substitution among workers with very different wages, and hence, different assumed marginal products. The method of cross-classifying workers by educational attainment, age and gender to distinguish between total hours and effective labor input is well known (see for example United Nations (1993) *System of National Accounts 1993*) and is used in the ICPA project. Our methods are described in detail in JHS (2005); here we summarize the special features of the US labor data.

We classify workers by gender, employment class (employee, self-employed and unpaid), seven age groups (16–17, 18–24, 25–34, 35–44, 45–54, 55–64, 65+), and six educational attainment classes (0–8 grade, some high school, high school diploma, some college, Bachelor's degree, MA and higher degrees).[17] There is a total of 2×2×7×6=168 types of workers for each of the 33 industries. For the whole economy there is thus a total of 168*33=5544 cells.

a) Methodology

Using subscript $l=1, 2,\ldots 168$ to denote the demographic types, we express the industry quantity of labor input as a translog index of the individual components:

$$\Delta \ln L_j = \sum_l \bar{v}_{l,j} \Delta \ln L_{l,j} \qquad (3.23)$$

where the share weights are:

$$\bar{v}_{l,j,t} = \frac{1}{2} \left(\frac{P_{L,l,j,t} L_{l,j,t}}{\sum_l P_{L,l,j,t} L_{l,j,t}} + \frac{P_{L,l,j,t-1} L_{l,j,t-1}}{\sum_l P_{L,l,j,t-1} L_{l,j,t-1}} \right) \qquad (3.24)$$

$P_{L,l,j,t}$ is the price of labor input of type l in industry j, and $L_{l,j}$ is the quantity.

This method assumes that labor input for each category $\{L_l\}$ is proportional to hours worked $\{H_l\}$:

$$L_{l,j,t} = Q_l H_{l,j,t} \qquad (3.25)$$

where the constants of proportionality Q_l are the same at all points of time.

Under this assumption, the labor quantity index in Equation (3.23) simplifies to:

$$\Delta \ln L_j = \sum_l \bar{v}_{l,j} \Delta \ln H_{l,j} \qquad (3.26)$$

The corresponding price of labor input is given implicitly by the value identity:

$$P_{L,j}L_j = \sum_l P_{L,l,j}L_{l,j} \tag{3.27}$$

Finally, the *labor quality index* measures the contribution of substitution among the components of labor input to the quantity obtained from a simple sum of industry hours, $H_j = \Sigma_l H_{l,j}$:

$$Q_{L,j} = \frac{L_j}{H_j} \tag{3.28}$$

b) Data

In order to describe our data construction it is more convenient to index the demographic types explicitly, for example H_{saecj} denotes the hours worked in the group sex s, age a, education e and employment class c, and P_{Lsaecj} denotes the corresponding price. We begin with the public use tapes from the decennial Censuses of Population for 1990, 1980 and 1970, covering 1% of the population in 1990 and 1980 and 0.1% of the population in 1970. We employ individual observations for about one million workers to construct benchmark matrices of employment (E_{saecj}), weekly hours (h_{saecj}), weeks per year (w_{saecj}), and labor compensation (c_{saej}). For each worker, we collect data on age, highest grade completed, class of employment, primary industry of employment, weekly hours worked, weeks worked the previous year, and wage and salary income of employees from the previous year. This dataset also provides population weights that allow us to derive national totals. The benchmark matrices are adjusted so that they equal the aggregate tables published by the Bureau of the Census, using the method of iterative proportional fitting (or RAS).

We make some additional refinements to deal with special features of labor data. First, there are multiple job holders working in more than one industry. We use detailed information on this from the May CPS to allocate hours for individual workers among industries and employment classes. Second, information on income is 'top-coded'. For each industry we fitted a lognormal distribution and used this to estimate the average income for the upper tail of the distribution. Third, the Census of Population for 1990 defines educational attainment as highest degree achieved. We used the estimates in Jaeger (1997) to bridge the new Census definition to the old definitions that apply prior to the 1992 data.

In the next step we employ the Current Population Survey (CPS) Annual Demographic File from the March surveys to estimate employment, hours and compensation matrices. For years 1977–91 we use the files reorganized by Unicon (2002) so that they have a convenient consistent structure through time. For years after 1991 we use the CPS March files directly. The data after 1991 are based on the new educational classifications of highest degree attained rather than the old number of years of schooling. These surveys have sample sizes of about 80 000 workers, only a tenth of the Census of Population. We thus do not use these annual data to estimate the matrix of 5544 cells directly, but only to estimate matrices of smaller dimension. For example, for employment we estimate three marginal matrices, (i) matrix with sex, class of employment, age and education; (ii) matrix with 66 industries and class of employment; and (iii) matrix with 19 industries and education. For weekly hours and annual weeks we cross-classify by sex, class, age and 10 industries. For hourly compensation of employees we estimate one matrix with sex, age and education, and another with 19 industries and education.

Our first step is to scale employment, hours, weeks and compensation matrices based on the March CPS so that the economy totals equal the BLS annual tabulations based on the monthly CPS.[18] These scaled matrices are then taken as marginal totals to interpolate and extrapolate the 1970, 1980 and 1990 Census benchmarks. An initial guess at the full matrix in the inter-censal years is derived from the nearest two Censuses and made consistent with these marginal totals for every year between 1970 and 1990. For years after 1990 we extrapolated the 1990 Census in the same way. The Census-based matrices are calibrated to the BLS totals for 1970, 1980 and 1990 in order to provide a smooth series.

The CPS covers only the civilian population; for measures of military workers we turn to data from the Defense Manpower Data Center which use classifications almost identical to ours.[19] The CPS top-codes income, but provides the average of the top-coded wages since 1996: for years prior to 1992 we use the estimates in BLS (1993), Appendix Table E-1. For the years 1992–95 we use averages from the 1990 Census.

From the time series of matrices on employment, hours, weeks and compensation based on individual data we generate a time series based on establishment data given in the National Income and Product Accounts. The NIPA gives the total number of employees and self-employed for detailed industries.[20] The number of workers is summed over the detailed sectors so that they match the ICPA industries for each class of employment. The NIPA does not include unpaid family workers and these are taken from a separate BLS tabulation and added to the self-employed total. We derive an establishment-based employment matrix, EE, by scaling each part of the individual-based employment E_{saecj} equally to these NIPA totals:

$$E_{saecj} \to EE_{saecj} \quad \text{such that} \quad \sum_{sae} EE_{saecj} = \text{NIPA total for } j$$

The NIPA gives the total annual hours worked by *employees* for 15 industry groups.[21] Using the hours/week and weeks/year matrices described above for *c=employee*, we generate the establishment-based hours matrix, *HE*, on a 52 weeks per year basis by scaling to this NIPA total for each industry group IND:

$$h_{saecj}, w_{saecj} \to HE_{saecj} \ni \sum_{sae,j \in IND} 52*EE_{saecj}HE_{saecj} = \text{NIPA total for IND}$$

For the self-employed and unpaid family workers, the BLS Division of Productivity Research provides an estimate of total non-farm hours for this group. We scale hours for these workers so that the sum over the non-farm sectors equals this total. For hours in agriculture the Economic Research Service of the US Department of Agriculture provides estimates of total hours.[22]

Finally, we control the compensation matrix to the NIPA's 'Compensation of employees by industry' and 'Wage and salary by industry', where the former includes wages and benefits.[23] We first adjust the labor compensation matrix c_{saej} for employees from the CPS data to the NIPA wage and salary totals for each industry. We then impute wage supplements and scale to the 'Compensation' totals to get the establishment-based compensation matrix, *CE*:

$$c_{saej} \to CE_{saecj} \ni \sum_{sae} 52*EE_{saecj}HE_{saecj}CE_{saecj} = \text{NIPA total for } j$$

For the self-employed and unpaid workers, we set wages equal to those of employees in each category. We then control the sum of capital and labor income to our estimate of proprietor's income as described in section III. This gives us all the pieces required to calculate the labor input in Equation (3.26), c_{saej} corresponds to $P_{L,l,j}$, and $H_{l,j}$ is given by $52* EE_{saecj} HE_{saecj}$.

c) Issues

The index number approach to measuring labor input has been subject to a number of criticisms. One objection is the identification of rates of labor compensation with marginal products since labor markets may be distorted by trade unions or labor monopsonies. Another subtle criticism arises from the 'signaling' hypothesis of Spence (1973) concerning asymmetric information about ability. These issues are discussed in JHS (2005) and BLS (1993, pp. 42–3).

d) **Results**

Table 3.5 gives the growth rate of labor input, hours and labor quality for the period 1980–2000. Recall that labor input is hours multiplied by quality. The fastest growth of labor input is in Other Private Services at 4.03% per annum, which also had the fastest growth rate in hours, 3.77%. This is the largest of the 33 industries and includes Computer Services, Business Services, Health, and Education. Health services are demanded by the aging, and growing, population; education services is what generated the large increase in college-educated workers; computer services is another essential element of the Information Age.

The next highest growth in labor input are Construction (2.87%), Transportation (2.63%), and Finance, Insurance & Real Estate (2.49%). These industries also had high growth of hours. At the other end of the spectrum of labor input and hours growth, the biggest shrinkage was in Coal Mining (−4.76%), Leather (−4.27%), Oil & Gas Extraction (−2.05), and Apparel (−2.14%). Textile, Petroleum Refining and Primary Metals all saw labor input falling at 1.8%. These industries consist of the group most exposed to low-wage international trade, and the energy-related group.

The close correlation between labor input growth and hours growth means that the range of labor quality change among the 33 industries is smaller compared to the wide range in the growth of capital quality described above in Section III. The industry with the most rapid growth of labor quality is Leather Products with 1.1% per year; however, this is an outlier since this industry shrank and shed many low-wage workers. The second most rapid growth of labor quality occurred in Miscellaneous Manufacturing at 0.83%, while the slowest growth was in Other Private Services at 0.26%. All but one of the industries had labor quality growth between 0.26% and 0.83% during 1980–2000. The supply of college-educated workers expanded during this period and all industries hired substantial numbers of them, even those that shrank and shed less-educated workers.

The other industries with high growth of labor quality are Oil & Gas Extraction (0.77%), Furniture (0.72%), and Coal Mining (0.70%), all small industries. The two IT manufacturing industries both saw above-average growth of labor quality, about 0.65% per year. The industries with slow growth of quality other than Other Private Services, are Gas Utilities (0.31%), Textiles (0.32%), Trade (0.33%), and Metal & Non-metal Mining

Table 3.5   Growth of labor input, hours and quality, 1980–2000

	Labor input	Hours	Labor quality
Agriculture	0.17	−0.37	0.54
Coal Mining	−4.76	−5.47	0.70
Metal and Non-metallic Mining	2.60	2.25	0.35
Oil and Gas Extraction	−2.05	−2.82	0.77
Construction	2.87	2.43	0.44
Food & Kindred Products	0.17	−0.10	0.36
Textile Mill Products	−1.78	−2.10	0.32
Apparel and Textiles	−2.14	−2.75	0.61
Lumber and Wood	1.83	1.24	0.60
Furniture and Fixtures	1.94	1.22	0.72
Paper & Allied	0.41	−0.09	0.50
Printing and Publishing	1.42	1.04	0.37
Chemical Products	0.23	−0.27	0.50
Petroleum Refining	−1.78	−2.07	0.29
Leather Products	−4.27	−5.41	1.13
Stone, Clay and Glass	0.40	−0.09	0.49
Primary Metals	−1.77	−2.36	0.59
Fabricated Metals	0.53	0.00	0.53
Machinery, non-electrical	−0.01	−0.67	0.66
Electrical Machinery	0.59	−0.05	0.64
Motor Vehicles	2.01	1.54	0.47
Other Transportation Equipment	−0.64	−1.08	0.44
Instruments	0.03	−0.57	0.60
Rubber and Misc. Plastic	2.08	1.68	0.40
Miscellaneous Manufacturing	1.00	0.17	0.83
Transport and Warehouse	2.63	2.24	0.39
Communications	1.44	0.88	0.56
Electric Utilities	−0.18	−0.63	0.45
Gas Utilities	−1.21	−1.52	0.31
Trade	1.84	1.51	0.33
FIRE	2.49	1.94	0.55
Other Private Services	4.03	3.77	0.26
Public Services	1.21	0.64	0.57

Note: All figures are average annual growth rates.

(0.35%). Two of the big industries with fast growth of output, Other Private Services and Trade, expanded in this period by hiring relatively more low-skilled workers, and saw slow growth in labor quality. This contributed to the low unemployment rates of low-wage workers during the economic boom period.

V. MEASURING PRODUCTIVITY

Our methodology for measuring productivity at the industry level begins
with an industry production function:

$$Y_j = f(K_j, L_j, E_j, M_j, T) \qquad (3.29)$$

where Y is output of industry j, and K, L, E, M are capital, labor, energy and
non-energy intermediate inputs, respectively, corresponding to the elements
in Equation (3.1). T is an indicator of efficiency. The variables K, L, and X
are each aggregates of the many components as described in the preceding
sections and the production function (3.29) is assumed to be separable in
these components.

Let P_{Y_j}, P_{K_j}, P_{L_j}, P_{E_j}, and P_{X_j} denote the prices for outputs and the four
inputs, respectively. All variables are also indexed by time, but the t sub-
script is suppressed wherever possible. Under the assumptions of constant
returns to scale and competitive markets, a translog index of *productivity
growth* is defined as:

$$v_{T,j} \equiv \Delta \ln Y_j - \bar{v}_{K,j} \Delta \ln K_j - \bar{v}_{L,j} \Delta \ln L_j - \bar{v}_{E,j} \Delta \ln E_j - \bar{v}_{M,j} \Delta \ln M_j \quad (3.30)$$

where $\bar{v}$ is the two-period average share of the input in the value of nominal
output. For example, the *value share* for capital is:

$$\bar{v}_{K,j} = \frac{1}{2} \left(\frac{P_{K,j,t} K_{j,t}}{P_{Y,j,t} Y_{j,t}} + \frac{P_{K,j,t-1} K_{j,t-1}}{P_{Y,j,t-1} Y_{j,t-1}} \right) \qquad (3.31)$$

and similarly for labor and intermediate inputs. Note that the assumptions
imply that value of output is equal to the sum of outlays on all inputs, as
given in Equation (3.1). In describing the results below, when we use the
term *contribution of capital to output growth* we are referring to the
$\bar{v}_{K,j} \Delta \ln K_j$ term in Equation (3.30), and similarly for the contributions of
labor and intermediate inputs.

Under these assumptions we decompose industry *labor productivity*
growth, or growth of output per hour worked, as follows:

$$\Delta \ln y_j = \bar{v}_{K,j} \Delta \ln k_j + \bar{v}_{L,j} \Delta \ln Q_{L,j} + \bar{v}_{E,j} \Delta \ln e_j + \bar{v}_{M,j} \Delta \ln m_j + v_{T,j}, \quad (3.32)$$

where lower-case letters refer to output and inputs per hour worked. The
terms on the right-hand side are, respectively, the contributions to growth
of labor productivity of capital deepening, labor quality, intermediate
input deepening, and total factor productivity growth.

a) Industry Growth Accounting Results, 1980–2000

In the Introduction we summarized the results in JHS (2005), which showed that, at the aggregate level, investments in information technology (IT) and other tangible assets are the most important sources of US economic growth during the boom period. Investments in these two classes of assets are about equally important in the economic resurgence of 1995–2000. Investments in human capital have also contributed significantly to growth and played a vital role in this revival. The substitution of college-educated workers for non-college workers has been an important mechanism for the restructuring of the US workforce. Aggregate total factor productivity gains essentially disappeared during the period 1977–90 but revived in the 1995–2000 period.

Now we describe the contribution of capital, labor and TFP at the industry level, which are quite different from the aggregate. At the industry level we are also concerned with the contributions of energy and non-energy intermediate inputs. We note that the fundamental element of IT hardware – semiconductor chips – is classified as an intermediate input produced by the Electrical Machinery industry. The dramatic fall in semiconductor prices is captured in our use of inter-industry transactions tables so we can get a correct accounting of industry productivity growth. In Table 3.6 we present the sources of growth for each industry based on Equation (3.30). The contributions of the factors are displayed graphically in Figures 3.3 to 3.6, where the contributions are ranked by size.

In the first line of Table 3.6 we see that that of the 2.56% annual growth of output in Agriculture, capital input growth contributed 0.05 percentage points, labor 0.06, energy intermediates −0.04, non-energy intermediates 0.26, and total factor productivity 2.22. This pattern, where TFP contribution dominates intermediate input, is not typical of US industries. Rapid TFP growth reflects the unusually good performance of US agriculture in this period, a feature often ignored in reviews of the Information Age.

The estimates for the two IT manufacturing industries show how their TFP growth dominated this period (see Figure 3.6). Of the 9.15% annual output growth in Electrical Machinery, TFP contributed 4.76 percentage points, non-energy materials 3.19, and capital 0.99. In Machinery, which makes computers and office equipment, TFP contributed 3.66 percentage points of the 7.30% growth rate, while non-energy materials contributed 3.20 and capital only 0.47.

A total of ten industries had TFP contribution bigger than input contribution, the others are Coal Mining, where the 1.30% output growth is decomposed to 3.14 percentage points for TFP and −1.59 for labor, and Textiles, where the 1.32% output growth is decomposed to 1.49 percentage

Table 3.6　Sources of growth of industry output, 1980–2000

	Output	Input contributions				Productivity
		Capital	Labor	Energy	Materials	
Agriculture	2.56	0.05	0.06	−0.04	0.26	2.22
Coal Mining	1.30	−0.05	−1.59	−0.19	−0.01	3.14
Metal and Non-metallic Mining	1.93	0.13	0.98	0.01	1.65	−0.84
Oil and Gas Extraction	−0.93	0.60	−0.34	−0.86	−0.07	−0.26
Construction	1.96	0.13	1.09	0.01	1.71	−0.99
Food & Kindred Products	1.68	0.26	0.03	−0.01	0.94	0.45
Textile Mill Products	1.32	0.13	−0.43	−0.03	0.17	1.49
Apparel and Textiles	0.39	0.15	−0.62	−0.02	0.24	0.63
Lumber and Wood	1.53	0.04	0.44	−0.03	0.80	0.28
Furniture and Fixtures	3.81	0.26	0.71	0.04	2.26	0.55
Paper & Allied	1.67	0.36	0.10	−0.02	0.88	0.36
Printing and Publishing	1.97	0.72	0.57	0.02	1.03	−0.37
Chemical Products	2.04	0.52	0.05	0.00	1.10	0.38
Petroleum Refining	0.48	0.06	−0.08	0.39	−0.31	0.42
Leather Products	−1.95	−0.11	−1.10	−0.03	−0.93	0.21
Stone, Clay and Glass	2.10	0.18	0.14	−0.03	1.01	0.80
Primary Metals	0.48	−0.01	−0.32	−0.19	0.12	0.88
Fabricated Metals	2.34	0.23	0.14	0.01	1.40	0.56
Machinery, non-electrical	7.30	0.47	−0.03	0.00	3.20	3.66
Electrical Machinery	9.15	0.99	0.18	0.01	3.19	4.76
Motor Vehicles	4.87	0.17	0.28	0.02	4.41	0.00
Other Transportation Equipment	1.21	0.29	−0.32	0.01	1.05	0.18
Instruments	3.21	0.61	0.02	0.00	1.72	0.87
Rubber and Misc. Plastic	4.61	0.42	0.70	0.05	2.00	1.43

Table 3.6   (continued)

	Output	Input contributions				Productivity
		Capital	Labor	Energy	Materials	
Miscellaneous Manufacturing	2.12	0.27	0.28	−0.01	1.04	0.53
Transport and Warehouse	2.92	0.26	0.97	0.04	1.23	0.42
Communications	3.17	1.49	0.41	0.06	1.49	−0.28
Electric Utilities	1.97	0.79	−0.05	0.26	0.40	0.55
Gas Utilities	−2.72	0.41	−0.11	−1.69	0.02	−1.36
Trade	3.50	0.93	0.86	0.02	1.05	0.64
FIRE	4.04	1.58	0.70	0.04	1.64	0.08
Other Private Services	4.06	0.86	2.05	0.02	1.61	−0.49
Public Services	1.62	0.73	0.88	0.00	0.00	0.00

Notes:
Output and productivity are average annual growth rates.
Capital, labor, and intermediate inputs are average annual contributions (share-weighted growth rates).

points for TFP, 0.17 for non-energy materials and −0.43 for labor. While the TFP growth in Primary Metals is not very large in absolute terms, it is larger than output growth; of the 0.48% output growth, TFP contributed 0.88 points, labor −0.32, and energy materials −0.12.

At the other end of the productivity performance scale there are seven industries with negative TFP growth (Public Services has zero TFP growth by definition). Gas Utilities has the worst with −1.36%, followed by Construction −0.99%, Metal and Non-metal Mining −0.84% and Other Private Services −0.49%. The perplexing phenomenon of negative productivity growth at the industry level in the US was a primary motivation for much research, for example, Gullickson and Harper (1999). One possible interpretation of negative productivity growth is a failure to account for changes in quality in the measurement of output. An alternative explanation is that negative productivity growth reflects worsening input efficiency due to such factors as rising barriers to entry, growing inflexibility in the allocation of labor, and health and safety regulations.

In the majority of industries, however, the dominant input contribution comes from non-energy intermediates. In the ranked contributions in Figure 3.3, Motor Vehicles is at the top with the highest materials contribution, 4.41 percentage points of the 4.87% annual growth in output. The

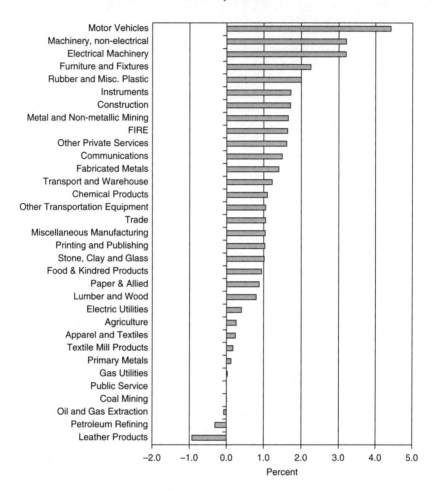

Figure 3.3   Non-energy materials contribution, 1980–2000

two IT manufacturers have the next largest materials contributions reflecting their purchases of semiconductors and other IT components. In Machinery, materials contributed 3.20 percentage points of the 7.3% output growth, just slightly less than 3.66 points for TFP. In Electrical Machinery, materials contributed 3.19 points and TFP 4.76 points to the 9.15% output growth rate. The other industries with large materials contributions are Furniture, Rubber and Instruments. At the other end, the two shrinking industries, Oil & Gas Extraction and Leather, had negative materials growth. The contribution of non-energy intermediates was also negative for Petroleum Refining.

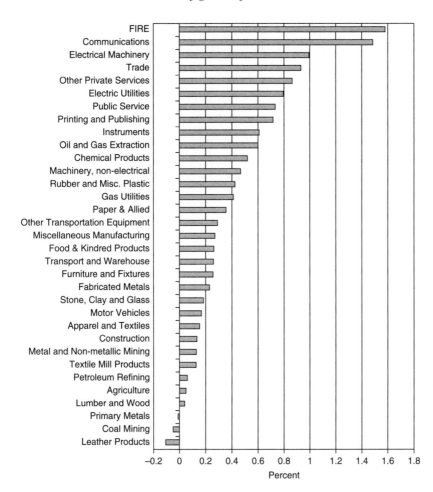

Figure 3.4   Capital contribution, 1980–2000

Energy intermediates are important for the energy-related industries and less so for the others. In Petroleum Refining, of the 0.48% growth in output, energy intermediates contributed 0.39 percentage points, non-energy intermediates −0.31, and TFP 0.42. In Electric Utilities, of the 1.97% output growth, energy intermediates contributed 0.26 percentage points, non-energy intermediates 0.40, capital 0.79 and TFP 0.55. A total of 13 industries had negative energy contributions.

We have noted that investment in tangible assets is an important contributor to the growth of aggregate GDP. As shown in Figure 3.4, the contributions of capital input are positive for every industry, except for Coal

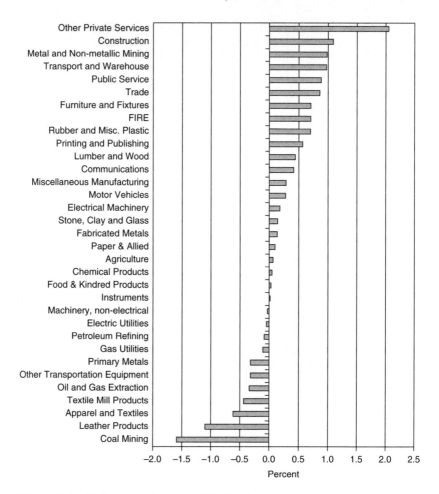

Figure 3.5   Labor contribution, 1980–2000

Mining, Leather, and Primary Metals. The contribution of capital input was largest in Finance, Insurance and Real Estate (1.58 points out of the 4.04% output growth), Communications (1.49 out of 3.17%) and Electrical Machinery (0.99 out of 9.15%). Industries where capital made a major contribution to output growth include Electric Utilities (0.79 out of 1.97%), Printing & Publishing (0.72 out of 1.97%), Public Services (0.73 out of 1.62%), Apparel (0.15 out of 0.39%), and Trade (0.93 out of 3.5%).

In Section 4 we noted the rise in the use of college-educated workers even though total hours grew only modestly in this period. In Figure 3.5 we see that labor input contribution is largest in Other Private Services where the

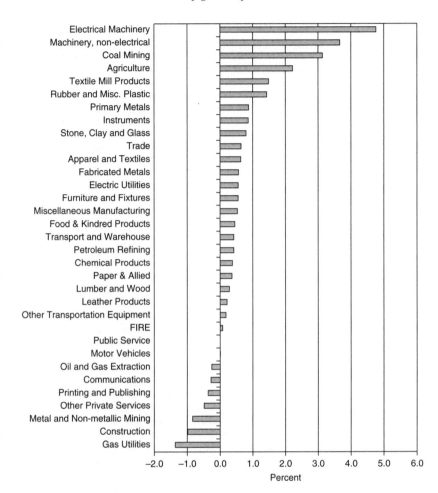

Figure 3.6   Total factor productivity growth, 1980–2000

4.06% output growth is decomposed to 2.05 for labor, 1.61 for materials, 0.86 for capital, and −0.49 to TFP. The other industries with large labor contributions are Construction (1.09 percentage points out of 1.96% output growth), Metal & Non-metal Mining (0.98 out of 1.93%), and Transportation (0.97 out of 2.92%). The contributions of labor input are negative for eleven industries: Coal Mining (−1.59 out of 1.30%), Apparel (−0.62 out of 0.39%), and Leather (−1.10 out of −1.95%).

In a competitive environment productivity gains would be passed on to the purchasers in the form of lower prices. In order to see how relative prices have changed we calculated the growth rate of industry output price relative

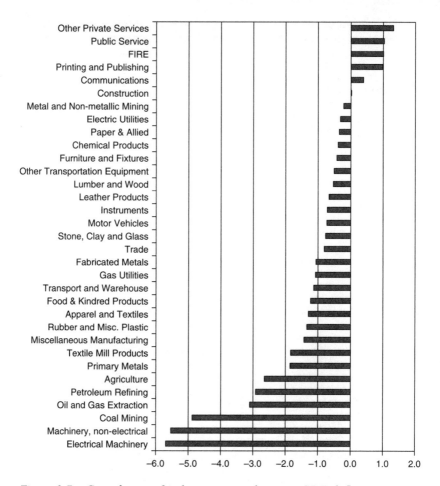

*Figure 3.7　Growth rate of industry price relative to GDP deflator,
1980–2000*

to the GDP deflator for the 1980–2000 period. This is shown in Figure 3.7,
ranked in order from the biggest decline to the biggest rise relative to the
aggregate price. The two IT industries with the largest TFP growth indeed
had the largest fall in prices; the price of Electrical Machinery fell at an
annual rate of 5.69% while the price of Machinery fell at 5.54%. Coal
Mining had the next fastest TFP growth (3.14% per year) and its price fell
at a remarkable pace of 4.88%. Agriculture had a 2.22% TFP rate and its
price fell at 2.65%. Note that these are domestic output prices; the price to
purchasers includes the imported component.

The industries with negative TFP growth have poor price performance, although not necessarily the worst. Other Private Services had the biggest price rise relative to the GDP deflator, at 1.32% per year (TFP was −0.49%), followed by Finance, Insurance & Real Estate at 1.01% (TFP 0.08%), Printing & Publishing at 0.98% (TFP −0.37), and Communications at 0.39% (TFP −0.28%). The industry with the infamous negative productivity growth, Construction (−0.99%), had price growth virtually equal to the GDP deflator. While the correlation between TFP and price behavior is not perfect, it is close and is consistent with a competitive view of the modern US economy. The link between market structure, innovation and price behavior is complex, but at the level of classification used here we may say quite definitively that poor TFP growth (due to whatever reason) led to high price growth.

b) Decomposing Labor Productivity

In addition to total factor productivity, Equation (3.32) gives the sources of *average labor productivity* (ALP) growth in terms of capital and intermediate input deepening, and labor quality growth. Capital deepening is the product of the value share of capital and the growth rate of capital input per hour worked. Energy and non-energy intermediate deepening is defined analogously. The contribution of labor quality to labor productivity growth is the product of the value share of labor and the growth rate of labor input per hour worked. Finally, productivity growth contributes point-for-point to labor productivity growth.

Our decomposition of industry labor productivity (ALP) growth for the period 1980–2000 is given in Table 3.7. Labor productivity is defined simply as output per hour worked, so the rate of ALP growth is rate of output growth (Table 3.2) minus the growth of hours worked (Table 3.5). Electrical Machinery and Machinery have the highest growth rates of output for this period 1980–2000, and also have the highest growth rates of labor productivity, 9.20% and 7.97% per year respectively. These are followed by Coal Mining (6.76%), Instruments (3.78%) and Leather (3.45%). Three industries had negative growth of ALP, Gas Utilities (−1.20%), Construction (−0.47%) and Metal & Non-metal Mining (−0.32%). The huge Other Private Services showed a small positive 0.29% growth in ALP; JHS (2005) showed that the many components of Services – Health, Legal, Education, and Business Services – had negative ALP growth in the 1977–2000 period. Ignoring the Public Services which had zero TFP growth by definition, the other poor performers are Lumber (0.29%), Transportation (0.68%) and Printing & Publishing (0.92%).

As the discussion of the sources of output growth in part (a) above indicates, we expect material input to have the largest contribution to labor

Table 3.7   Sources of growth in industry labor productivity, 1980–2000

	ALP	Capital deepening	Energy deepening	Materials deepening	Labor quality	TFP
Agriculture	2.93	0.13	−0.02	0.47	0.12	2.22
Coal Mining	6.76	1.36	0.68	1.35	0.24	3.14
Metal and Non-metallic Mining	−0.32	−0.03	−0.04	0.45	0.13	−0.84
Oil and Gas Extraction	1.89	1.54	−0.17	0.68	0.10	−0.26
Construction	−0.47	−0.02	−0.03	0.39	0.17	−0.99
Food & Kindred Products	1.87	0.27	0.00	1.09	0.06	0.45
Textile Mill Products	3.42	0.29	0.04	1.52	0.08	1.49
Apparel and Textiles	3.14	0.37	0.02	1.93	0.18	0.63
Lumber and Wood	0.29	−0.14	−0.05	0.05	0.15	0.28
Furniture and Fixtures	2.59	0.14	0.02	1.61	0.27	0.55
Paper & Allied	1.76	0.37	−0.02	0.92	0.12	0.36
Printing and Publishing	0.92	0.56	0.00	0.57	0.15	−0.37
Chemical Products	2.31	0.56	0.03	1.24	0.10	0.38
Petroleum Refining	2.55	0.20	1.88	0.03	0.01	0.42
Leather Products	3.45	0.54	0.06	2.35	0.29	0.21
Stone, Clay and Glass	2.19	0.18	−0.01	1.05	0.18	0.80
Primary Metals	2.84	0.23	0.00	1.64	0.11	0.88
Fabricated Metals	2.35	0.20	0.02	1.40	0.17	0.56
Machinery, non-electrical	7.97	0.54	0.01	3.53	0.22	3.66
Electrical Machinery	9.20	1.00	0.02	3.20	0.21	4.76
Motor Vehicles	3.33	0.05	0.01	3.20	0.07	0.00
Other Transportation Equipment	2.29	0.36	0.02	1.55	0.19	0.18
Instruments	3.78	0.66	0.01	1.94	0.31	0.87
Rubber and Misc. Plastic	2.93	0.26	0.00	1.10	0.14	1.43
Miscellaneous Manufacturing	1.95	0.25	−0.01	0.94	0.24	0.53
Transport and Warehouse	0.68	−0.06	−0.09	0.26	0.14	0.42
Communications	2.29	1.21	0.03	1.15	0.17	−0.28
Electric Utilities	2.59	1.13	0.30	0.53	0.09	0.55

Table 3.7 (continued)

	ALP	Capital deepening	Energy deepening	Materials deepening	Labor quality	TFP
Gas Utilities	−1.20	0.72	−0.82	0.23	0.02	−1.36
Trade	1.99	0.72	−0.03	0.50	0.16	0.64
FIRE	2.10	0.91	0.02	0.94	0.15	0.08
Other Private Services	0.29	0.36	−0.04	0.32	0.13	−0.49
Public Services	0.98	0.55	0.00	0.00	0.42	0.00

Notes:
Average labor productivity and TFP are average annual growth rates.
Capital deepening, intermediate deepening, and labor quality are average annual
contributions (share-weighted growth rates).

productivity growth in most industries. We indeed see this, as no industry
had a negative material input contribution. The largest material contribution to ALP is in Machinery (3.53 percentage points), Electrical Machinery
(3.20) and Motor Vehicles (3.20). The smallest materials contribution is in
Petroleum Refining and Lumber. The roles of TFP in Equations (3.30) and
(3.32) are identical, giving a point for point contribution, and no separate
discussion is needed here for ALP.

The contribution of capital deepening to labor productivity growth is
positive for all industries except for Metal & Non-metal Mining, Lumber
and Transportation. The greatest contributions are in Coal Mining (1.36
percentage points), Communications (1.21) and Electric Utilities (1.13). As
shown in Table 3.5, labor quality growth was positive in all industries and
so the contribution to LP is also positive for all 33 industries. Ignoring
Public Services, the industry with the largest labor quality contribution is
Instruments, with 0.31 percentage points, followed by Leather (0.29) and
Furniture (0.27).

c) Sources of acceleration in 1995–2000

We now turn to the sources of growth in various sub-periods in order to
identify the proximate causes of the remarkable growth resurgence during
1995–2000. In Section II we have already discussed Table 3.2 giving the
output growth for the 1980–90, 1990–95, 1995–2000 sub-periods. Tables 3.8
to 3.12 give the contributions of capital, labor, energy, materials and TFP
to output growth for these three sub-periods, respectively.

Let us begin with productivity growth, shown in Table 3.12 for the sub-
periods. During the resurgence of economic growth after 1995, Machinery

Table 3.8   Contribution of industry capital input by sub-period

	1980–2000	1980–90	1990–95	1995–2000
Agriculture	0.05	−0.16	0.15	0.38
Coal Mining	−0.05	−0.34	0.21	0.27
Metal and Non-metallic Mining	0.13	−0.07	0.10	0.54
Oil and Gas Extraction	0.60	1.33	−0.62	0.37
Construction	0.13	−0.06	0.10	0.55
Food & Kindred Products	0.26	0.20	0.23	0.43
Textile Mill Products	0.13	0.06	0.20	0.18
Apparel and Textiles	0.15	0.16	0.23	0.06
Lumber and Wood	0.04	−0.08	0.02	0.29
Furniture and Fixtures	0.26	0.27	0.12	0.38
Paper & Allied	0.36	0.44	0.26	0.30
Printing and Publishing	0.72	0.78	0.37	0.92
Chemical Products	0.52	0.35	0.61	0.77
Petroleum Refining	0.06	0.06	0.20	−0.07
Leather Products	−0.11	−0.05	−0.25	−0.06
Stone, Clay and Glass	0.18	−0.03	−0.09	0.89
Primary Metals	−0.01	−0.14	0.01	0.22
Fabricated Metals	0.23	0.13	0.16	0.49
Machinery, non-electrical	0.47	0.36	0.36	0.79
Electrical Machinery	0.99	0.78	0.86	1.56
Motor Vehicles	0.17	0.07	0.22	0.30
Other Transportation Equipment	0.29	0.42	−0.08	0.41
Instruments	0.61	0.59	0.48	0.78
Rubber and Misc. Plastic	0.42	0.26	0.46	0.73
Miscellaneous Manufacturing	0.27	0.22	0.22	0.41
Transport and Warehouse	0.26	−0.04	0.25	0.86
Communications	1.49	1.32	1.31	2.00
Electric Utilities	0.79	1.28	0.20	0.42
Gas Utilities	0.41	0.28	0.41	0.68
Trade	0.93	0.84	0.78	1.26
FIRE	1.58	1.62	1.00	2.07
Other Private Services	0.86	0.83	0.66	1.13
Public Services	0.73	0.89	0.61	0.54

Note: All figures are average annual contributions (share-weighted growth rates).

and Electrical Machinery achieve double-digit output growth rates.
Productivity growth in Electrical Machinery accelerated steadily throughout the period 1980–2000, but the industry emerged as the leader in productivity growth only after 1990. Coal Mining had the fastest TFP growth
during 1980–90 with 3.24% per annum, followed by Agriculture, with

Table 3.9   Contribution of industry labor input by sub-period

	1980–2000	1980–90	1990–95	1995–2000
Agriculture	0.06	−0.07	0.31	0.08
Coal Mining	−1.59	−1.32	−1.87	−1.85
Metal and Non-metallic Mining	0.98	0.88	0.47	1.68
Oil and Gas Extraction	−0.34	−0.29	−0.46	−0.33
Construction	1.09	1.00	0.56	1.79
Food & Kindred Products	0.03	−0.03	0.15	0.03
Textile Mill Products	−0.43	−0.33	−0.07	−1.02
Apparel and Textiles	−0.62	−0.29	0.05	−1.95
Lumber and Wood	0.44	0.34	0.71	0.37
Furniture and Fixtures	0.71	0.74	0.66	0.68
Paper & Allied	0.10	0.27	0.07	−0.21
Printing and Publishing	0.57	0.97	0.29	0.05
Chemical Products	0.05	0.14	−0.14	0.05
Petroleum Refining	−0.08	−0.08	−0.07	−0.12
Leather Products	−1.10	−1.06	−0.65	−1.63
Stone, Clay and Glass	0.14	−0.14	0.28	0.57
Primary Metals	−0.32	−0.61	−0.08	0.02
Fabricated Metals	0.14	−0.22	0.51	0.48
Machinery, non-electrical	−0.03	−0.29	0.18	0.27
Electrical Machinery	0.18	0.19	−0.04	0.38
Motor Vehicles	0.28	0.13	0.66	0.18
Other Transportation Equipment	−0.32	0.68	−3.02	0.38
Instruments	0.02	0.51	−1.16	0.21
Rubber and Misc. Plastic	0.70	0.83	0.83	0.31
Miscellaneous Manufacturing	0.28	0.17	0.61	0.19
Transport and Warehouse	0.97	0.79	1.37	0.94
Communications	0.41	0.33	0.27	0.73
Electric Utilities	−0.05	0.33	−0.40	−0.43
Gas Utilities	−0.11	−0.03	−0.07	−0.30
Trade	0.86	0.97	0.77	0.74
FIRE	0.70	0.86	0.29	0.81
Other Private Services	2.05	2.46	1.30	1.99
Public Services	0.88	1.15	0.49	0.75

Note: All figures are average annual contributions (share-weighted growth rates).

3.15%. The two IT manufacturers were ranked third and fourth before 1990. The well-known remarkable improvement in Electrical Machinery is seen in our data; its TFP growth rose from 2.29% during 1980–90, to 5.89% during 1990–95, to 8.60% during 1995–2000. A slightly more muted, but

Table 3.10 Contribution of industry energy input by sub-period

	1980–2000	1980–90	1990–95	1995–2000
Agriculture	−0.04	−0.09	−0.04	0.08
Coal Mining	−0.19	0.31	−0.85	−0.54
Metal and Non-metallic Mining	0.01	0.00	0.00	0.03
Oil and Gas Extraction	−0.86	−0.95	−1.33	−0.21
Construction	0.01	−0.02	0.04	0.04
Food & Kindred Products	−0.01	−0.02	−0.02	0.02
Textile Mill Products	−0.03	−0.05	−0.03	0.00
Apparel and Textiles	−0.02	−0.01	−0.04	−0.02
Lumber and Wood	−0.03	−0.10	0.02	0.04
Furniture and Fixtures	0.04	0.02	0.00	0.12
Paper & Allied	−0.02	−0.02	0.03	−0.06
Printing and Publishing	0.02	0.02	−0.01	0.04
Chemical Products	0.00	−0.02	0.04	0.02
Petroleum Refining	0.39	−1.15	−1.07	4.94
Leather Products	−0.03	−0.06	−0.07	0.07
Stone, Clay and Glass	−0.03	−0.19	−0.05	0.30
Primary Metals	−0.19	−0.35	−0.03	−0.01
Fabricated Metals	0.01	−0.02	0.00	0.09
Machinery, non-electrical	0.00	−0.02	0.01	0.04
Electrical Machinery	0.01	−0.02	0.04	0.06
Motor Vehicles	0.02	0.02	0.02	0.03
Other Transportation Equipment	0.01	0.03	−0.07	0.04
Instruments	0.00	0.00	−0.02	0.03
Rubber and Misc. Plastic	0.05	0.03	0.07	0.07
Miscellaneous Manufacturing	−0.01	−0.03	−0.01	0.03
Transport and Warehouse	0.04	−0.13	0.01	0.41
Communications	0.06	0.01	0.08	0.12
Electric Utilities	0.26	0.34	0.11	0.25
Gas Utilities	−1.69	−2.51	−0.39	−1.33
Trade	0.02	−0.02	0.01	0.10
FIRE	0.04	0.06	0.01	0.04
Other Private Services	0.02	−0.01	0.02	0.08
Public Services	0.00	0.00	0.00	0.00

Note: All figures are average annual contributions (share-weighted growth rates).

still remarkable, pattern held for Machinery. The closest performer among manufacturing industries is Primary Metals, with TFP growth rates of 0.36%, 0.50% and 2.29% during these sub-periods. Electric Utilities also had rapid improvement from −0.58% to 1.09%, to 2.29%. Other industries

Table 3.11   Contribution of industry materials input by sub-period

	1980–2000	1980–90	1990–95	1995–2000
Agriculture	0.26	−0.31	0.57	1.09
Coal Mining	−0.01	0.31	−0.63	0.00
Metal and Non-metallic Mining	1.65	1.22	0.59	3.58
Oil and Gas Extraction	−0.07	0.00	−0.67	0.37
Construction	1.71	1.26	0.64	3.69
Food & Kindred Products	0.94	0.93	0.98	0.93
Textile Mill Products	0.17	0.33	0.94	−0.90
Apparel and Textiles	0.24	0.44	2.67	−2.60
Lumber and Wood	0.80	0.53	2.35	−0.22
Furniture and Fixtures	2.26	1.52	1.64	4.35
Paper & Allied	0.88	1.44	1.65	−1.03
Printing and Publishing	1.03	1.77	0.13	0.45
Chemical Products	1.10	1.33	0.86	0.86
Petroleum Refining	−0.31	−0.84	−0.33	0.79
Leather Products	−0.93	−1.37	−2.01	1.02
Stone, Clay and Glass	1.01	0.17	0.80	2.90
Primary Metals	0.12	−1.06	2.09	0.52
Fabricated Metals	1.40	0.52	1.56	3.01
Machinery, non-electrical	3.20	1.56	4.38	5.31
Electrical Machinery	3.19	1.16	5.12	5.34
Motor Vehicles	4.41	3.40	5.63	5.21
Other Transportation Equipment	1.05	1.13	−2.30	4.26
Instruments	1.72	1.19	1.58	2.92
Rubber and Misc. Plastic	2.00	2.21	2.65	0.95
Miscellaneous Manufacturing	1.04	0.41	1.77	1.57
Transport and Warehouse	1.23	1.31	1.34	0.95
Communications	1.49	0.89	1.52	2.67
Electric Utilities	0.40	0.54	0.20	0.34
Gas Utilities	0.02	0.06	−0.04	0.01
Trade	1.05	0.89	1.02	1.39
FIRE	1.64	1.46	1.12	2.51
Other Private Services	1.61	1.39	1.46	2.22
Public Services	0.00	0.00	0.00	0.00

Note: All figures are average annual contributions (share-weighted growth rates).

with steady progress are Apparel, Furniture, Leather, Fabricated Metals, and Other Transportation Equipment.

Moving in the opposite direction are Construction where the TFP growth fell from −0.48% to −1.41%, to −1.59%; Metal & Non-metal Mining which

68   *Productivity in Asia*

Table 3.12   Growth of industry total factor productivity by sub-period

	1980–2000	1980–90	1990–95	1995–2000
Agriculture	2.22	3.15	0.88	1.71
Coal Mining	3.14	3.24	3.13	2.93
Metal and Non-metallic Mining	−0.84	−0.33	−1.24	−1.46
Oil and Gas Extraction	−0.26	−1.93	1.95	0.89
Construction	−0.99	−0.48	−1.41	−1.59
Food & Kindred Products	0.45	0.47	0.71	0.15
Textile Mill Products	1.49	1.06	1.64	2.21
Apparel and Textiles	0.63	0.19	0.21	1.94
Lumber and Wood	0.28	1.59	−2.14	0.09
Furniture and Fixtures	0.55	−0.12	0.38	2.07
Paper & Allied	0.36	0.02	−0.39	1.80
Printing and Publishing	−0.37	−0.57	−0.84	0.51
Chemical Products	0.38	0.51	−0.02	0.50
Petroleum Refining	0.42	1.96	1.80	−4.04
Leather Products	0.21	−1.22	−0.11	3.39
Stone, Clay and Glass	0.80	1.00	0.24	0.94
Primary Metals	0.88	0.36	0.50	2.29
Fabricated Metals	0.56	−0.11	0.95	1.52
Machinery, non-electrical	3.66	2.39	4.01	5.85
Electrical Machinery	4.76	2.29	5.89	8.60
Motor Vehicles	0.00	0.04	−0.45	0.35
Other Transportation Equipment	0.18	−0.11	0.05	0.90
Instruments	0.87	1.03	0.57	0.84
Rubber and Misc. Plastic	1.43	1.53	1.28	1.39
Miscellaneous Manufacturing	0.53	0.96	0.13	0.08
Transport and Warehouse	0.42	0.73	0.56	−0.36
Communications	−0.28	−0.46	0.05	−0.26
Electric Utilities	0.55	−0.58	1.09	2.29
Gas Utilities	−1.36	−1.79	−2.15	0.29
Trade	0.64	0.78	0.33	0.67
FIRE	0.08	−0.16	0.72	−0.09
Other Private Services	−0.49	−0.49	−0.44	−0.52
Public Services	0.00	0.00	0.00	0.00

Note: All figures are average annual contributions (share-weighted growth rates).

fell from −0.33% to −1.24%, to −1.46%; and Transportation which fell from 0.73% to 0.56%, to −0.36%. Other Private Services had negative TFP growth of about −0.5% in all three sub-periods. The pattern of negative productivity growth is discussed by JHS (2005). We note here that we find negative TFP growth in all sub-periods. JHS (2005) argue that this requires an explanation beyond the popular allegation of persistent errors of measurement.

Since the contribution of non-energy intermediate input is the most important one for most industries, the change in its contribution is also an important component of the change in output growth (see Table 3.11). In Electrical Machinery, its contribution rose from 1.16 percentage points in 1980–90, to 5.12 in 1990–95, to 5.34 in 1995–2000, tracking the changes in output (4.39% to 11.9% to 15.9%). Machinery had a similar pattern change in material contribution. In the largest industry, Other Private Services, the materials contribution rose from 1.39 to 1.46 to 2.22 percentage points, which is not exactly parallel to output growth (4.17% to 3.01% to 4.88%).

As output growth accelerated from the 1980–90 period to the boom period, energy input contributions also rose significantly, as shown in Table 3.10. In the 10-year period after the second oil shock, 21 industries had negative energy input contributions, but in the boom period when oil prices were much lower, only six industries had negative contributions. There was continual energy conservation in the Electric Utilities sector where energy input growth was slower than output growth; the energy contributions were 0.34, 0.11 and 0.25 percentage points during the three sub-periods when output growth was 1.91%, 1.19% and 2.87% per year respectively.

The contribution of capital input rose noticeably during this period, as shown in Table 3.8. During 1980–90, nine industries had negative capital contribution whereas only two were negative during 1995–2000 (Petroleum Refining and Leather). Finance, Insurance and Real Estate has the biggest capital contributions, 1.62 percentage points during 1980–90, 1.00 during 1990–95, and 2.07 during 1995–2000. Following close behind is Communications with 1.32, 1.31 and 2.00 percentage points. The other industries with large capital contributions during 1995–2000 were Electrical Machinery, Trade and Other Private Services.

The change in labor input is quite varied among the 33 industries as shown in Table 3.9. Negative labor input contributions were seen in all periods. Even in the booming Electrical Machinery sector, the labor input contribution changed from 0.19 points in 1980–90 to −0.04 in 1990–95, to 0.38 in 1995–2000. The substitution away from labor is illustrated by the pattern in Printing & Publishing, where labor contribution was 0.97 points when output growth was 2.97% during 1980–90, and was 0.05 points when output growth was 1.97% during 1995–2000. The big service sectors which had above-average growth rates saw positive labor contributions in all three sub-periods – Transportation, Trade, FIRE, Other Private Services and Public Services.

Table 3.13   Growth of industry labor productivity by sub-period

	1980–2000	1980–90	1990–95	1995–2000
Agriculture	2.93	3.56	1.30	3.30
Coal Mining	6.76	6.62	6.29	7.52
Metal and Non-metallic Mining	−0.32	−0.15	−0.75	−0.23
Oil and Gas Extraction	1.89	1.22	2.34	2.80
Construction	−0.47	−0.36	−0.90	−0.27
Food & Kindred Products	1.78	2.06	1.53	1.49
Textile Mill Products	3.42	3.43	3.54	3.30
Apparel and Textiles	3.14	1.81	3.90	5.03
Lumber and Wood	0.29	1.45	−1.17	−0.57
Furniture and Fixtures	2.59	1.20	1.99	5.97
Paper & Allied	1.76	1.52	2.04	1.96
Printing and Publishing	0.92	0.79	0.01	2.10
Chemical Products	2.31	2.18	2.65	2.25
Petroleum Refining	2.55	1.90	2.25	4.15
Leather Products	3.45	1.26	0.85	10.45
Stone, Clay and Glass	2.19	1.69	1.21	4.17
Primary Metals	2.84	2.27	3.63	3.21
Fabricated Metals	2.35	1.32	2.44	4.31
Machinery, non-electrical	7.97	5.58	8.94	11.79
Electrical Machinery	9.20	4.82	12.24	14.90
Motor Vehicles	3.33	2.91	2.44	5.05
Other Transportation Equipment	2.29	0.93	1.78	5.51
Instruments	3.78	3.04	4.23	4.82
Rubber and Misc. Plastic	2.93	2.68	3.66	2.69
Miscellaneous Manufacturing	1.95	2.22	1.27	2.10
Transport and Warehouse	0.68	0.96	0.38	0.41
Communications	2.29	1.61	2.85	3.09
Electric Utilities	2.59	0.90	3.37	5.19
Gas Utilities	−1.20	−3.29	−1.06	2.84
Trade	1.99	1.75	1.79	2.69
FIRE	2.10	1.47	2.71	2.75
Other Private Services	0.29	−0.23	0.36	1.27
Public Services	0.98	1.09	1.11	0.62

Note: All figures are average annual contributions (share-weighted growth rates).

Finally, to complete the record, Table 3.13 gives the labor productivity growth rates by sub-periods. There is the same steady acceleration in labor productivity growth as in the growth of TFP in Machinery and Electrical Machinery. Coal Mining had the fastest ALP growth during the first sub-period 1980–90, followed by the two IT manufacturers and Agriculture.

In the boom period 1995–2000, the IT leaders had ALP growth rates above 11% per year, followed by Leather, with 10.4%, Coal Mining, with 7.52%, and Furniture, with 5.97%. Construction and Metal & Non-metal mining are the only industries that exhibited a decline in ALP growth for all three sub-periods.

VI. CONCLUSIONS

We have given an account of the sources of growth for the 33 industries in the International Comparison of Productivity (ICPA) Project. Our approach embodies internationally recommended standard practices for productivity measurement, as presented by Schreyer (2001) in the *OECD Productivity Manual*. We have incorporated data on output and intermediate input from a time series of inter-industry transactions tables, allowing us to track the remarkable decline in the prices of electronic components. We identified the role of the changing composition of capital and labor by employing detailed capital flow data and demographic data.

Jorgenson, Ho and Stiroh (2005) concluded that the gross output methodology is key to identifying the role of IT intermediate inputs, something that could not be done with a value added approach. It also concluded that using capital stock as a measure of capital input and hours worked as a measure of labor input, misses important compositional changes. Our results reinforce those conclusions.

Investments in capital assets and higher education stand out as the most important sources of growth at the industry level, reflecting our previous work on measuring the aggregate economy (Jorgenson et al., 2004). The changes in the quality of capital show that almost all sectors invested heavily in IT assets, but the total capital contribution also indicates the role of large investments in non-IT assets. Labor input grew slowly on average but it was an important source of growth for the biggest services industries. The rise in labor quality in all industries also indicates the widespread shift towards college-educated workers, even in industries usually labeled as low-skilled.

The growth of total factor productivity is an important source of growth, but less significant in economic terms than capital and labor. While the amazing TFP growth of the IT industries makes headlines, many of the largest industries had low, or even negative productivity growth. Even in the boom period of 1995–2000, seven of the 33 industries had negative TFP growth.

In this brief period of twenty years we see substantial restructuring of the American economy in response to the progress of information technology, changing consumption demands, and expanding international trade. The structure of output is shifting away from low-skilled manufacturing toward the IT-producing industries, but even more substantially toward the IT-using industries. The service industries are expanding to meet the demand of an older, richer, population for health services and income-elastic personal services. The capital deployed in the economy is moving rapidly toward short-lived assets such as information technology equipment and software. Finally, the composition of the workforce is evolving toward more college-educated workers as investments in higher education continue to rise. We can expect these changes to continue.

At the international level, it will be interesting to trace the diffusion of IT technology as it moves across countries for a particular industry, and to explore how the changes in the pattern of international trade affect productivity growth in each country. The rapid productivity gains of the IT producers in the US affected the other US industries with some lag, and will certainly affect IT users in other countries. This study is a first step in this research.

NOTES

*   This chapter has been prepared for the International Comparison of Productivity among Pan-Pacific Countries (ICPA) Project of the Research Institute of Economy, Trade and Industry, Tokyo. The authors thank Jon Samuels for excellent research assistance. The views expressed are those of the authors and do not necessarily reflect those of the Federal Reserve System or the Federal Reserve Bank of New York.

1.   Models of the interactions among semiconductor, computer, and other industries are presented by Triplett (1996) and Oliner and Sichel (2000).

2.   In Jorgenson et al. (2005), Figure 6.6, we show that the average wage of those with four years of college education rose from 136% of the high school wage in 1980 to 146% in 1991, and 153% in 2000.

3.   The Standard Industrial Classification (SIC 1987) codes for these items are: coal (12), oil and gas (13), refining (29), electricity (491, part 493), gas (492, part 493, 496).

4.   The same subscript *i* is used in the numerator and denominator of Equation (3.3) to avoid the proliferation of symbols; the different references should be obvious. This applies to similar expressions throughout the chapter.

5.   For example, the hotel industry produces the services of both 'hotels' and 'restaurants'.

6.   The 1992 tables are described in *Survey of Current Business*, November 1997, p. 36. There is a set of I/O tables for 1997; however, it uses a different classification, NAICS, and is not included in our work.

7.   We are grateful to Charles Bowman, Carl Chentrens and James Franklin of the BLS for providing these data. The I/O data are available at www.bls.gov/emp/.

8.   The aggregation process involves reallocating special sectors like scrap, rest of the world, inventory valuation adjustment, general government, and so on. These are reallocated to the 33 sectors and final demand in accord with both Use and Make matrices.

9.   These data were kindly provided by Jay Berman of the BLS. The data are available at www.bls.gov/emp/empind2.htm.

10. These data are available from the 'Gross Output by Detailed Industry' file on the BEA's website www.bea.gov/bea/dn2/gpo.htm. The data are described in Lum and Moyer (2000).

11. These GDP by Industry data are described in Lum and Moyer (2000), and are available at www.bea.gov/bea/dn2/ gdpbyind_data.htm. A major issue is that they are not consistent with the value added data in the benchmark inter-industry transactions tables (see BEA, 1997). We maintain the total of value added for each industry estimated in the BLS tables and allocate it in the same proportions as those in GDP by Industry. This gives us values of capital income, labor income, and taxes that sum to the BLS values.
12. Another difficulty with the GDP by Industry data is that the series prior to 1987 is based on SIC-1972 while recent data are based on the SIC-1987. Data are provided for both classifications in 1987 and we have adjusted the old classification to the new one, using the shares of each of the old industries in the new industries for 1987.
13. This formulation of the cost of capital means that assets with higher depreciation rates, or where capital losses are expected ($\pi_{k,j,t} < 0$), have higher service prices. Jorgenson and Stiroh (2000) and Oliner and Sichel (2000) discuss the importance of incorporating asset-specific revaluation terms for information technology assets experiencing rapid downward revaluations.
14. More precisely, Equation (3.14) applies to estimates for the corporate sector. As discussed in Jorgenson and Yun (2001, Chapter 2), tax considerations vary by legal form of ownership – corporate, non-corporate and household – and our empirical work takes this into account.
15. In our earlier work in Jorgenson et al. (1987) this allocation assumed that the nominal rate of return in the non-corporate sector matched the estimated nominal after-tax rate of return in the corporate sector. Non-corporate labor income was then estimated as residual. For many of the small industries, however, this led to unstable estimates of average wages and labor quality.
16. We comment more on the pattern on capital input growth after a discussion of TFP growth in Section V.
17. These classes are for 1992+; for years prior to 1992 we follow the official system and have (0–8 years, 1–3 years HS, 4 years HS, 1–3 years college, 4 years college, 5+years college). For the link year 1992 we use both classifications.
18. The BLS reports include *Employment and Earnings, Special Labor Force Reports* and *BLS Bulletins*. Other unpublished tabulations such as the educational attainment of self-employed and unpaid family workers were kindly provided by Tom Hale and Tom Nardone of the BLS.
19. We thank Mike Dove and Scott Segerman of the DMDC for making these data available to us.
20. *Survey of Current Business*, August 2001, Tables 6.4C, 6.7C, 6.8C give the most recent data. The time series is available at www.bea.gov. The industry classification in NIPA was revised from the 1972-SIC to the 1987-SIC. To obtain a consistent time series we transformed all the data prior to 1987 to the new basis using the 1987 data which is provided for both classifications.
21. *Survey of Current Business*, August 2001, Table 6.9C. Kurt Kunze kindly provided separate information for total military hours.
22. We are grateful to Larry Rosenblum of the BLS and Eldon Ball of the ERS for generously sharing their unpublished data with us.
23. *Survey of Current Business*, August 2001, Table 6.2C, 6.3C.

REFERENCES

Baily, Martin N. (2002), 'The new economy: post mortem or second wind', *Journal of Economic Perspectives*, **16**, 3–22.
Bartelsman, Eric J. and J. Joseph Beaulieu (2004), 'A consistent accounting of US productivity growth', FEDS Discussion Series 2004–55, Federal Reserve Board, Washington.

Berndt, Ernst R. and Melvyn A. Fuss (1986), 'Productivity measurement with adjustments for variations in capacity utilization and other forms of temporary equilibrium', *Journal of Econometrics*, **33**, 7–29.

Blades, Derek (2001), *Measuring Capital: A Manual on the Measurement of Capital Stocks, Consumption of Fixed Capital, and Capital Services*, Paris: OECD.

Bonds, Belinda and Tim Aylor (1998), 'Investment in new structures and equipment in 1992 by using industries', *Survey of Current Business*, December, pp. 26–33.

Bureau of Economic Analysis (BEA) (1999), *Fixed Reproducible Tangible Wealth in the United States, 1925–94*, Washington: US Department of Commerce.

Bureau of Economic Analysis (BEA) (1997), 'Note on alternative measures of gross product by industry', *Survey of Current Business*, November, pp. 84–5.

Bureau of Labor Statistics (BLS) (1993), 'Labor composition and US productivity growth, 1948–90', *Bureau of Labor Statistics Bulletin 2426*, Washington: US Department of Labor.

Federal Reserve Board (1995), 'Balance sheets for the US economy', Release C.9, June.

Federal Reserve Board (1997), 'Flow of funds accounts of the United States', Release Z.1.

Fernald, John G. and Shanthi Ramnath (2004), 'The acceleration in US total factor productivity after 1995: The role of information technology', *FRB Chicago Economic Perspectives*, **28**, Q1 2004, pp. 52–66.

Fraumeni, Barbara (1997), 'The measurement of depreciation in the US national income and product accounts', *Survey of Current Business*, July, pp. 7–23.

Gullickson, William (1995), 'Measurement of productivity growth in US manufacturing', *Monthly Labor Review*, July, pp. 13–37.

Gullickson, William and Michael J. Harper (1999), 'Possible measurement bias in aggregate productivity growth', *Monthly Labor Review*, February, pp. 47–67.

Herman, Shelby W. (2000a), 'Fixed assets and consumer durable goods', *Survey of Current Business*, April, pp. 17–30.

Herman, Shelby W. (2000b), 'Fixed assets and consumer durable goods for 1925–99', *Survey of Current Business*, September, pp.19–30.

Jaeger, David A. (1997), 'Reconciling the old and new census bureau education questions: recommendations for researchers', *Journal of Business and Economic Statistics*, **15**, 300–309.

Jorgenson, Dale W. (1995), 'Productivity and economic growth', in Dale W. Jorgenson (ed.), *International Comparisons of Economic Growth*, Chapter 1, Cambridge: The MIT Press, pp. 1–88.

Jorgenson, Dale W. (2001), 'Information technology and the US economy', *American Economic Review*, **91**, 1–32.

Jorgenson, Dale W. and Kevin J. Stiroh (2000), 'Raising the speed limit: US economic growth in the information age', *Brookings Papers on Economic Activity*, **1**, 125–211.

Jorgenson, Dale W. and Kun-Young Yun (2001), *Lifting the Burden: Tax Reform, the Cost of Capital and US Economic Growth*, Cambridge: The MIT Press.

Jorgenson, Dale W., Frank M. Gollop and Barbara M. Fraumeni (1987), *Productivity and US Economic Growth*, Cambridge: Harvard University Press.

Jorgenson, Dale W., Mun S. Ho and Kevin J. Stiroh (2004), 'Will the US productivity resurgence continue?', *Federal Reserve Bank of New York Current Issues in Economics and Finance*, **10**(13), December.

Jorgenson, Dale W., Mun S. Ho and Kevin J. Stiroh (2005), *Information Technology and the American Growth Resurgence*, Cambridge: The MIT Press.

Lane, Richard N. (1999), 'Appraisal report "Large Aerospace Firm" Personal Property', Los Angeles County, 1 March, 1995, Revised 1 February.
Lum, Sherlene K.S. and Brian C. Moyer (2000), 'Gross domestic product by industry for 1997–99', *Survey of Current Business*, December, pp. 24–35.
Oliner, Stephen D. (1993), 'Constant-quality price change, depreciation, and the retirement of mainframe computers', in Murray F. Foss, Marilyn E. Manser and Allan H. Young (eds), *Price Measurement and Their Uses*, Chicago: University of Chicago Press, pp. 19–61.
Oliner, Stephen D. (1994), 'Measuring stocks of computer peripheral equipment: theory and application', Washington: Board of Governors of the Federal Reserve System, May.
Oliner, Stephen D. and Daniel E. Sichel (2000), 'The resurgence of growth in the late 1990s: is information technology the story?', *Journal of Economic Perspectives*, **14**, 3–22.
Oliner, Stephen D. and Daniel E. Sichel (2002), 'Information technology and productivity: where are we now and where are we going?', *Economic Review*, Federal Reserve Bank of Atlanta, July, pp. 15–44.
Schreyer, Paul (2001), *OECD Productivity Manual: A Guide to the Measurement of Industry-Level and Aggregate Productivity Growth*, Paris: OECD.
Spence, A. Michael (1973), 'Job market signaling', *Quarterly Journal of Economics*, **87**, 355–74.
Triplett, Jack E. (1996), 'High-tech industry productivity and hedonic price indices', *Industry Productivity, International Comparison and Measurement Issues*, Paris: OECD, pp. 119–42.
Triplett, Jack E. and Barry Bosworth (2002), 'Services industries and US productivity acceleration: contributions of IT and MFP', presented at the *New Economy Conference*, Texas A&M, 19 April.
Unicon Research Corporation (2002), 'CPS Utilities', Santa Monica: Unicon Research Corporation.
United Nations (1993), *System of National Accounts 1993*, New York: United Nations.
Whelan, Karl (2002), 'Computers, obsolescence, and productivity', *Review of Economics and Statistics*, **84**, 445–62.

4. Total factor productivity growth in Chinese industries, 1981–2000

Ruoen Ren and Lin lin Sun[1]

I. INTRODUCTION

China has become an important trading nation over the last two decades. Its exports rose from US$9.7 billion in 1978 to US$593 billion in 2004, boosting its share of world exports from 0.8% to 6.7%. While 6.7% may seem a small number, it is instructive to note that this is enough to put China at the forefront of the East Asian export powerhouses. China is now the largest exporter in the community of non-oil developing Asian economies. It had ranked fifth within this community in 1978, behind South Korea, Taiwan, Hong Kong and Singapore.[2]

China's integration into the international trade and finance systems, and its growing stature in them, has transformed both the international economic landscape as well as its own domestic economic situation. This point is clearly seen in present-day Southeast Asia. With the accession of China into the World Trade Organization (WTO), some foreign companies are moving more of their production operations from Southeast Asia to China. The surprise is that relocation is occurring even though the 1997–98 financial crises in these countries greatly devalued their currencies against China's currency.

After China becomes a member of the WTO, China's industry will face severe challenges from foreign companies both in the domestic and world markets. So the key issue is to improve China's sectoral international competitiveness in order to sustain its economic development and obtain a strong position in the international segmentation of production processes.

The purpose of this study is to analyze the sources of output growth in Chinese industries for 1981–2000. At the industry level, we estimate capital input index by aggregating capital stocks across different asset types, using the share of property income as the weight for each type. At the same time, we combine hours worked by each type of worker using their share of labor compensation to reflect labor quality.

In this study the KLEMS framework is used to assess China's economic performance at the industry level and investigate sectoral international competitiveness based on the total factor productivity analysis.

The chapter is structured as follows: section II outlines the progress in economic reform in China for the past two decades. Section III discusses the construction of output and input data for the sectoral and aggregate growth accounting. Section IV reports the growth rate of productivity in 33 industries of the Chinese economy between 1981–2000. Section V presents the allocation of the growth in aggregate value-added between growth in capital and labor input and changes in TFP. The discussion about the implication of the growth rate of productivity is given in the concluding remarks.

II. THE PROGRESS IN ECONOMIC REFORM

China is undergoing two simultaneous economic processes: it is moving from an autarkic, centrally-planned economy to a market economy that is integrated into the international division of trade; and it is developing from an agriculture-based economy to a modern industrialized economy with a large service sector.

Analyses that have focused only on China's transition from central planning have led to erroneous diagnoses of the mechanisms behind its post-1978 growth. On the other hand, analyses that focus only on the development process will arrive at results that are widely at odds with the predictions of standard neoclassical economic theory, and hence may wrongly conclude that standard economic theory is inapplicable to developing economies. The two key analytical points to remember for comparative analysis are that:

1. Unlike Poland and the Russia Federation, which were urbanized, industrialized economies, on the eve of their respective market reforms, China had a subsistence agricultural economy.
2. Compared with Indonesia and India, China's private sector faced much more severe legal discrimination (it was in fact largely illegal until the mid-1980s); regulation of economic activities in China was both much more pervasive and stringent, and China's state-owned sector was proportionately much bigger.

Table 4.1 shows that China's growth pattern displays the features of a developing economy in transition. China began as an overwhelmingly subsistence peasant economy with 70.5% of its workforce in 1978 in agriculture. The subsequent growth of the industry-dominated secondary industry is

Table 4.1   Transformation of production and employment pattern (%),
            1978–1999

	Structure of GDP			Distribution of Employment		
	Primary	Secondary	Tertiary	Primary	Secondary	Tertiary
1978	41.3	34.0	24.7	70.5	17.3	12.2
1988	28.2	38.8	33.0	59.3	22.4	18.3
1999	17.4	51.8	30.8	50.1	23.0	26.9
2000	15.2	51.3	33.5	50.0	22.5	27.5

typical of a developing economy undergoing industrialization; the share of GDP from agriculture fell from 41.3% in 1978 to 15.2% in 2000, and the secondary sector's share surged from 34.0% to 51.3%.

The dramatic increase in the employment share of the tertiary sector is also typical of a transition economy, because of the suppression of the service sector under central planning. When the suppression of service activities started being relaxed in 1979, the eruption of retail, commercial and transportation firms pushed the tertiary sector share of employment from 12.2% in 1978 to 27.5% in 2000, an increase that exceeded the employment growth of the fast-growing secondary sector. In fact, the preliminary statistics delivered recently from the 2004 Economic Census have indicated that official statistics under-reported the output in the service sector by a quite substantial margin.

The Development and Major Components of China's Economic Reform

Sachs and Woo (1997) described the development and major components of China's economic reform for the past two decades. China's reform strategy after 1978 has best been described as a dual-track approach: the establishment of a market track in parallel to the pre-existing plan track, with the market track increasing in importance over time. The dual-track approach pervades almost every aspect of policy-making: sectoral reform, policy deregulation, enterprise restructuring, regional development, trade promotion, foreign exchange management, central–local fiscal arrangement and domestic currency issuance.

We divided the two decades of China's economic development and reform covered in the current study into four phases. We described the institutional changes during these four phases according to the discussion presented in Qian (1999). Table 4.2 shows the average GDP growth rate in the four main phases of China's economic history, and the contribution of

Table 4.2 Average annual contribution of each sector to structural transformation (%)

Period	GDP growth	Contribution of each sector to GDP growth				Total growth of each sector			
		Primary	Secondary		Tertiary	Primary	Secondary		Tertiary
			Industry	Construction			Industry	Construction	
1979–84	9.1	2.9	2.6	0.6	3.1	29.6	29.7	6.9	33.9
1985–88	10.6	1.0	4.2	1.0	4.4	9.9	39.3	9.0	41.8
1989–91	5.5	1.2	2.5	0.0	1.8	27.6	41.4	−2.4	33.4
1992–99	10.2	0.9	5.7	0.7	2.9	9.0	55.7	6.4	29.0

each sector, measured in percentage points, to the average growth rate. It confirms that industrialization is not only the biggest engine of growth since 1984, it is also getting bigger over time. The industry component of the secondary sector accounted for 39% of the growth in 1985–88, 41% in 1989–91, and 56% in 1992–99. The fact that the composition of China's export swung sharply toward manufactured goods over 1978–99 indicates that the growing access to international trade spurred the growth of industrial firms.

1979–84: Growth led by agriculture sector reforms

In 1979 the government increased the gain procurement price by 20% and also decreased agricultural input prices. During the period of 1970–84, five major reforms are pursued: agricultural reform, opening up the economy, fiscal decentralization, state-owned enterprise reform, and support for commune-brigade enterprises.

In the agricultural sector, the major change was the introduction of the 'household responsibility system', which emerged spontaneously in poor areas, introduced by the peasants themselves. By the end of 1982, 80% of households adopted the 'household responsibility system', and by 1984, almost all of them had done so.

In the external sector, in 1979 the government decided to expand foreign trade and welcome foreign investment. In 1979, the central government decided that two provinces (Guangdong and Fujian) should pursue reform 'one step ahead' of other regions in the country. In 1980 China established four special economic zones. These zones could enjoy lower tax and a special institutional and policy environment and gained more authority over their economic development.

In 1980, a major fiscal reform known as the 'fiscal contracting system' began, which was concerned with the central and provincial relationship. Under the fiscal contracting system, budgetary revenue income was first divided between 'central fixed income', all of which was remitted to the central government, and 'local revenue', which was shared. The contracted share-rates varied from province to province. The new fiscal system was designed to increase the incentives from the local governments for revenue collection and local economic development.

The experiment of state-owned enterprise (SOE) reform started even earlier than agricultural reform. There had been some experiments in reform in some provinces since 1978. In 1979, the central government issued five documents to promote the experience of those provinces nationwide. By 1980, about 60% of SOEs had joined the experiments and obtained some limited autonomy. In 1981, the first document implementing the 'Economic Responsibility System' in industrial SOEs was issued.

In 1983, encouraged by the outstanding performance of the agricultural household contracting system, the responsibility system got a boost in the cities.

In 1979, the central government issued a document to allow provinces to grant tax holidays of 2–3 years to new commune and brigade enterprises. They were no longer restricted to the industries that served agriculture, and included most industries unrelated to agriculture, where previously only state enterprises had had access. They also no longer used only local resources and could sell beyond local markets.

By 1984 the extraordinary success of the agricultural reform had become apparent. In comparison, the SOE reform was disappointing. The industrial sector was much too complicated, involving prices, taxes, finances and enterprises employment, all of them under central planning. From 1984 onwards, the central government started to pursue reform in urban areas by promoting 'dual-track market liberalization' and 'contract responsibility system' in SOEs as two major reform programs.

In 1983, the central government granted the People's Bank of China the authority of a central bank and subsequently transferred commercial operations to four specialized banks: the Agricultural Bank of China, the Industrial and Commercial Bank of China, the People's Construction Bank of China, and the Bank of China. Since 1984, the four specialized banks have been allowed to compete for deposits and loans in each other's previously monopolized markets, and enterprises are allowed to open accounts with more than one bank.

1985–88: Growth led by industrial sector reforms
In 1985, the 'dual-track' was formally in place with the restriction of price ranges of the market track to be within 20% of the planned price removed. Under this system, goods legally carried two prices; a planned price as before, and a true market price, which was not regulated by the government.

From 1987 the government promoted the 'contract responsibility system'. In this system, contracts lasted for at least three years to avoid annual bargaining. By the end of 1987, about 80% of large and medium-sized SOEs adopted the contract responsibility system, and by 1989, almost all SOEs adopted it, which continued through to 1993.

During this period of time, local government at provincial, municipal and county levels gained great influence over credit decisions through the regional branches of the central bank and state specialized banks. As reform proceeded, local government carried more weight. It was directly involved in credit plan formulation, imposed loans on specialized banks, and had the authority to decide whether an enterprise should pay back a loan.

The central government has declared an additional 14 coastal cities as 'coastal open cities', which gave them new authority similar to that of the special economic zones. Each of these open cities also has the authority to set up 'development zones' inside their regions to implement more liberal policies for attracting foreign capital and technology. In 1988, Hainan was added as the largest special economic zone when it became a separate province.

The most significant achievement in this period was made by the fast entry and expansion of urban and rural non-state enterprises. These firms were under harder budget constraints and had better internal incentive structures. They also indirectly benefited from the various reforms aimed at the state sector, such as fiscal decentralization, financial reform, the dual-price system, and expanding the SOEs' autonomy. Joint ventures between domestic and foreign investors mushroomed, especially in the development zones, to take advantage of the more liberal policy. By the end of the 1980s, rural enterprises had already become the pillars of national industry.

1989–91: Growth under the freezing of the 1979–88 growth strategy

An austerity program was implemented in 1989 and 1990 to cool down the over-heated economy. During that period, the conservatives gained political, ideological and military power for a possible reversal of reform. However, all of these efforts failed. Because of the previous decentralizations, some reforms actually accelerated, but in a decentralized way.

Some rural enterprises suffered greatly during the 1989–90 austerity program, when they experienced substantial credit cuts. About three million rural enterprises went bankrupt or were taken over by other enterprises in 1989.

1992 onward: Growth guided by the new doctrine of a socialist market economy with Chinese characteristics

The process of conversion to a private market economy was accelerated. Nationwide reforms reached a new high in 1992. All the price caps imposed on stocks on the Shanghai Stock Exchange were removed, and within three days the stock price index soared by 570%.

Because of the tight monetary policy, market price levels in 1990 declined, and the difference between the planned and market price was also reduced. By 1993, dual-prices had almost ended for most industrial products. In retail, the plan track accounted for only 5%, while in agricultural procurement it accounted for about 10%.

In 1992, most cities along the Yangtze River and the borders of the country were also granted special privileges as coastal cities, and in addition,

Shanghai was granted even more autonomy. As a result, numerous 'development zones' were established to attract foreign and domestic investment, which also gave rise to a real estate boom. Foreign direct investment (FDI) increased from US$4.4 billion in 1991, to US$11 billion in 1992, and further to US$28 billion in 1993 when China became the second largest country to attract FDI, next to the US.

In 1992, the central government issued a new document to enhance the contract responsibility system in SOEs by granting enterprise managers the '14 Rights' of control, covering foreign trade, investment, labor, wages, and so on.

The total employment in township and village enterprises fell from 48.9 million in 1988 to 47.2 million in 1989 and to 45.9 million in 1990, reversing the trend of expansion of more than 10 years. However, because rural enterprises were market oriented and were under hard budget constraints, they adjusted themselves quickly. Rural enterprise employment increased by 10% and 17% in 1992 and 1993 respectively, and the industrial output increased even more, leading the economic recovery.

During the past two and half decades of reform, the most profound structural change came from the entry and expansion of the non-state sector, despite the fact that major reform efforts had been concentrated in the state sector.

The big ideological breakthrough occurred at the Fourteenth Party Congress in 1992 when the Party, for the first time, endorsed the 'socialist market economy' as China's reform goal. In 1993, the central government issued a landmark document on issues concerning the establishment of a socialist market economic structure, which made four major advances in the areas of reform strategy including a rule-based system, building market-supporting institutions, and property rights and ownership.

In 1997, a major breakthrough was made on ownership issues: state ownership was downgraded to a 'pillar of the economy' and private ownership was elevated to an 'important component of the economy'. At this time, the official ideology toward private ownership finally became friendly.

In 1999, private ownership and the rule of law were incorporated into the Chinese Constitution by issuing an amendment of Article 11 of the Constitution which places private businesses on an equal footing with the public sector. The constitutional amendments demonstrated China's commitment to a full market system based on the rule of law (Qian, 1999).

The Process of Economic Opening in China

Chow (2000) has discussed the process of economic opening in China in his 2000 speech as follows:

The open-door policy is an essential element of the economic reform process. It encourages foreign investment and promotes foreign trade. Foreign investment has provided capital, new technology, managerial skill, and training for labor to China. It has introduced a modern managerial system, business practices and a legal framework for conducting business transactions. In addition it has provided competition in the domestic market, and competition has forced domestic enterprises to become more efficient. Foreign trade has enabled the low-cost and high-quality labor in China to produce goods to be sold at higher prices in the world market, thus increasing the compensation to Chinese labor. It has also enabled the import of technology and high-quality capital goods for use in production in China, as well as the import of high-quality consumer goods. The availability of high-quality capital goods improves productive efficiency. The availability of high-quality consumer goods not only increases consumer welfare directly; it also acts as an important competitive force in the Chinese consumer market that stimulates the improvement of the quality of domestically manufactured products.

This process of economic opening has been carried out for the past two decades.

The evolution of trade policy

The first 'Customs Import and Export Tariff Schedule of the People's Republic of China' was issued in 1951 and was in force until 1984. The average tariff rate was 52.9%, with the tariff rate for agricultural products at 92.3%, and the tariff rate for industrial products at 47.7%. The second 'Customs Import and Export Tariff Schedule' was introduced in 1985. The new average tariff rate was 38%, with a rate of 43.6% for agricultural products and a rate of 36.9% for industrial products. The tariff structure was also adjusted. The new tariff rates were 27.2% for intermediate goods, 31.2% for capital goods and 62.6% for consumer goods. Table 4.3 summarizes the deregulation of trade from 1986 to 1996.

Table 4.4 shows the tariff structure for the 1982–98 period, showing that the average tariff rate has declined from 55.6% in 1982 to 17.1% in 1998.

Integration into the global trade and financial systems

The exchange rate was unified at the prevailing swap-market rate in 1994, which led to a depreciation of the official exchange rate of about 50%. The value of trade (exports plus imports of goods and services) was US$20.64 billion in 1978 and US$289.9 billion in 1996. In real terms, the value of trade in 1996 was 4.8 times the value of exports and imports in 1978. The growth and composition of exports are displayed in Tables 4.5 and 4.6. Table 4.7 reports the proportion of production that is exported, and the two most export-oriented manufacturing industries are

Table 4.3   Changes in tariffs, taxes and non-tariff barriers, 1986–1996

	Tariffs and taxes	Non-tariff barriers
1986–91	Rates reduced by 30–85% for 81 of 6300 tariff lines.	
1992	Rates reduced by an average of 7.3% in January and by the same amount again in December for 3596 tariff lines.	Reduction in the number of export goods subject to quota license regulation from 212 to 183.
	Elimination of adjustment tax levied since 1985 on 15 classes of imports.	Eliminated import-quota license requirements for 16 classes of goods.
1993	Rates reduced by an average of 8.8% for 2898 tariff lines.	Elimination of import-quota license requirement for 9 categories of goods (i.e., 283 goods).
1994	Rates reduced for sedans from 220% and 180% (depending on the model) to 150% and 110%.	Stopped issuing mandatory plans for imports and exports.
	'Temporary tariff rates' (tariff reductions) stipulated for 282 tariff lines.	Eliminated import license requirements for 195 goods.
1995		Elimination of import license requirements for 120 goods.
1996	Rates reduced for 4997 tariff lines by an average of 35%.	Elimination of 30% of remaining quotas.
	Rates reduced for all goods to a simple rate of 23%.	

Notes:
Information before 1997 from Zhang Shuguang, Zhang Yansheng and Wan Zhongxin, 1998, *Measuring the Cost of Protection in China*, Institute for International Economics, Washington DC.
Information since 1997 was collected by the authors.

wearing apparel (17.2%), and machinery (10.1%). Table 4.8 shows the destinations of exports, and (excluding Hong Kong because of its middle-man role) the biggest export markets for China are Japan and the United States.

China's capital inflows have mainly been in the form of foreign direct investment (FDI). FDI inflow averaged US$1 billion a year during 1981–86, and grew quite rapidly after that. In 1992, FDI went beyond

Table 4.4   Tariff and its structure in China, %

Goods Category	1982	1985	1988	1991	1996	1998	Decrease rate
1	55.92	43.88	43.88	43.88	31.56	20.6	53.1
2	104.91	39.15	39.56	40.18	23.93	16.9	57.9
3	100.63	40.25	42.93	42.93	28.22	22.7	47.1
4	40.25	62.54	62.68	63.39	41.37	28.7	54.7
5	52.01	22.77	22.75	22.75	5.82	4.5	80.2
6	61.09	34.45	35.82	36.89	18.34	10.9	70.5
7	66.06	36.98	37.29	37.11	23.06	15.2	59.0
8	43.72	66.81	66.81	66.71	34.24	18.1	72.9
9	55.76	47.11	46.95	47.62	18.01	10.4	78.2
10	50.36	19.84	21.78	21.78	21.05	14.3	34.3
11	80.54	61.87	61.89	61.86	30.41	26.6	57.0
12	24.79	90.83	90.83	90.83	46.51	24.3	73.2
13	39.38	46.38	46.17	46.08	25.62	18.3	60.3
14	23.30	23.64	21.67	21.67	23.36	13.8	36.3
15	49.88	29.39	29.49	30.09	14.52	10.5	65.1
16	19.09	28.39	29.33	30.22	19.02	15.0	50.4
17	77.48	19.17	19.88	19.88	33.87	27.0	35.8
18		45.29	47.19	48.39	32.18	15.2	68.6
19		60.00	60.00	60.00	43.24	15.0	75.0
20		71.86	72.37	72.37	41.86	21.4	70.6
21		20.00	20.00	20.00	12.75	10.1	69.5
Average	55.61	43.34	43.77	44.05	27.09	17.1	61.4

Notes:
Simple arithmetic average tariff.
  In 1982, there are 17 categories: 1. Food; 2. Beverages; 3. Marine products; 4. Medicinal materials, rubber and plant products; 5. Wood products; 6. Animal products; 7. Leather products; 8. Mineral products, glass and pottery products; 9. Oil and fats; 10. Chemical products; 11. Textiles and apparel; 12. Paper and products; 13. Metal products; 14. Machinery and electrical products; 15. Instruments; 16. Transport equipment; 17. Miscellaneous goods.
  Since 1985 there have been 21 categories: 1. Animal products; 2. Plant products; 3. Oil and fats; 4. Food and beverages; 5. Mineral products; 6. Chemical products; 7. Plastic and rubber products; 8. Leather products; 9. Wood products; 10. Paper and products; 11. Textiles and apparel; 12. Footwear and caps; 13. Glass and pottery products; 14. Precious metals; 15. Metal products; 16. Machinery and electrical products; 17. Transport equipment; 18. Optical instruments; 19. Weapons; 20. Miscellaneous goods; 21. Artistry products.
  The decrease rates were estimated by comparing the tariff level in 1998 with that in 1991 because the figures in 1982 were not comparable to the figures in the other years.
  The tariffs for 1982–1996 were estimated by Yin Xiangshuo based on *Customs Import and Export Tariffs* (various versions) in his study, while the tariff in 1998 was from the published data issued by China's customs.

Source: Yu, Xiangshuo, 1998, *Process and Consequence of Trade Reform in China*, Shanxi Publisher, Taiyuan, China.

Table 4.5   Growth of trade

	Export & import (US$ billions)	Export (US$ billions)	Purchasing power of US$	Growth rate of export, %
1978	20.64	9.745	1.532	
1979	29.33	13.658	1.38	26.2
1980	38.14	18.191	1.215	17.3
1981	44.02	22.007	1.098	9.3
1982	41.60	22.321	1.035	−4.4
1983	43.61	22.226	1.003	−3.5
1984	53.55	26.139	0.961	12.7
1985	69.6	27.35	0.928	1
1986	73.84	30.942	0.913	11.3
1987	82.65	39.437	0.88	22.8
1988	102.80	47.516	0.846	15.8
1989	111.68	52.538	0.807	5.5
1990	115.44	62.093	0.766	12.2
1991	135.63	71.842	0.734	10.9
1992	165.53	84.94	0.713	14.8
1993	195.71	91.763	0.692	4.9
1994	236.73	121.011	0.674	28.4
1995	280.85	148.78	0.656	19.7
1996	289.90	151.07	0.638	−1.2
1997	202.51	113.82	0.623	−24.6
1998	194.358	110.256	0.600	−3.1
1999				

Note: The purchasing power of the US dollar was calculated based on CPI, 1982–84=1.00.

Source: The Editorial Board of the Almanac of China's Foreign Economic Relations and Trade, *Almanac of China's Foreign Economic Relations and Trade*, China National Economy Publishing House, Beijing, China, various issues.

US$10 billion, which was over 20% of total FDI inflow into developing countries. China is the second largest FDI inflow country after the United States. Table 4.9 shows the distribution of FDI by manufacturing sector.

The great extent to which China's economy has been internationalized is captured succinctly in Table 4.10. It shows that China's exports have risen from 7% of GDP in the 1979–84 period to 19.3% in 1992–99, and imports have climbed from 7.1% of GDP to 17.3%. Trade in manufactured products is becoming the primary channel of international economic interaction. Manufactured exports have increased from 4% of GDP in 1979–84 to 16.5%

Table 4.6 The values of export of goods and services classified by Chinese manufacturing industries in 1973–1992 (in US$ millions)

	Food	Textiles	Wood	Paper	Chemicals	Non-metallic	Metal	Machinery	Other	Total
1973	938	1,354	44	65	251	121	219	129	129	3,250
1974	1,269	1,278	50	76	400	143	343	177	134	3,870
1975	1,287	1,405	48	59	402	146	263	235	163	4,009
1976	1,038	1,674	64	74	450	161	293	275	200	4,230
1977	1,099	1,840	85	70	509	183	283	256	230	4,554
1978	1,336	2,478	111	90	675	211	400	349	261	5,911
1979	1,464	3,566	156	121	1,369	261	555	475	334	8,302
1980	1,862	4,653	199	165	2,498	331	775	551	486	11,519
1981	1,932	5,591	232	187	2,745	344	1,211	725	598	13,566
1982	2,005	5,702	268	164	2,888	319	1,199	675	606	13,826
1983	2,042	6,392	219	176	2,834	288	836	697	601	14,085
1984	1,958	6,811	158	182	2,925	190	761	1,396	915	15,296
1985	2,013	5,953	124	160	2,830	155	739	608	616	13,199
1986	2,519	8,485	170	217	2,680	241	1,027	1,137	1,047	17,524
1987	2,989	11,148	300	273	3,419	352	1,889	1,764	1,224	23,358
1988	4,025	15,900	412	305	4,271	510	2,931	6,010	2,730	37,095
1989	4,330	16,379	541	344	5,185	751	2,495	3,981	2,081	36,087
1990	4,666	20,796	673	350	5,500	1,168	3,428	11,175	4,583	52,340
1991	4,901	25,135	927	384	5,851	1,616	4,104	14,253	5,223	62,394
1992	5,544	32,550	1,490	547	7,242	1,627	4,695	13,479	8,403	75,578

Source: Robert C. Feenstra, Robert E. Lipsey and Harry P. Boen, 1997, 'World trade flows, 1970–1992, with production and tariff data', *NBER Working Paper No. 5910, January*.

Table 4.7   The ratios of export in each industry to the export in total manufacturing (%), 1985–1995

	1985	1986	1987	1988	1989	1990	1991	1992	1993	1994	1995
Food	14.09	13.46	11	10.71	9.86	9.37	8.15	6.49	6.06	5.74	5.53
Beverages	2.39	2.2	1.96	1.57	1.49	1.24	1.08	0.85	0.74	0.54	0.46
Tobacco	0.24	0.23	0.24	0.27	0.35	0.36	0.56	0.58	0.77	0.61	0.71
Textiles	28.36	29.12	29.8	23.94	21.96	17.6	16.55	12.65	11.59	11.56	10.48
Wearing apparel	13.3	15.87	15.3	19.17	20.47	20.5	22.18	22.1	22.26	21.12	17.18
Leather	2.18	2.26	2.3	3.16	3.78	4.85	4.69	5.92	6.68	5.85	5.18
Wood	2.17	2.18	2.27	2.07	2.17	2.13	2.35	2.52	2.66	2.64	2.6
Paper	1.05	0.93	1.14	0.85	0.82	0.71	0.68	0.7	0.77	0.66	0.79
Chemicals	18.89	14.13	12.9	10.94	10.63	10.5	9	7.25	6.74	6.25	7.18
Rubber	0.84	0.86	0.72	0.75	1.03	1.09	1.23	1.9	2.1	2.17	2.23
Non-metallic	1.46	1.72	1.79	1.67	1.99	2.78	3.02	2.26	1.88	2.24	2.45
Metal	4.84	5.3	7.38	8.17	5.95	7.02	7.12	5.91	5.53	5.99	8.44
Machinery	3.58	3.63	3.68	4.07	4.8	5.57	6.24	7.97	8.15	8.19	10.09
Electrical	1.36	2.37	3.42	3.92	4.91	6.26	6.7	9.47	10.24	11.25	12.32
Other	5.24	5.74	6.03	8.75	9.78	10.1	10.45	13.44	13.83	15.18	14.34

Sources: The Editorial Board of the Almanac of China's Foreign Economic Relations and Trade, Almanac of China's Foreign Economic Relations and Trade, China National Economy Publishing House, Beijing, China, various issues; and Customs General Administration of the People's Republic of China, Custom Statistics Year Book of China, Goodwill Information Ltd, Hong Kong, various issues.

Table 4.8 Direction of China's trade (export) (%) (10 largest export destinations)

Country (region) 1979	Share	Country (region) 1980	Share	Country (region) 1981	Share	Country (region) 1982	Share
Hong Kong	0.244	Hong Kong	0.2393	Hong Kong	0.23511	Hong Kong	0.223
Japan	0.202	Japan	0.2217	Japan	0.20889	Japan	0.2178
US	0.044	US	0.0539	US	0.06842	US	0.0725
Romania	0.036	West Germany	0.0391	West Germany	0.03569	West Germany	0.0305
UK	0.035	UK	0.031	UK	0.03228	Singapore	0.0283
West Germany	0.034	Romania	0.0282	Singapore	0.02324	UK	0.0199
North Korea	0.023	Singapore	0.0231	Brazil	0.01575	Brazil	0.017
Italy	0.022	North Korea	0.0206	France	0.01548	France	0.0167
Singapore	0.022	Italy	0.0193	Romania	0.01476	Romania	0.0132
Former Soviet Union	0.018	France	0.0187	Italy	0.01301	Italy	0.0129

Country (region) 1983	Share	Country (region) 1984	Share	Country (region) 1985	Share	Country (region) 1986	Share
Hong Kong	0.243	Hong Kong	0.2244	Hong Kong	0.2217	Hong Kong	0.2799
Japan	0.201	Japan	0.2193	Japan	0.2164	Japan	0.1616
US	0.077	US	0.0942	US	0.1023	US	0.0913
Jordan	0.071	Jordan	0.0518	Singapore	0.0808	Former Soviet Union	0.0447
West Germany	0.038	Singapore	0.0499	Jordan	0.0409	Singapore	0.0396
Singapore	0.028	West Germany	0.0292	Former Soviet Union	0.0374	Jordan	0.0348

Country (region) 1987	Share	Country (region) 1988	Share	Country (region) 1989	Share	Country (region) 1990	Share
Hong Kong	0.349	Hong Kong	0.3844	Hong Kong	0.417	Hong Kong	0.429
Japan	0.162	Japan	0.1663	Japan	0.16	Japan	0.145
US	0.077	US	0.0711	US	0.084	US	0.083
Jordan	0.034	West Germany	0.0312	Former Soviet Union	0.035	Former Soviet Union	0.036
Singapore	0.034	Singapore	0.0311	Singapore	0.032	Singapore	0.032
Former Soviet Union	0.032	Former Soviet Union	0.031	West Germany	0.031	West Germany	0.03
West Germany	0.031	Zaire	0.0205	Netherlands	0.015	Korea	0.0203
Zaire	0.018	Netherlands	0.0157	Italy	0.0136	Netherlands	0.015
Netherlands	0.015	Italy	0.0156	France	0.01	Italy	0.0134
Italy	0.014	Jordan	0.0152	Thailand	0.0095	Thailand	0.0133
UK	0.022	Former Soviet Union	0.0252	West Germany	0.0262	West Germany	0.0313
Brazil	0.018	UK	0.0189	UK	0.0174	UK	0.0192
Former Soviet Union	0.015	Brazil	0.0167	Brazil	0.0163	Poland	0.0152
Italy	0.013	Syria	0.0156	Switzerland	0.0136	Italy	0.0123

Country (region) 1991	Share	Country (region) 1992	Share	Country (region) 1993	Share	Country (region) 1994	Share	Country (region) 1995	Share
Hong Kong	0.447	Hong Kong	0.442	Hong Kong	0.2403	Hong Kong	0.267	Hong Kong	0.242
Japan	0.142	Japan	0.138	US	0.1849	Japan	0.178	Japan	0.191
US	0.086	US	0.101	Japan	0.172	US	0.177	US	0.166
Germany	0.033	Germany	0.0289	Germany	0.04325	Germany	0.039	Korea	0.045

Table 4.8 (continued)

Country (region) 1991	Share	Country (region) 1992	Share	Country (region) 1993	Share	Country (region) 1994	Share	Country (region) 1995	Share
Korea	0.030	Korea	0.0283	Korea	0.03118	Korea	0.0364	Germany	0.038
Singapore	0.028	Russian Federation	0.0275	Russian Federation	0.02934	Singapore	0.021	Singapore	0.024
Former Soviet Union	0.025	Singapore	0.0239	Singapore	0.02447	UK	0.02	Netherlands	0.022
Netherlands	0.015	Netherlands	0.0141	UK	0.02102	Netherlands	0.0187	Taiwan	0.021
Italy	0.013	Italy	0.0129	Netherlands	0.01754	Taiwan	0.0185	UK	0.019
Thailand	0.012	UK	0.011	Taiwan	0.01593	Italy	0.013	Thailand	0.0139

Sources: The Editorial Board of the Almanac of China's Foreign Economic Relations and Trade, *Almanac of China's Foreign Economic Relations and Trade*, China National Economy Publishing House, Beijing, China, various issues.

Table 4.9   Distribution of FDI by economic sectors in manufacturing (%)

	1995	1996	1997	Average
Food manufacturing	7.83	7.59	7.99	7.81
Beverages	3.65	3.78	3.95	3.79
Tobacco	0.1	0.13	0.12	0.12
Textile products	8.59	7.28	6.94	7.60
Wearing apparel	5.01	4.25	4.17	4.48
Leather and footwear	3.34	2.92	2.73	2.99
Wood products & furniture	2.07	1.79	2.14	2.00
Paper products	3.35	3.41	3.78	3.51
Chemicals	9.50	9.88	10.56	9.98
Rubber & plastic	5.65	5.08	5.36	5.36
Non-metallic products	6.55	6.14	6.13	6.27
Metals	8.91	7.59	7.76	8.09
Machinery & transport	14.85	18.62	14.91	16.13
Machinery, electrical	17.34	18.74	20.53	18.87
Other manufacturing	3.26	2.79	2.95	3.00
Total	100	100	100	100

Source: Numbers calculated based on the data from State Statistical Bureau, *China Statistical Yearbook*, China Statistical Publishing House, Beijing, China, various issues.

Table 4.10   Share of China's exports and imports in GDP (%)

Period	Total exports	Manufactured exports	Total imports	Manufactured imports
1979–84	7.0	4.0	7.1	5.1
1985–88	10.9	6.9	14.0	11.9
1989–91	15.1	11.3	14.2	11.6
1992–99	19.3	16.5	17.3	14.4

in 1992–99, and manufactured imports have moved up from 5.1% of GDP to 14.4%.

Throughout this process of economic integration, China has been experiencing an unprecedented period of sustained high growth. This correlation between economic opening and a higher rate of sustained growth in China was no accident. The international development experience leaves no doubt that causality runs powerfully from economic opening to economic growth. Sachs and Warner (1995) showed in a seminal paper on the trade-growth nexus that 73% of (economically) open developing economies had GDP per capita growth rates of more than 3% a year while only 5% of (economically) closed developing economies had annual growth rates higher than 3%. More importantly, Sachs and Warner also showed that open developing economies were catching up with the developed economies, while the closed developing economies were not.

The major approach used in the international comparisons of TFP is the KLEM approach. The KLEM project is a long-term and multinational research cooperation based on the approach which is described in detail in many books and papers (see Jorgenson, Gollop and Fraumeni, 1987; Jorgenson and Stiroh, 2000; Gu and Ho, 2000; and OECD, 2001) and Chapter 2 in this volume. So we will not discuss methodology further here, and will instead further concentrate on data used in the study. In order to apply the KLEM approach to China, we need to construct an internationally comparable database including output, capital, labor, intermediate input and energy data.

III.   CONSTRUCTING OUTPUT AND INPUT INDICES FOR SECTORS

In this section we will describe the construction of the sectoral input and outputs on China for the ICPA (International Comparison of the Productivity among Pan-Pacific Countries (Asian Countries)) project, which is a part of International Comparisons of Productivity and Economic Growth (KLEM).

Output and Intermediate Input

We have estimated the output and intermediate input indices based on a time series of input–output tables specifically compiled for this project. The project has been conducted in a collaborative way, including professional staff from the National Bureau of Statistics of China, who have high level expertise in the statistical methods and data used for the study, and researchers from the academic community who have been working on data issues for China for a long time (Szirmai and Ren, 1995; Szirmai and Ren, 2000; Woo and Ren, 2002).

Because China's national accounting system has been transformed gradually to SNA since 1987, this study used different methods to compile time series of input–output tables before and after 1987. The time series of China's Use tables in this period were constructed in the following three phases.

In the first phase, we compiled aggregate data series including total inputs, total value-added and its components, and final use.

In the second phase, we constructed current price benchmark Use tables for 1981, 1987, 1992 and 1997. From 1987, all tables are in the SNA format, however the industrial classification, statistical coverage and definition have been improved gradually, so all the tables except those for 1997 should be adjusted to conform to the 1997 I/O table in terms of coverage and definition, and scaled to the latest GDP series.

The I/O tables before 1987 are material product input and output tables in the MPS format which only can provide limited information for this study. Therefore, we mainly used the structure of the 1987 Use table as well as the changes of technical parameters between 1981 and 1987 to construct a current price Use table for 1981. We compiled a direct input coefficient for the 1981 Use table in section 33 using this information.

In the third phase, we constructed the 1987–2000 current price Use tables based on the four comparable benchmark tables. The intermediate use was extrapolated using the Kuroda approach.

The value-added of agriculture, manufacture, construction, transportation, communications, trade and other sectors can be derived from national accounting data of gross domestic product. But some of these should be calculated by relevant data such as statistical yearbooks and financial and fiscal data, and then adjusted to conform to national accounting data of gross domestic product. There are two approaches to compile the components of value-added. One approach is to calculate the components of value-added by income approach according to the relevant statistical, accounting and operating data. The other approach is to calculate the components of value-added using the data on the structure of value-added from the input/output survey.

Total final use can be derived from national accounting data of gross domestic product by expenditure approach which include rural household consumption, urban household consumption, government consumption, gross fixed capital formation, changes in inventories, exports, imports and errors. But some of these data need to be appropriately adjusted before the data can be used. For example, imputed consumption of finance and insurance by rural and urban households should be included in rural household consumption and urban household consumption while import duties should be included in imports.

The items in final use were mainly compiled by using rural and urban household surveys, financial accounting, extra-budget data, special investigations on fixed-asset investment composition, custom statistics, balance of payments statistics and related statistical, accounting and operating data.

Sectoral price indices for 33 sectors from 1981–2000 for China (Year 1995=100) were compiled in a way similar to the methods used in the sectoral GDP estimation at constant prices in the current Chinese statistical practice, documented in detail in OECD (2000). On some occasions, the current approach was adjusted according to the ICPA framework.

The sectoral price indices discussed above are commodity price indices. We also constructed V tables (commodity×industry tables) from 1981 to 2000 in order to compile commodity and industry price indices. We have converted commodity price indices to industry price indices using V tables. By using current price Use tables, sectoral commodity and industry indices, we can construct the 1981–2000 constant price Use tables. Xu Xian chun et al. (2005) give the detailed discussion about the study.

Based on the data on output and intermediate input in constant prices by sector from the time series of the input–output table, we have estimated the index of output growth for each sector. To get an index of the growth of intermediate inputs used in industry 'i', we assumed that total intermediate input could be written as a translog function of the various individual inputs. Hence the corresponding index of intermediate input is a translog quantity index of the individual intermediate inputs. Data on real growth of each input, and the current price share of each particular input in the total value of intermediate inputs are needed. This information can be derived from input–output tables.

The Measurement of Labor Input Index

We conducted a sub-project to estimate China's labor input by industrial sector for 1981–2000 based on a KLEM framework formulated in Jorgenson, Gollop and Fraumeni (1987), and an OECD productivity manual (OECD, 2001). Because of the data sources limitation, we have had to start with an estimate of labor input on several benchmark years. Based on the benchmark studies, eventually we will complete the time series of labor input for the whole period of time.

It is important to take into account heterogeneity of the workforce for compiling a labor input index. Hours worked or the numbers in employment are sometimes used as a proxy for labor input. However, labor is heterogeneous in the sense that the different types of labor have different forms of productivity, and labor input could increase if share of hours worked by skilled labor increased, even if total hours worked remained unchanged. The objective of constructing labor input is to measure services provided by labor during the production process by taking into account different qualities among different types of labor.

Labor is typically subdivided into different types by demographical characteristics such as sex and age, and other attributes, like education, employment status, occupation of workers and industrial sectors that the workers are working for. In the ICPA project, four attributes of sex, age, education and industrial sector are employed for the cross-classification of labor.

Three categories of educational attainments are specified in ICPA, (1) junior high school or less, (2) high school and (3) college or above. The problem with these categories in the Chinese case is their inability to capture the major educational improvement of employees, which is reflected in an increase in workers with junior high school education as a share of total employees, and a sharp decline in the share of illiterate and semi-illiterate workers throughout the entire workforce. It is evident that the main educational improvement of workers cannot show up if workers with junior high school education or less are combined into one category, like ICPA does. We therefore modified the categories of educational attainment in ICPA by subdividing the category of lowest education attainment in ICPA into three categories, (1) illiteracy and semi-illiteracy, (2) elementary school and (3) junior high school. The total number of types of employment amounts to 990.

The data on the number of laborers used in the study came from 1982, 1990 and 2000 population censuses and the 1987 and 1995 Sample Population Survey. The data on employment in the population censuses for some years are displayed by four attributes of labor, which are consistent with the cross-classification required in the ICPA project. Therefore an employment matrix by the four attributes can be obtained simply by re-grouping the original data from the population census. For some benchmark years, the population census gives several datasets on employment cross-classified by attributes less than four. In these cases, we applied the iterative proportional fitting technique proposed by Bishop et al. (1975) to obtain most likely estimates of cells in the employment matrix.[3]

Compiling an annual labor input index needs annual data on the number of employed, especially the data on employment breakdown by some attributes. There are two series of data on total number of employed available in current Chinese statistics. One comes from the population censuses and sampling population surveys. The data for years other than benchmark years of the censuses and sampling population surveys are estimated using the annual Population Change Survey. This estimation has been made since 1990.

Another dataset comes from the so-called 'labor force of society' series. These statistics give a breakdown of employment into about 15 sectors, and the summation of employment over sectors has served as the total number of employed for the entire Chinese economy before 1989. But the total number of employed is replaced by figures obtained from population censuses, sampling population surveys and population change survey since 1990. This means that the series of the total number of employed is discontinued in 1990. Young (2003) argued that the 'labor force of society' series is better equipped, albeit not perfectly, than the series from population censuses to track the movement of sectoral distribution of employment, especially the breakdown of the total of those employed in the agricultural and non-agricultural sectors. But as shown in Yue et al. (2005), this might not be the case.[4]

This study relies entirely on population censuses and sampling population surveys, not only for detailed breakdown of employment, but also for the total number in employment. The employment matrices for years other than census years and sampling survey years are derived by interpolation. The interpolated employment matrices are scaled up so that the summation of all types of interpolated employed equals the number of total employed for the years after 1991. This scaling up is impossible for years prior to 1989, as already mentioned above. So for the total number of employed before 1989, the sum of all cells of interpolated employment matrices are actually used as total number in employment in the study.

Hours worked is one of the most important indicators that are lacking in current Chinese statistics. Perhaps the only available data source for hours worked is a 1995 sampling population survey, which gives average working hours by sector (15 sectors) and gender for the week under survey. Average hours worked daily are estimated by sector and gender as average hours worked weekly, divided by six days. The resulting hours worked daily, multiplied by total number of working days for each type of employment, produces hours worked matrices for every year. The total number of working days for each year is estimated by taking into account the total number of holidays, changes in institutional arrangements for hours worked (weekly working days have been reduced from six days to five days since May Day of 1999), and so on. The estimates of hours worked are no doubt error-prone, as institutional arrangements largely dictate working times.

Estimations for the compensation matrix are different for different benchmark years, due to data availability. For 1987, 1995 and 2000 the matrix is compiled based on two sets of labor data. One dataset comes from three rounds of household surveys of income distribution conducted by a team consisting of researchers from The Institute of Economics of Chinese Academy of Social Sciences (CASS) and from other countries. This series of datasets is usually called CHIP (China Income Project) data and gives information on labor compensation by gender, age, education and economic sector. The CHIP data contains information on compensation of both urban and rural workers. Only urban data is used in the study, as income, rather than wages which are specific to individual members of households, is usually earned jointly by family members in rural areas, and it is impossible to allocate the share of jointly earned income to each of the family members.

The other dataset is average compensation of employment by sectors, derived by sector as the ratio of the total compensation from input–output tables compiled for this project to the total number of workers estimated above. Combining the two datasets to generate a full dimension of compensation matrix involves reconciliation of sectoral breakdowns between the two datasets. While sectoral wage rates employ the same sectoral breakdown as in the ICPA project, the breakdown of sectors in CHIP data is rather coarse. In the CHIP data, the total economy is only subdivided into 14 or 15 sub-sectors and there is further breakdown for sectors like mining, manufacturing and public utilities.

Given data availability, our strategy for obtaining a full dimension of compensation matrix is to compile the compensation matrix for every part of the total 33 sectors in the ICPA sectoral classification as a first step, and then to merge them to form a full dimension of compensation matrix. For instance, there are 20 sub-sectors in ICPA classification for manufacturing, from sector 6, Food and dried products, to sector 25, Miscellaneous manufacturing. Compilation of a compensation matrix for the 20 sectors is accomplished by using wage rate by gender, age and education from CHIP and wage rate by sector from ICPA, as mentioned above, and applying the iterative proportional fitting technique.

Two adjustments must be carried out to CHIP data before running the iterative proportional fitting. The first comes from the fact that the CHIP data does not provide a full dimension of compensation matrix by gender (2), age (3) and education (5) and wage range, because some cells are missing, mainly due to the small size of sample in the CHIP survey. The missing figures are fulfilled by predicted values from regression of wage on dummy variables for gender, age and education. The R-squared from such a regression is as high as above 0.80. The second adjustment that needs to be made to the CHIP data is that the wage rates by gender, age and education, after fulfilling the above, are scaled up so that the summation of compensation over gender, age and education for manufacturing is equal to total compensation of manufacturing given in the input–output table.

The method used for manufacturing is also applied to mining and public utilities. For each of the rest of the sectors in ICPA, it either corresponds exactly to a sector in CHIP, for instance, agriculture, construction, finance insurance and real estate and so on, or to a combination of some sectors in CHIP. Finally, we adjusted the wage rates by gender, age and education from CHIP so that the summation of compensation over workers by gender, age and education is identical to the total compensation given in the input–output table for the corresponding sector.

For two other benchmark years of 1982 and 1990, we only have sectoral wage rates, which are derived as a ratio of total compensation by sector from input–output tables to total number in employment of the corresponding sectors. In deriving a full dimension of compensation matrix for 1982, the compensation matrix for 1987 is rescaled so that total compensation for each sector is equal to the compensation of corresponding sectors given in the 1982 input–output table. The same method is used to obtain a compensation matrix for 1990.

The hourly wage matrix is derived by total compensation (wage multiplied by the number in employment from the employment matrix) divided by total hours worked from the matrix of hours worked for each type of employment. Yue et al. (2005) give a detailed discussion about the measurement of labor input.

The Measurement of Capital Input Index

We have estimated data on capital stock and the rental price of capital services for each, cross-classified by asset type-structure, equipment and automobiles. In order to estimate the capital stock under the PIM, we need the investment time series; the capital stock of base period; the depreciation rate and the investment price deflator. The main sources of the investment data used in the current study are the *China Statistical Yearbook on Investment in Fixed Assets* and the *China Statistical Yearbook* for each year.

We used an indirect way to estimate the capital stock of the base period. Based on the indices provided in Maddison's 1995 OECD study (Maddison, 1995a), the GDP time series for 1940–51 in the 1952 prices was estimated. A ratio between investment and GDP for 1933 was estimated in Kung-chia Yeh (1979), which is 0.05. On the other hand, based on his analysis, Feuerwerker (1977) believed that the ratio between the investment and GDP had not exceeded 0.05 before 1949. So we used the ratio of 0.05 to estimate the investment from GDP data for 1940–51. The procedure adopted here depends on the analysis in Feuerwerker (1977). The data for construction and investment for 1931–36 provided in Kung-chia Yeh (1979) were used to estimate the investment on construction for 1940–49. The war damage was allowed for by making reference to the assumption of war damage by Japan made in Maddison (1995a).

We chose the geometrically declining pattern and assumed an asset life of 16 years for equipment, 40 years for structure, and 8 years for automobiles according to the experience in the study on estimation of capital stock in other countries. With our assumption of asset life, the depreciation rate of equipment is 17%, of structure is 8% and of automobiles is 26%.

Although data on investment in auto vehicles is rare, we have estimated the capital stock of auto vehicles by KLEM sector based on limited data. Due to the small amount of data on investment in auto vehicles, we can not obtain the initial capital stock of auto vehicles on a PIM basis. Under the assumption that the gross value of the fixed asset ratio is the same as the capital stock ratio between the auto vehicle industry and the state-owned firms, the initial capital stock is given by: Initial capital stock for auto vehicle in 1980=the gross value of fixed asset of auto vehicle/the gross value of fixed of fixed asset of stated-owned firms * the initial capital stock for state-owned firms in 1980.

We have estimated the initial capital stock for stated-owned firms, which is 426.278 billion yuan. The *China Statistical Yearbook* gives us the gross value of fixed assets of state-owned firms; the gross value of fixed assets for auto vehicles is not available in the official statistical sources, so this has to be estimated. The total auto vehicle volume data in 1980 is 1 782 900 based on the *China Statistical Yearbook*. The revenue of the auto vehicle industry in 1980 (8 601 980 000 yuan), is divided by the sales volume of auto vehicles (222 288) to obtain the average price of autos in 1980: 38 700 yuan. Then we obtain the approximate gross value of fixed asset of auto vehicles, that is, 38 700*1 782 900 yuan. At last, we have the initial capital stock, which is 69 billion yuan.

The investment data published in Chinese statistics publications were divided into three categories: the structure investment, the equipment investment, and other investment. The investment data for auto vehicles is not available. We used the annual domestic revenue for auto vehicles plus the net import value of auto vehicles as the domestic consumption value of auto vehicles.

Since the domestic consumption value of auto vehicles can be divided into two parts: auto consumption by household (which should not be included in the figures for investment in auto vehicles), and auto consumption by businesses, we need further adjustment to the data. At the beginning of the 1980s, auto consumption by household was quite low; however, in recent years auto consumption by household has become more and more important. So, the annual auto volume increment ratio between the households and the whole economy is applied to estimate the consumption by household and by the whole economy. Then we can deduct the auto consumption by household from the auto consumption by the whole economy, and obtain the annual auto vehicle investment. As to the assumption of relative efficiency pattern of auto vehicles, we still use the geometrically declining relative efficiency.

Because land is an important capital input for the agriculture sector, we have estimated the land capital stock for agriculture. We can obtain the infield quantity data from the *China Statistical Yearbook*, but there is no land price data. The official data on land is known to be inaccurate. Various new estimates indicate that official figures under-reported actual acreage by as much as 30–40%. However, it is difficult to judge how this under-reporting varies over time, so in this study we simply use the official data.

Since there has been no land market in China, we have to estimate the land price ourselves. The ordinary methods of estimating the price of land include: surplus method, market comparison method, shadow price method, and the profit discount method. We adopted the profit discount method, which denotes the price of land as:

$$P = a/r \qquad (4.1)$$

where P refers to the land price, a refers to the annual profit, that is the difference between annual cost (including production cost and human cost etc) and the annual revenue, and r refers to the annual discount rate.

From the *China Agriculture Statistical Yearbook*, we can obtain the data about the profit and cost for land. As for the annual discount rate, we select the one-year deposit interest rate. Moreover, as land is used for different purposes, it has different rates of profit associated with it. In order to obtain the price of land in China, we weight land prices according to purpose.

Then the capital stock of land is equal to the land price multiplied by the total sown area of farm crops. For some years (1981, 1982, 1984, 1990), we could not find the price of land, so we used the average price of land for similar years.

The expression for the rental price of capital services can be modified to incorporate property taxes, corporate income tax, value-added tax, and the present value of capital consumption allowances.

$$c = \{[rq_{t-1} + \delta q_t - (q_t - q_{t-1})](1 + h - u(1 + h)z)\}/(1 - u) + q_i^t \tau^t \quad (4.2)$$

where u^t is the corporate income tax rate; τ^t is the property tax rate; h is the value-added tax rate; and z^t is the present discounted value of depreciation allowances of a 1 yuan investment. In order to estimate the capital rental price, we need the data for the depreciation rate, capital gain and return rate. The depreciation rate of assets should be consistent with the depreciation rate used in the estimation of capital stock. As for capital gains, the most common approach consists of approximating expected asset price inflation by the observed change in the price index for assets. The implication is that the asset price changes have been perfectly anticipated by agents. We estimated the internal rate of return with the help of an accounting method that was introduced by Hall and Jorgenson (1967).

For the aggregation of capital services over different asset types, it is assumed that aggregate services are a translog function of the services of individual assets, where weights are given by the average shares of each component in the value of property compensation:

$$V_k = \frac{1}{2}(V_k^t + V_k^{t-1}), \quad \text{with } V_k^t = \frac{p_k^t k_k^t}{\sum_k p_k^t k_k^t}, \tag{4.3}$$

where P_k is the rental price of capital services from asset type k. Sun and Ren (2005) provided a detailed discussion about the measurement of capital input.

IV. SECTORAL OUTPUT AND TFP GROWTH

Output and TFP Growth

In this section, we examine output growth in the 33 industries over the four periods: 1981–84; 1984–88; 1988–94; 1994–2000. The four periods are not chosen arbitrarily. The endpoints of each period are years in which a cyclical peak occurred. We then analyze growth in TFP, capital input, labor input and intermediate inputs. Output growth averaged 9.62% per year across 33 industries during 1981–84. That figure increased to 15.14% per year during 1984–88 and then declined to 11.58% per year during 1988–94 and to 8.3% per year during 1994–2000. TFP growth slowed down from 2.57% annually during 1981–84 to 2.64% during 1984–88 and 1.49% during 1989–94 to 0.17% during 1994–2000.

Table 4.11 summarizes the patterns of output and TFP growth by period. Output growth is negative for lumber and furniture during 1981–84, for oil and gas extraction, coal products during 1984–88, for oil and gas extraction during 1988–94, for finance insurance and real estate during 1994–2000. The number of industries with output growth exceeding 15% per year increased from 7 during 1981–84 to 18 during 1984–88, then declined to 8 during 1988–94 and 2 during 1994–2000. Only electrical machinery experienced growth in output, at rates exceeding 10% in all four periods.

The slowdown in TFP growth became widespread over the course of the four periods. The number of industries experiencing negative TFP growth went from 7 during the period 1981–84 and 1984–88, to 8 over the years 1988–94, and to 16 during 1994–2000. The number of industries with annual TFP growth exceeding 5% declined from 14 during 1981–84 to 10

Table 4.11   Classification of industries by annual rate of growth of output and productivity

Growth rate (%)	1981–84		1984–88		1988–94		1994–2000	
	Output	TFP	Output	TFP	Output	TFP	Output	TFP
<0	2	7	2	7	1	8	1	16
0–5	2	12	2	16	0	22	2	16
5–10	13	14	5	7	12	3	25	1
10–15	9	0	6	3	12	0	3	0
>15	7	0	18	0	8	0	2	0

during 1984–88, to 3 during 1988–94, and to 1 during 1994–2000. Two industries suffered negative TFP over the entire periods – oil and gas extraction; finance insurance and real estate.

Although the slowdown in both output and TFP growth became widespread over the last three periods, some industries did expand. Twenty-one industries saw their output grow faster during 1984–88 than 1981–84, 13 industries experienced faster output growth over 1988–94 than 1984–88, 9 industries experienced faster output growth over 1994–2000 than 1988–94. However, only the communication industry experienced faster output growth in 1984–88, 1988–94 and 1994–2000 relative to the immediately preceding period. On the TFP side, 19 industries experienced faster growth in the second period compared to the first, 10 industries experienced faster growth in the third period compared to the second, and 9 industries experienced faster growth in the last period compared to the third. No industry posted faster TFP growth in each successive period.

The Aggregate Shift in Technology

The aggregate shift in technology can be represented as a weighted sum of industry-level productivity change. Each industry's productivity change is weighted by the ratio of its gross output to total value-added. This is Domar's Aggregation Formula. China has not experienced obvious TFP growth during 1981–2000; on the contrary, many years have negative Domar-weighed TFP. We can measure the Domar-weighted productivity contributions of each industry as the product of the share of that industry's gross output to total value-added and its productivity change (see Table 4.12). Agriculture made the biggest contribution to aggregate TFP during 1981–2000, because the average share of agriculture gross output to total value-added is the largest over the 33 industries during 1981–2000.

Table 4.12   The Domar aggregation TFP index (%)

	Aggregation TFP		Aggregation TFP
1981–82	2.35	1991–92	9.82
1982–83	4.66	1992–93	5.20
1983–84	12.22	1993–94	7.87
1984–85	15.72	1994–95	6.47
1985–86	1.96	1995–96	−1.53
1986–87	1.82	1996–97	2.99
1987–88	0.59	1997–98	−0.50
1988–89	−9.46	1998–99	−0.85
1989–90	−2.55	1999–2000	−4.02
1990–91	10.19		

Input Growth and Its Contribution to Output Growth

Now we attribute growth in output to the growth of capital, labor and intermediate input. Table 4.13 ranks industries by pattern of input growth rate for each period.

The capital input grew quickly during the whole period. Considering the four periods in chronological order, 5, 7, 2 and 7 industries, respectively, experienced annual rates of growth of the capital input in excess of 15%. In 1981–84, 22 industries had a negative capital input growth rate. The number of industries with negative capital input growth declined to 3, 4, 0 industries, during 1984–88, 1988–94, 1994–2000, respectively. Finance insurance and real estate, other private services, and public services had an annual rate of capital growth in excess of 15% during three periods. In China, service and extraction had a high capital accumulation speed during the past years. The average capital input growth across industries was 2.66%, 7.82%, 5.49% and 10.93% during 1981–84, 1984–88, 1988–94 and 1994–2000, respectively.

The average annual labor input growth across industries was 4.41%, 4.02%, 2.15% and 3.87% over the periods 1981–84, 1984–88, 1988–94 and 1994–2000, respectively. In the four periods, 4, 3, 3, 10 had negative labor input growth, and 3, 1, 0, 5 experienced a labor growth rate greater than 10%. Only gas utilities had a labor input growth rate in excess of 5% during the four periods. Among the 33 industries, lumber and wood, furniture and fixtures and gas utilities recorded annual rates of labor input growth exceeding 10% during 1981–84, gas utilities in the period 1984–88, but no industry reached that level during 1988–94; in the last period apparel, leather, gas utilities, trade, finance insurance and real estate experienced labor growth in excess of 10%. Only instruments experienced a labor input decline in excess of 2% per year during 1981–84 and 1984–88, but in 1988–94 lumber and wood, and furniture and fixtures were in that category; during 1994–2000 coal mining, metal and non-metal mining, textile mill products, non-electrical machinery, and instruments all experienced a labor input decline in excess of 2%.

Intermediate input experienced stronger growth than capital input and labor input. Intermediate inputs grew at an annual average of 9.75%, 15.55%, 12.78%, 10.82%, respectively, over the four periods across industries. During 1981–84, 8 industries recorded intermediate input growth in excess of 15% per year. That number increased to 15 during 1984–88 and declined to 8 during 1988–94 and 4 during 1994–2000. Lumber and wood and furniture and fixtures experienced negative intermediate input growth during 1981–84. Oil and gas extraction, petroleum and coal products, and transportation suffered a decline of intermediate input during 1984–88. But no industry had a negative intermediate input growth during 1988–94 and 1994–2000. Electrical machinery, rubber and plastics, and other private services had intermediate input growth rates in excess of 15% over the four periods.

The output growth for each industry is the sum of the contributions of the three inputs (capital, labor and intermediate inputs) and of TFP growth. The contribution of each input is measured as the product of the share of that input in the value of output and of its growth rate. Table 4.14 compares TFP growth with the sum of the contributions of all three inputs to output growth. It shows that input growth is the predominant source of output growth in China for most years. By comparing the contribution of TFP growth with that of each of the three inputs, Table 4.15 provides further insight into these developments. Intermediate input growth is the primary source of output growth in most industries over 1984–88, 1988–94 and 1994–2000. In 1981–84, TFP growth is the primary source of output in most industries. The contribution of capital input becomes more important over the four periods, as this factor was the primary source of output growth in 4 industries during 1981–84, in 4 industries during 1984–88, in 7 industries during 1988–94, and in 6 industries during 1994–2000. The industries that relied on the contribution of the labor input as their primary source of expansion are few; only 1 industry over 1984–88, 1988–94 and 1994–2000.

V. SOURCES OF VALUE-ADDED GROWTH

In this section, we allocate the growth in aggregate value-added between growth in capital and labor inputs and changes in TFP. Our analysis is based on the premise that there exists an aggregate function. As discussed in Jorgenson, Gollop and Fraumeni (1987), this requires a number of restrictive assumptions, but it provides a useful framework for identifying the sources

Table 4.13 Classification of industries by annual rate of growth of three input categories

| Growth rate (%) | Number of industries | | | | | | | | | | | |
| | Labor input | | | | Capital input | | | | Intermediate input | | | |
	1981–84	1984–88	1989–94	1994–2000	1981–84	1984–88	1989–94	1994–2000	1981–84	1984–88	1989–94	1994–2000
<0	4	3	3	10	22	3	4	0	2	3	0	0
0–5	16	16	25	8	2	10	10	4	3	2	0	2
5–10	10	13	5	10	3	10	15	12	13	2	7	15
10–15	2	1	0	5	1	3	2	10	7	11	18	12
>15	1	0	0	0	5	7	2	7	8	15	8	4

Table 4.14   Predominant source of output growth among 33 industries

	Number of industries			
	1981–84	1984–88	1988–94	1994–2000
Input contribution	18	25	27	26
TFP contribution	15	8	6	7

Table 4.15   Primary source of output growth in 33 industries

	Number of industries			
	1981–84	1984–88	1988–94	1994–2000
Capital input contribution	4	4	5	6
Labor input contribution	0	1	1	1
Intermediate input contribution	16	20	20	18
TFP growth	13	8	7	8

Table 4.16   Sources of output growth (%)

	1981–84	1984–88	1988–94	1994–2000	1981–2000
Output growth	9.56%	10.69%	9.07%	8.29%	9.26%
Capital input contribution	1.94%	5.82%	4.20%	5.84%	4.56%
Labor input contribution	1.17%	1.73%	1.04%	1.93%	1.47%
TFP growth	6.45%	3.14%	3.83%	0.52%	3.22%

of economic growth in the aggregate economy. We construct data on the TFP growth by combining price and quantity data for value-added, capital input and labor input. We employ a translog quantity index of TFP growth equal to the difference between the growth rate of value-added and a weighted average of the growth rates of capital and labor inputs. The weights are given by average shares of each input in value-added for the two periods. The contribution of each input is the product of its average share in value-added and its growth rate. Table 4.16 compares the average annual growth of value-added with the contributions of the two primary-factor inputs and the average annual rate of TFP growth for four sub-periods: 1981–84, 1984–88, 1988–94 and 1994–2000, and for the period 1981–2000.

The contribution of capital input is the most significant source of growth for the period 1981–2000 as a whole. Capital input is the most important source for 1984–88, 1988–94 and 1994–2000, and TFP growth is the most important source for only one, 1981–84. The contribution of capital input exceeds the contribution of labor input for all four periods, while the contribution of labor input exceeds TFP growth in only one period. Our overall conclusion is that growth in capital input is the most important source of growth in value-added, TFP growth is the next most important source, and labor input growth is the least important.

VI. CONCLUDING REMARKS

The results of our aggregate function analysis show that the contribution of capital input is the most significant source of value-added growth for the period 1981–2000 as a whole. Capital input is the most important source for 1984–88, 1988–94 and 1994–2000, and TFP growth is the most important source for only one, 1981–84. The contribution of capital input exceeds the contribution of labor input for all four periods, while the contribution of labor input exceeds TFP growth in only one period. Our overall conclusion is that growth in capital input is the most important source of growth in value-added, TFP growth is the next most important source, and labor input growth is the least important.

Intermediate input growth is the primary source of output growth in most industries over the four periods. The contribution of capital input becomes more important over the four periods, as this factor was the primary source of output growth in 4 industries over 1981–84 and 1984–88, in 5 industries over 1988–94, and in 6 industries over 1994–2000. The number of industries that relied on the contribution of labor input as the primary source of expansion is low; only 1 industry over 1984–88, 1988–94 and 1994–2000.

Ho and Jorgenson (2001) attempted to apply the method developed in Jorgenson, Gollop and Fraumeni (1987) to the Chinese data. That was a new step in that direction. The current study should be regarded as an update of those efforts in terms of time covered, and because Jorgenson and Ho have been greatly involved in the current study. During the current project, we have made a great effort to tackle these issues. We have addressed some of the data problems, for example the new time series of input and output tables, capital stocks and labor input data. However, some problems, such as producer price indices, remain unsolved.

NOTES

1. This project was funded by the Research Institute of Economy, Trade and Industry, Tokyo, Japan, National Natural Science Foundation of China (grant no. 70173029) and

Productivity in Asia

the US Environmental Protection Agency (EPA Work Order 3W-0258-NASX). We thank
Dale Jorgenson, Mun Ho, Masahiro Kuroda, Kazuyuk Motohashi, Kazushige Shimpo,
Hiroki Kawai, Hak K. Pyo, Chi-yuan Liang and Marcel Timmer for their advice and com-
ments. E-mail: ruoen8324@vip.sina.com

2. If we regard the bulk of Hong Kong exports to be re-exports of China's products, then
   China ranked third in 1978.
3. In the 2000 Population Census, two types of questionnaire were used: a long form and a
   short form. Data from the long form gives total number of employed, and its detailed information is used in this study. The ratio of number of population from the long table to total
   population which comes from an aggregate of the long form and short form tables is 0.095.
   Original figures on employment from *Tabulation on the 2000 Population Census of People's
   Republic of China* Volume 2 are scaled up by multiplying by 1.0181*(1/0.095) before applying iterative proportional fitting calculations.
4. See Yue et al. (2005) for the reason.

REFERENCES

Bishop, Y., S.E. Feinberg, P.W. Holland, R.J. Light and F. Mosteller (1975), 'Discrete
multivariate analysis: theory and practice', *Contemporary Sociology*, **4**(5), 507–9.
Chow, Gregory (2000), 'China's economic reform and politics at the beginning of
the 21st Century', an invited speech at the Fourth International Investment
Forum on 8 September.
Christensen, L., D. Cummings and D.W. Jorgenson (1980), 'Economic growth,
1947–1973: An international comparison', in J.W. Kendrick and B. Vaccara (eds),
New Development in Productivity Measurement, New York: Columbia University
Press, pp. 595–698.
Conrad, K. (1992), 'Inter-country changes in productivity in the manufacturing
sector of five OECD countries, 1963–86', in B.G. Hickman (ed.), *International
Productivity and Competitiveness*, New York: Oxford University Press.
Feuerwerker, Albert (1977), 'Economic trends in the Republic of China,
1912–1949', *Michigan Papers in Chinese Studies*, no. 31.
Gu, Wulong and Mun Ho (2000), 'A comparison of productivity growth in Canada
and the US', *American Economic Review*, May.
Hall, Robert E. and Dale W. Jorgenson (1967), 'Tax policy and investment behav-
ior', *American Economic Review*, **57**(3) (June), 391–414.
Ho, Mun S. and Dale W. Jorgenson (2001), 'Productivity growth in China,
1981–95', Kennedy School of Government, unpublished draft.
Jorgenson, D.W. and L. Frank (2001), 'Industry-level productivity and inter-
national competitiveness between Canada and the United States', Industry
Canada Research Monograph, Ottawa.
Jorgenson, D.W. and Z. Griliches (1967), 'The explanation of productivity change',
Review of Economic Studies, **34**(3) (July), 249–83.
Jorgenson, D.W. and M. Kuroda (1992), 'Productivity and international competitive-
ness in Japan and the United States, 1960–85', in B.G. Hickman (ed.), *International
Productivity and Competitiveness*, New York: Oxford University Press.
Jorgenson, D.W. and M. Nishimizu (1978), 'US and Japanese economic growth,
1952–1974: An international comparison', *Economic Journal*, **88**(352), 707–26.
Jorgenson, Dale and Kevin Stiroh (2000), 'US economic growth at the industry
level', *American Economic Review*, May.

Jorgenson, D.W., F.M. Gollop and B.M. Fraumeni (1987), *Productivity and US Economic Growth*, Cambridge, MA: Harvard University Press.
Jorgenson, D.W., M. Kuroda and M. Nishimizu (1987), 'Japan–US industry-level comparisons, 1960–79', *Journal of Japanese and International Economies*, 1 (March), 1–30.
Kung-chia, Yeh (1979), 'China's National Income, 1931–1936', in Chi-ming Hou and Tzong-shian Yu (eds), *Modern Chinese Economic History*, Taipei: Academia Sinica.
Maddison, A. (1995a), *Monitoring the World Economy 1820–1992*, Paris: OECD Development Centre.
Maddison, A. (1995b), 'Standardized estimates of fixed capital stock: A six country comparison', in A. Maddison (ed.), *Explaining the Economic Performance of Nations: Essays in Time and Space*, Aldershot, UK and Brookfield, US: Edward Elgar.
Maddison, A. (1998), *The Chinese Economy in the Long Run*, Paris: OECD Development Centre.
OECD (2000), *National Accounts for China. Sources and Methods*, Paris: OECD Centre for Cooperation with Non-Members.
OECD (2001), *Productivity Manual: A Guide to the Measurement of Industry-level and Aggregate Productivity Growth*, Paris: OECD.
Qian, Yingyi (1999), 'The process of China's market transition (1978–98): The evolutionary, historical, and comparative perspectives', paper prepared for the *Journal of Institutional and Theoretical Economics* Symposium on 'Big-bang transformation of economic systems as a challenge to new institutional economics', 9–11 June, Wallerfangen/Saar, Germany.
Ren, R. (1997), *China's Economic Performance in an International Perspective*, Paris: OECD.
Sachs, Jeffrey D. and Andrew Warner (1995), 'Economic reform and the process of global integration', *Brookings Papers on Economic Activity*, Vol. 1, pp. 1–118.
Sachs, Jeffrey D. and Wing Thye Woo (1997), 'Understanding China's economic performance', NBER working paper 5935.
Sun, Lin lin and Ruoen Ren (2005), 'Estimates of capital input index by industries: The People's Republic of China (1980–1999)', paper prepared for the International Comparison of Productivity among Pan-Pacific Countries (Asian Countries), ICPA Project No. 5.
Szirmai, A. and Ruoen Ren (1995), 'China's manufacturing performance in comparative perspective, 1980–1992', *Research Memorandum 581 (GD-20)*, Groningen: Groningen Growth and Development Centre.
Szirmai, A. and R. Ren (2000), 'Comparative performance in Chinese manufacturing, 1980–1992', *China Economic Review*, 11(1), 16–53.
Szirmai, A., M. Bai and R. Ren (2001), 'Labour productivity trends in Chinese manufacturing, 1980–1999', paper prepared for the International Conference on 'The Chinese Economy, Achieving Growth with Equity', 4–6 July, Beijing.
Woo, Wing Thye and Ruoen Ren (2002), 'Employment, wage and income inequality in the internationalization of China's economy', *Employment paper, the International Labor Organization, 2002/39*.
Xu Xian chun et al. (2005), 'A study on an internationally comparable time series of China's use tables: 1981–2000', 15th International Input–Output Conference, Beijing, China PR, 27 June–1 July.
Young, Alwyn (2003), 'Gold into base metals: productivity growth in the People's

Republic of China during the reform period', *Journal of Political Economy*, **111** (6), 1220–61.

Yue, Ximing, Yukun Lin and Ruoen Ren (2005), 'Labor input in China: 1982–2000', paper prepared at the International Comparison of Productivity among Pan-Pacific Countries (Asian Countries), ICPA Project. No.3.

STATISTICAL SOURCES

Census 1985: National Bureau of Statistics (1987–88), *Industrial Census 1985, Vol. I–X*, Office of Leading Group of the National Industrial Census under the State Council, People's Republic of China, China Statistics Press, Beijing (in Chinese).

Census 1995: National Bureau of Statistics (1997), *Census of the People's Republic of China in 1995*, Office of the Third Industrial Census, China Statistics Press, Beijing (in Chinese).

State Statistical Bureau, *China Statistical Yearbook*, China Statistics Press, Beijing, various issues.

State Statistical Bureau, *China Labor Statistical Yearbook*, China Statistics Press, Beijing, various issues.

CIESY: National Bureau of Statistics, *Zhongguo Gongye Jingji Tongji Nianjian*, (Chinese Industrial Economy Statistics Yearbook), Beijing, various issues.

I/O Table 1987: National Bureau of Statistics (1987), Department of Balances of National Economy and Office of the National Input–Output Survey, *Input–Output Table of China 1987*, China Statistics Press, Beijing.

I/O Table 1990: National Bureau of Statistics (1993), Department of Balances of National Economy and Office of the National Input–Output Survey, *Input–Output Table of China 1990*, China Statistics Press, Beijing.

I/O Table 1992: National Bureau of Statistics, P.R. China, Department of National Accounts, *Input–Output Table of China, 1992*, China Statistics Press, 1995.

I/O Table 1995: National Bureau of Statistics, P.R. China, Department of National Accounts, *Input–Output Table of China, 1995*, China Statistics Press, 1997.

I/O Table 1997: National Bureau of Statistics (1999), P.R. China, Department of National Accounts, *Input–Output Table of China, 1997*, China Statistics Press, 1999.

National Bureau of Statistics, Department of National Economic Accounting, *The Gross Domestic Product of China, 1952–1995*, Donghei University of Finance and Economics Press, 1997.

National Bureau of Statistics (State Statistical Bureau)/Institute of Economic Research Hitotsubashi University (1997), *The Historical National Accounts of the People's Republic of China*, 1952–1995, September 1997.

SCIT 2000: National Bureau of Statistics Department of Industry and Transport, *Statistics of China's Industry and Transport, 1949–1999*, China Statistics Press, Beijing, November, 2000.

TVE (1996), The Editing Committee of the Township and Village Owned Enterprises Yearbook of China, *Township and Village Owned Enterprises' Yearbook of China*, 1996 and various issues.

5. Growth accounting and productivity analysis by 33 industrial sectors in Korea (1984–2002)

Hak K. Pyo, Keun-Hee Rhee and Bongchan Ha*

1. INTRODUCTION

In recent years, both growth accounting and productivity analysis by sector have attracted renewed attention on a global scale. The breakdown of inputs into capital (K), labor (L), energy (E), and intermediate materials (M) for detailed industry-level analysis of productivity growth was first applied to the postwar US economy by Jorgenson, Gollop and Fraumeni (1987). The basic KLEM methodology has been extended to cover eight European countries through the European KLEM project as in Timmer (2000) and the Canada–Japan–USA database. In addition, the number of inputs has increased to include imported goods (I), and services (S), forming the framework of the KLEMS methodology as carried out by Forsgerau and Sorenson (1999).

Earlier studies along the lines of the KLEM approach in Korea such as Kwon and Yuhn (1990), the main interests of which were limited to estimating elasticity of substitution and productivity growth, used data in the manufacturing sector only or value-added accounting. More recent empirical works such as Kim and Hong (1997), Pyo (2001), Timmer and van Ark (2000), and Rhee (2001) have also applied value-added accounting. The earlier exception of applying gross-output accounting was Kim and Park (1985), but this study was also limited to the manufacturing sector. Therefore, it would be desirable to attempt a growth accounting of gross output in a consistent KLEM framework approach. In addition to growth accounting, the international comparison of productivity among countries requires a consistent database for purchasing power parity (PPP) at industrial level by country.

The purpose of this chapter is to discuss the application of the KLEM methodology to the Korean database and to present the results of gross output growth accounting and productivity analysis. After a review of available data, a detailed database of consistent output and input data for the Korean economy for the period of 1984–2002 was constructed. According to gross output growth accounting, the Korean economy has recorded a significant growth of gross output at an average rate of 8.04 per cent during the period of 1984–2002. On the other hand, capital (K), labor (L), energy (E), and material input (M) have grown at a rate of 9.36 per cent, 3.15 per cent, 6.68 per cent, and 8.65 per cent respectively during the period. The average estimated share of the four inputs were 0.20 (v_K), 0.20 (v_L), 0.08 (v_E) and 0.52 (v_M) respectively. As a consequence, the total factor input and total factor productivity have increased at an average annual rate of 7.49 per cent and 0.55 per cent respectively. Therefore, the relative contribution of total factor productivity to gross output growth is estimated to be only 6.84 per cent, which is rather insignificant, reconfirming both Krugman's (1994) proposition, and empirical findings by Young (1994) and Lau and Kim (1994). It has also been noted that there was a discernable structural turning point after the 1997 economic crisis in Korea: both capital–gross output coefficient and capital–value-added coefficient started to fall after 1998.

The chapter is organized as follows: section 2 examines the database on Korea, including gross output, four inputs and value-added from national accounts and input–output tables, and other sources of data. Section 3 presents the result of growth accounting and productivity analysis. The last section concludes.

2.   DATABASE FOR KOREA (1984–2002)

2.1   Gross Output Data from National Accounts and Input–Output Tables

National accounts by the Bank of Korea (1999, 2004) report annual series (1970–2002) of gross output, intermediate consumption, GDP, indirect taxes, consumption of fixed capital, domestic factor income, compensation of employees, and operating surplus of 21 industries (including 9 manufacturing industries and 3 sub-sectors of government services) in current prices, following the 1993 UN System of National Accounts.

The Bank of Korea has also published input–output tables since 1960. Its most recent – the 2000 input–output table – is the nineteenth table. A detailed description of the input–output tables for 1970–2000 is given in Table 5A.1 in the appendix. The table for 2000 has 404, 168, 77 and 28 industrial sectors in basic, small, medium and large classifications, respectively. Therefore, if a KLEM model with more than 21 industrial classifications is to be estimated, an estimation of time series input–output tables following those methods described in Kuroda (2001) would be required, since input–output tables are available only in selected years. The I/O tables have been reclassified in Tables 5A.2 and 5A.3 in the appendix.

For the present study, gross output and value-added by 33 industries were generated through the RAS method. The generated annual data of both gross output and value-added have been adjusted to match the National Income Accounts, which contain neither indirect tax nor subsidy. Since the RAS method is sensitive to the I/O coefficients' benchmark year values, the closest years' I/O table data has been used as a benchmark value.

A V-Table (commodity×industry table) was used to generate commodity prices by 33 sectors and then the generated commodity prices were used to estimate output prices by 33 sectors.

2.2 Measurement of Capital Stocks

The success of late industrialization by newly industrializing economies would not have been possible had the rapid accumulation of capital and its changing distribution among sectors not been realized in their development processes. However, it is difficult to identify these factors empirically because the time series data of capital stocks in fast-developing economies, both by types of asset and by industry, are not readily available. The lack of investment data for a period of time long enough to apply the perpetual inventory estimation method is the main cause of the problem. However, the National Statistical Office of the Republic of Korea has conducted nation-wide wealth surveys four times since 1968. Korea is one of a few countries to have conducted economy-wide national wealth surveys at regular intervals. Since the first National Wealth Survey (NWS) was conducted in 1968, surveys were subsequently made every ten years, in 1977, 1987 and 1997. Since such regular surveys with nationwide coverage are very rare in both developed and developing countries, an analysis on the dynamic profile of national wealth seems warranted to examine how national wealth in a fast-growing economy is accumulated and distributed among different sectors.

The estimation of national wealth by types of asset and by industry was made by Pyo (1998) and updated in Pyo (2003) by modified perpetual inventory method and polynomial benchmark-year estimation method, using four benchmark-year estimates. The latter study modifies and extends the earlier one in two respects. Firstly, the results of the 1997 NWS were released in 1999, so additional benchmark-year estimates could be made use of. Secondly, the estimates of capital stocks were re-based from 1990 prices to 1995 prices, which was inevitable as the Bank of Korea had re-based their national accounts accordingly.

2.2.1 National Wealth Survey in Korea

In the National Wealth Survey (NWS), the gross capital stock (*GK*) was evaluated by multiplying the purchase price of the fixed tangible asset by the appropriate price index by type of asset, which had been compiled and prepared by the Bank of Korea dating back to the year 1910, as follows:

$$GK_i = P_i^t \times PI_i^t,$$

where GK_i is the value of gross capital stock of asset *i* evaluated at a certain benchmark year *m* (*m*>*t*), P_i^t is the purchase price of the asset *i* in year *t*, and PI_i^t is the price index to reflect the value of the asset *i* in year *t*. In other words, the gross capital stock is supposed to reflect the repurchase value or re-acquisition value of the fixed tangible asset.

The net capital stock (*NK*) was deduced by multiplying the gross capital stock by the residual cost ratio as follows:

$$NK_i = GK_i \times (S/P_i^t)^{n/N} = P_i^t \times PI_i^t \times (S/P_i^t)^{n/N},$$

where *S* is the value of survived assets, *N* is average service life of the asset, and *n* is the number of years elapsed. In other words, a proportional depreciation method is adopted. The value of survived assets is assumed to be 10 per cent of the purchase value when it reaches the assumed average service life, and 1 per cent of the purchase value when it reaches double the assumed average service life.

Suppose, for example, the average service life of a certain asset such as a personal computer is five years and it was purchased three years ago at a price of \$3000. In addition, assume that the inflation rate of the computer price since the purchase year is 20 per cent. Then the following calculations can be made:

$$GK = 3000 \times 1.2 = 3600, \tag{5.1}$$

$$NK = 3000 \times 1.2 \times \left(\frac{300}{3000}\right)^{\frac{3}{5}}. \tag{5.2}$$

Korea's NWS assumes shorter average lives than BEA (1993). For example, BEA's are 32–80 years for residential structures and 31–48 years for non-residential structures, while Korea's NWS assumes an average service life of 23–60 years for residential buildings and 8–60 years for non-residential buildings. For automobiles, Korea's assumed average life (4–5 years) is shorter than BEA's (10 years). The shorter average life and, therefore, higher depreciation rate are typical in the process of late industrialization.

2.2.2   Estimation of net and gross capital stock

Estimation method for 1968–97   In principle, the existence of four bench-mark year estimates of gross and net capital stocks makes it possible for us to apply the polynomial benchmark year estimation method. In Pyo's earlier studies (1988, 1992 and 1998), he estimated proportional retirement rates and depreciation rates both by types of asset and by industry, based on the polynomial equations.

When the polynomial benchmark year equation was applied to estimate the proportional retirement rates for the sub-periods of 1977–87 and 1987–97, most estimates became negative, including the average economy-wide retirement rates (–3.0 per cent for 1977–87 and −3.1 per cent for 1987–97), except other construction (0.6 per cent) and transport equipment (3.4 per cent) in 1977–87, and non-residential building (0.9 per cent) in 1987–97. Therefore, following Pyo (1998) the polynomial benchmark year estimation method has been applied to estimate depreciation by types of asset only. Thus, net stocks by types of asset for the period of 1968–97 were generated first and then distributed over different sectors of industries by using interpolated industrial weights between the respective benchmark years.

It has been decided that net capital stock will be estimated first, and then gross capital stock will be estimated by using interpolated net–gross conversion ratios. The reason for this is that the margin of prediction error from the polynomial benchmark year equation turns out to be larger with gross capital stock than with net capital stock, as observed in Pyo (1992).

Estimation method for 1953–1967   Since it has been decided that 1968 NWS values will be used as the first benchmark year estimates, capital stocks for the period of 1953–67 must be estimated using the perpetual inventory equation backwards. The net stock data of the 1968 NWS in current prices was deflated into 1995 prices using the implicit GDP deflator of capital formation. Then, capital–output coefficients by industry were estimated by regressing net capital stock in 1995 constant prices on real GDP by industry and a linear time trend variable during the period of 1968–87, in order to generate estimates of net stocks by industries during 1953–67, in 1995 prices. The 1968 NWS weights of different types of asset for the period of 1953–1967 have also been used.

In order to estimate net stocks by industry for the period of 1968–76, both the 1968 NWS and 1977 NWS have been used to estimate interpolated industrial weights by each type of asset. Then, for the period of 1953–67, both cumulated weights of capital formation by industry from old National Accounts by the Bank of Korea (1984) and the industrial weights of the 1968 NWS have been used.

Estimation method after 1997   The National Statistical Office of Korea
decided to terminate the National Wealth Survey in 1997 and to switch
from direct estimation to indirect estimation of national wealth, following
the method of the BEA and OECD. The cost of such direct national wealth
surveys has increased significantly as the size of the national economy has
expanded considerably. In addition, some of the participating institutions,
such as Kookmin Bank for unincorporated business enterprises, have been
privatized, so that the National Statistical Office alone can no longer afford
the national wealth survey. Japan terminated its National Wealth Census in
1970 for almost the same reasons.

   Therefore, for the period after the last national wealth survey in 1997,
capital stocks must be estimated by a modified perpetual inventory method
using 1997 NWS values as benchmark estimates. First, net stocks are estimated by type of asset in constant prices by using the depreciation rates estimated from the period of 1987–97 and distributed across industries using
both industrial weights in the 1997 NWS and those in subsequent Mining &
Manufacturing Censuses and Surveys, and Wholesale and Retail Surveys. In
the long run, the estimated depreciation rates by type of asset may need to be
updated and revised by the micro data-based studies. Second, the generated
net stocks by type of asset and by industry have to be converted into gross
stock by using the net–gross conversion ratio of the 1997 NWS, for the time
being. But, ultimately, further studies on the trend of net–gross conversion
ratio by type of asset and industry and average asset life may be required.

2.2.3   Reconciliation with Pyo (2003) database

Since the database in Pyo (2003) covers 10 broad categories of industrial
sector, together with 28 sub-sectors of manufacturing, it can be reclassified
and reconciled with the 33-sector classification for the ICPA project using
other sources such as the Mining & Manufacturing Censuses and Surveys,
the Wholesale and Retail Surveys, and so on. Pyo (2003) classified assets
into five categories: residential building, non-residential building, other
construction, transportation vehicles, and machinery, while excluding large
animals and plants, household durables, and inventory stocks. Assuming
that the flow of capital service is proportional to capital stock, the average
capital stock of two years was used as the capital service.[1]

   In order to make quality adjustments to the capital input data, the
following steps have been taken:

1.   Following Kuroda (2001), the capital service of asset i in industry j is
     defined as

$$K^{ij}(t) = b^{ij}(t)\bar{A}^{j}(t) \qquad i = 1,..,n; j = 1,...m$$

$$= b^{ij}(t) \cdot \frac{1}{2} [A^j(t) + A^j(t-1)], \tag{5.3}$$

where $b^{ij}(t)$ denotes the proportion of the ith asset type on the jth sector's total capital service input $\bar{A}^j(t)$, which is the average of unweighted sum over all assets during the tth and $(t-1)$th period.

2. The growth rate of capital service input is defined as

$$\ln K^j(t) - \ln K^j(t-1) = [\ln \bar{A}^j(t) - \ln \bar{A}^j(t-1)]$$
$$+ \sum_i \bar{v}_i^j [\ln b^{ij}(t) - \ln b^{ij}(t-1)]$$
$$j=1, 2, \ldots . J, \tag{5.4}$$

where $\bar{v}_i^j$ is the average share of an individual component in the value of property compensation. The first term on the right-hand side is the change in the quantity of capital service and the second term is the change in the quality of the capital service.

The growth rate of the quality of capital was very small in comparison to the growth rate of the quantity of capital. There was no substantial change in the structure of capital in Korea during 1984–2002.

2.2.4 Measurement of capital input price

Following Jorgenson et al. (1987) and Timmer (2000), the aggregate index of capital services over the different types of asset in j-sector ($K_j(t)$) can be assumed as a translog function of the services of individual assets ($\bar{A}_i^j(t)$) as follows:

$$\ln K^j(t) - \ln K^j(t-1) = \sum_i \bar{v}_i^j [\ln \bar{A}_i^j(t) - \ln \bar{A}_i^j(t-1)],$$

where weights are given by the average shares of each type of capital in the value of property compensation, $\bar{v}_i^j = [v_i^j(t) + v_i^j(t-1)]/2$ and $v_i^j(t) = p_i^j(t)K_i^j(t)/\Sigma_i p_i^j(t)K_i^j(t)$ with $P_i(t)$ the rental price of capital services from asset type i.

In order to apply the above aggregation formula, it is necessary to impute the rental prices of capital services. In the absence of taxation, Hall and Jorgenson (1967), Jorgenson et al. (1987) and Jorgenson and Yun (1991) have derived the following formula for imputing the rental price of capital services from asset type i:

$$P_i(t) = \{r(t) + \delta_i - \Pi_i(t)\} q_i(t-1), \tag{5.5}$$

where $r(t)$ is the rate of return, $q_i(t)$ is the acquisition price of investment good i with $\Pi_i(t) = [q_i(t) - q_i(t-1)]/[q_i(t-1)]$ as the rate of inflation in the price of investment good i. The nominal rate of return after tax is usually assumed to be the same for all assets in an industry so that $r(t)$ does not have a subscript i.

The acquisition prices of each asset in different industries are not usually available and, therefore, investment deflators are frequently used as substitutes for the acquisition prices. But, investment deflators in National Accounts are available either by type of asset or by industry, not by both. Estimates of depreciation rates in Pyo (2003) are also available either by type of asset or by industry, not by both.

In the case of Korea, there have been studies by Yun and Kim (1997) and Won and Hyun (2000) on the estimation of effective marginal tax rates following methods developed by King and Fullerton (1984) and Jorgenson and Landau (1993). Since they have used the above formula for cost of capital, they must have generated the imputed cost of capital. But their estimates are based on *whole* industries, not for *each* industry, and even those estimates are not available. Faced with this lack of data and consistent estimates for the variables to impute rental price of capital in each industry, the following approach has been adopted.

In order to get capital input prices that are different both for each asset i and each industry j, Equation (5.5) has been slightly changed to Equation (5.5′), which is the formula of the capital input price both for each asset i and each industry j:

$$P_j^i(t) = \{r_j(t) + \delta_i - \Pi_i(t)\}q_i(t-1). \tag{5.5′}$$

In Equation (5.5′) it has been assumed that the price of investment asset $i(q_i)$, the rate of depreciation of asset $i(\delta_i)$, and the inflation rate of investment asset $i(\Pi_i)$, are identical across all industries, but it has been assumed that the rate of return can be different in each industry.

The application of Equation (5.5′) requires data on the rate of return by industry $j(r_j)$, the acquisition price of investment asset $i(q_i)$, and the rate of depreciation of asset $i(\delta_i)$. As there was no data for the nominal rate of return for each industry, only for the nominal value of capital services summed over all types of asset in the jth industry, the rate of return for each industry $r_j(t)$ was estimated by using the equality between the nominal capital income in the jth industry (CI_j) and nominal value of capital services summed over all types of asset in the jth industry $(\Sigma_i P_j^i(t) \cdot K_i^j(t))$. From this equality the rate of return for each industry, $r_j(t)$, was estimated as follows:

$$CI_j(t) = \sum_i P_j^i(t) \cdot K_i^j(t)$$

$$= \sum_{i} \{r_j(t) + \delta_i - \Pi_i(t)\} q_i(t-1) K_i^j(t)$$

$$r_j(t) = \frac{CI_j(t) - \sum_{i} \{\delta_i - \Pi_i(t)\} q_i(t-1) K_i^j(t)}{\sum_{i} q_i(t-1) K_i^j(t)}. \tag{5.6}$$

Using these nominal rates of return of each industry ($r_j(t)$), the rental price of capital services of each asset and industry could be calculated by adding the depreciation rate and subtracting the inflation rate of capital, and multiplying the result by the price of capital.

2.3 Measurement of Labor Input

In order to measure labor input for the KLEM model, both quantity data of labor input, such as employment by industries and hours worked, and quality factors such as sex, education and age must be obtained. Both availability and reliability of labor statistics in Korea have improved since 1980, but the measurement of labor input by industry cannot be readily made because the statistics of employment by industry are not detailed enough to cover the 33 sectors.

Following the characteristics of labor input described in Kuroda (2001), the sources of labor statistics are presented in Table 5.1. The *Economically Active Population Yearbook* by the National Statistical Office reports the numbers of employed, unemployed, not-economically-active and economically active members of the population by 10 categories of age groupings (15–19, 20–24, 25–29, 30–34, 35–39, 40–44, 45–49, 50–54, 55–59, and over 60). Employment by different industries is available in nine broad categories: (1) Agriculture, Forestry and Fishing; (2) Mining; (3) Manufacturing; (4) Construction; (5) Wholesale, Retail, Restaurants and Hotels; (6) Electricity and Gas; (7) Transportation, Storage and Communication; (8) Finance, Insurance, Real Estate, and Business Services; and (9) Other Services. More detailed classifications of employment will have to rely on the employment table, which is published as a supporting table to the input–output table, but is available only every five years when the main input–output tables are published. The Mining and Manufacturing Census (Survey) by the National Statistical Office also reports employment statistics, but is limited only to mining and manufacturing. Statistics on unemployed persons by gender and educational attainment are also available from the Economically Active Population Survey.

The Monthly Labor Survey by the Ministry of Labor shows figures for the monthly earnings and working days of regular employees by 12–15

Table 5.1   Characteristics of Korean database for KLEM model

(1) Gross output	Number of Sectors
• National Accounts	21
• Input–Output Tables (1980, 1985, 1990, 1995, 2000)	392–402
• U-Table and V-Table Annual Tables (1985–2002)	22
(2) Capital stock (capital services)	
• Gross and Net Stock Data: National Wealth Survey (1987) (1997)	5 types of asset and 10 large industries
• Capital Formation Data: National Accounts (1999, 2004)	with 28 sub-manufacturing
• Annual Gross and Net Stock by Industry and by Type of Asset, and Estimated Depreciation Rates are available in Pyo (2001)	industries
• Net stock and Investment data: Mining and Manufacturing Census; Mining and Manufacturing Survey	
• Type of asset: residential building, nonresidential building, other construction, transport equipment, machinery equipment	
(3) Labor input (hours worked)	18 types
• Survey Report on Wage Structure (Ministry of Labor)	
• Economically Active Population Survey (NSO)	
– *sex* (male/female)	2 types
– *educational attainment* (middle school and under, high school, college and/or above)	3 types
– *age classes* (16–34, 35–54, 55 and above)	3 types
(4) Intermediate inputs	
• National Accounts	
• Input–Output Tables (1980, 1985, 1990, 1995, 2000)	
• U-Table and V-Table Annual Tables (1985–2002)	
• Energy Input: sectors 2, 4, 14, 28, and 29	

broad categories of industry. The Survey Report on Wage Structure (or Basic Statistics of Wage Structure) by the same ministry previously reported wages in six categories of occupational classification (1980–1992) and then changed to report in nine categories (1993–1999): (1) Senior Officials and Managers; (2) Professionals; (3) Technicians; (4) Clerks; (5) Service and Sales Workers; (6) Skilled Agriculture and Fishery Workers; (7) Craftsmen and Assemblers; (8) Plant and Machine Operators; and (9) Other Laborers. Nominal and real wage indices are also available from the Monthly Labor Survey by the Ministry of Labor.

For the present study, the raw-data file of the Survey Report on Wage Structure was obtained from the Ministry of Labor, and the Economically Active Population Survey from the National Statistical Office for the period of 1984–2002. The data are classified into two gender categories (male and female), three age categories (16–34, 35–54, 55 and above), and three education categories (middle school and under, high school, college and/or above); making a total of 18 categories of labor.

Since the raw-data file of the Survey Report on Wage Structure contains a more detailed industrial classification than that of the Economically Active Population Survey, the quantity of labor was calculated from the Economically Active Population Survey and the quality of labor from the Survey Report on Wage Structure. This allowed self-employed workers to be included, as well as allowing the use of more detailed data. However, since the Survey Report on Wage Structure does not include the agriculture and government sectors, the average value of the entire economy had to be used for the quality measure of these two sectors.

In order to make quality adjustments to the employment data, the following steps have been taken:

1. Defining P^j_{Ll} as wage rate for j-sector and l-type category of labor, the share of labor income by l-type category of labor in j-sector can be expressed as:

$$v^j_{Ll} = \frac{p^j_{Ll}L^j_l}{\sum p^j_{Ll}L^j_l}.$$ (5.7)

The average weight of j-sector and l-type labor income during the period of $(t-1)$ and t can be generated as:

$$\bar{v}^j_{Ll} = \frac{1}{2}[v^j_{Ll}(t) + v^j_{Ll}(t-1)].$$ (5.8)

2. In order to make a quality adjustment to labor input data, the labor input of j-sector and l-type have been further decomposed as follows:

$$L^j_l(t) = d^j_l(t)M^j(t)H^j(t),$$ (5.9)

where d^j_l denotes relative weight of working hours of l-type in j-sector. In other words, $L^j_l(t)$ measures labor input of l-type labor in j-sector. M^j and H^j denote the employment and average working hours of j-sector respectively.

3. Finally, the growth rate of *j*-sector labor input has been computed as follows:

$$\ln L^j(t) - \ln L^j(t-1) = [\ln M^j(t) - \ln M^j(t-1)]$$

$$+ [\ln H^j(t) - \ln H^j(t-1)] + \sum_l \bar{v}_{Ll}^j [\ln d^j(t) - \ln d^j(t-1)]$$

$$j = 1, 2, \ldots\ldots 33, \qquad\qquad (5.10)$$

where the first bracket on the right-hand side measures change in employment, the second bracket measures change in average working hours, and the third bracket measures the change in quality of labor through change in weighted working hours.

2.4   Measurement of Energy Input and Material Input

In order to separate energy input from intermediate input, intermediate inputs have been broken down into two input categories following ICPA criteria. For this purpose, I/O tables have been used to identify five sectors (sectors 2, 4, 14, 28 and 29) as energy input sectors, and the remaining 28 sectors as material input sectors.

2.5   Deflators for Gross Output and Inputs

The 21-sector gross output data from the Bank of Korea's national accounts are available only in current prices. For the period after 1985, a V-Table in both constant and current prices has been used to generate implicit gross output deflators by sector. For the period before 1985, a linked I/O table in constant prices has been used to generate implicit gross output deflators by sector for 1985 and interpolate the data for 1984. For the deflators of energy input and material input, the same sources of data have been used; a V-Table for the period after 1985 and a linked I/O table for before 1985. The basic characteristics of the KLEM database for Korea (1984–2002) in 1995 prices are presented in Table 5.2. During the period 1984–2002, Korea's gross output grew at an average annual rate of 8.04 per cent. The four inputs grew at a rate of 9.36 per cent (K), 3.15 per cent (L), 6.68 per cent (E), and 8.65 per cent (M).

2.6   Input Shares

Regarding shares of inputs, 'Compensation of Employees in Gross Domestic Product and Factor Income by Kind of Economic Activity' in the national accounts and Operating Surplus have been used to generate the relative share of labor input and capital input respectively in total value-added, and then adjusted into shares in total gross output. The amount of energy input and material input have been divided by gross output to generate shares of energy input and material input respectively.

3. GROWTH ACCOUNTING AND PRODUCTIVITY ANALYSIS

A growth accounting and a productivity analysis for Korea has been conducted for the period 1984–2002. The input data have been quality-adjusted. In other words, education, sex and age have been used for labor input and individual assets data for capital input to consider the changes of the input shares.

In Table 5.2, average growth rates of gross output and four inputs are presented in 1995 constant prices. The gross output of whole industries has grown at an average annual rate of 8.04 per cent while capital (K), labor (L), energy (E), and material input (M) have grown at a rate of 9.36 per cent, 3.15 per cent, 6.68 per cent, and 8.65 per cent respectively during the period. The average estimated shares of the four inputs were 0.20(v_K), 0.20 (v_L), 0.08 (v_E), and 0.52 (v_M) respectively. Total factor productivity based on both gross output growth accounting and value-added growth accounting have been estimated.

3.1 Gross Output Growth Accounting

The economy-wide growth rate of TFP during the pre-crisis period (1984–97) has been estimated as 0.21 per cent, as shown in Table 5.3, and the growth rate during the post-crisis period (1998–2002) has been estimated as 1.47 per cent. After the economic crisis in 1997, the growth rate of gross output declined, and the growth rates of input factors such as capital, labor, energy and material also reduced compared to rates before the crisis. Accordingly, the growth rate of TFP during the post-crisis period has been relatively higher than that of the pre-crisis period.

The relative contribution of TFP to gross output growth increase in the post-crisis period (22.14 per cent) seems to reflect structural adjustments made after the financial crisis of 1997–98. Idle capacities were cut-off and the level of employment was also drastically reduced.

The relative contribution ratio of the input factors to the output growth can be examined. The contribution ratio to output growth during the post-crisis period reduced from pre-crisis period levels. Capital reduced

Table 5.2   KLEM data in Korea (1984–2002) (1995 prices)

Year	Gross Output (bill. won)	K (bill. won)	L (100,000 hours)	E (bill. won)	M (bill. won)
1984	320640	273246	41711	28576	145281
1985	339199	301366	43116	24885	158202
1986	384485	331320	43556	29246	179567
1987	439153	366098	47350	34362	207712
1988	486723	408891	48921	38819	230433
1989	514333	460284	49911	42292	244819
1990	569375	523683	50585	27729	296468
1991	622993	599730	51736	31184	324144
1992	657020	677878	52080	33933	343405
1993	696338	755237	52971	37269	362548
1994	754081	838348	54336	41352	392516
1995	829403	930893	56097	48772	430735
1996	905645	1031360	57127	54132	474389
1997	978101	1130389	57246	57184	514881
1998	918702	1208037	52486	70490	457315
1999	1034499	1270100	53264	77940	525203
2000	1162277	1339583	55659	86816	600586
2001	1241612	1427315	56627	90451	628288
2002	1363415	1530471	58221	95153	689711
Growth (%)	8.04	9.36	3.15	6.68	8.65

Notes:
Capital (K) and labor (L) are the values without quality.
The growth rates are the average growth rates.
The growth rates of capital and labor include both growth rates of quantity and quality.

(to 18.37 per cent), as did labor (to 2.41 per cent), and material (to 45.48 per cent); the exception being energy, which increased (to 11.60 per cent). Hence, the contribution ratio of TFP to output growth increased to 22.14 per cent during the post-crisis period.

The economy-wide growth rate of TFP has been estimated as 0.55 per cent during the entire period of our analysis, 1984–2002, and the contribution ratio of TFP to output growth is 6.84 per cent, which is rather insignificant. The relative magnitude of contribution to output growth is in the order of: material, capital, labor, TFP, then energy. The quality of capital has not affected the growth of output at all, but the quality of labor has affected the growth of output by about 3.36 per cent.

The total factor productivity growth in gross output growth accounting is lower than that without quality adjustment in input data. This reconfirms

Table 5.3   Gross output growth accounting of TFP in whole industry in Korean economy

	Gross output	Capital input			Labor input			Energy	Material	TFP
		Total capital	Quality of capital	Quantity of capital	Total labor	Quality of labor	Quantity of labor			
				Average Growth Rate (%)						
'84–'97	8.58	2.20	0.00	2.20	0.81	0.33	0.48	0.36	5.00	0.21
'98–'02	6.64	1.22	0.00	1.22	0.16	0.12	0.04	0.77	3.02	1.47
'84–'02	8.04	1.93	0.00	1.93	0.63	0.27	0.36	0.48	4.45	0.55
				Contribution Ratio to Output Growth (%)						
'84–'97	100.00	25.64	0.00	25.64	9.44	3.85	5.59	4.20	58.28	2.45
'98–'02	100.00	18.37	0.00	18.37	2.41	1.81	0.60	11.60	45.48	22.14
'84–'02	100.00	24.00	0.00	24.00	7.84	3.36	4.48	5.97	55.35	6.84

Note: The growth rates of inputs are weighted by each share of income.

Krugman's (1994) proposition and empirical findings by Young (1994) and Lau and Kim (1994).

Secondly, the growth rate of TFP in manufacturing's gross output during the pre-crisis period (1984–97) has been estimated as 1.21 per cent, as shown in Table 5.4, and the growth rate of TFP during the post-crisis period (1998–2002) has been estimated as 1.73 per cent. The pattern of the growth rate of TFP is similar to that of the entire economy. But, quantity of labor input in manufacturing has reduced during the post-crisis period. It reflects a drastic structural adjustment in Korea's labor market after the financial crisis of 1997–98. As a consequence, the contribution rate of labor to output growth has become negative.

In manufacturing, the growth rate of TFP has been estimated as 1.36 per cent during the entire period of 1984–2002. The contribution ratio of TFP to output growth is estimated as 15.16 per cent.

Thirdly, the growth rate of TFP in the service sectors during the pre-crisis period (1984–97) has been estimated as −0.25 per cent, as shown in Table 5.5. During the pre-crisis period the growth rate of capital in the service sectors (3.07 per cent) was much higher than that in manufacturing (1.17 per cent), so its growth may have been adversely affected by the overall efficiency in the service sectors.

But the growth rate of TFP during the post-crisis period (1998–2002) changed to 1.04 per cent. The growth rates of both input factors and gross output slowed down during the post-crisis period.

As a result the growth rate of TFP has been estimated as 0.11 per cent in service during the entire period. The relative contribution of TFP on output growth in service has become lower than that of manufacturing. The relative magnitude of the contribution to output growth is in the order: material, capital, labor, energy, TFP.

3.2 Value-added Growth Accounting

Next, the growth of TFP has been analyzed by value-added growth accounting. In Table 5.6 the economy-wide growth rate of TFP during the pre-crisis period (1984–97) has been estimated as 0.36 per cent, and the rate during the post-crisis period (1998–2002) has been estimated as 0.71 per cent. As a whole, the growth rate of TFP is estimated to be 0.46 per cent. So, the pattern of TFP growth from value-added accounting is similar to that from gross output growth accounting, but the absolute levels of TFP growth rates are lower in value-added growth accounting than those in gross output growth accounting.

Again, the effect of quality change in capital input was almost negligible, but the growth and contribution ratio of labor quality to value-added

Table 5.4 Gross output growth accounting of TFP in manufacturing

	Gross output	Capital input			Labor input			Energy	Material	TFP
		Total capital	Quality of capital	Quantity of capital	Total labor	Quality of labor	Quantity of labor			
Average Growth Rate (%)										
'84–'97	9.28	1.17	0.07	1.10	0.21	0.19	0.02	0.33	6.36	1.21
'98–'02	8.15	0.86	0.11	0.75	-0.04	0.07	-0.11	0.98	4.62	1.73
'84–'02	8.97	1.08	0.08	1.00	0.15	0.16	-0.01	0.51	5.87	1.36
Contribution Ratio to Output Growth (%)										
'84–'97	100.00	12.61	0.75	11.85	2.26	2.05	0.22	3.56	68.53	13.04
'98–'02	100.00	10.55	1.35	9.20	-0.49	0.86	-1.35	12.02	56.69	21.23
'84–'02	100.00	12.04	0.89	11.15	1.67	1.78	-0.11	5.69	65.44	15.16

Note: The growth rates of inputs are weighted by each shares of income.

Table 5.5 Gross output growth accounting of TFP in services

	Gross output	Capital input			Labor input			Energy	Material	TFP
		Total capital	Quality of capital	Quantity of capital	Total labor	Quality of labor	Quantity of labor			
		Average Growth Rate (%)								
'84–'97	8.82	3.07	0.04	3.03	1.66	0.24	1.42	0.45	3.89	−0.25
'98–'02	5.50	1.61	0.01	1.60	0.64	0.36	0.28	0.60	1.61	1.04
'84–'02	7.90	2.67	0.04	2.63	1.37	0.27	1.10	0.49	3.26	0.11
		Contribution Ratio to Output Growth (%)								
'84–'97	100.00	34.81	0.45	34.35	18.82	2.72	16.10	5.10	44.10	−2.83
'98–'02	100.00	29.27	0.18	29.09	11.64	6.55	5.09	10.91	29.27	18.91
'84–'02	100.00	33.80	0.51	33.29	17.34	3.42	13.92	6.20	41.27	1.39

Note: The growth rates of inputs are each weighted by shares of income.

were considerable. The contribution ratio of labor quality to the growth of value-added was about 10 per cent, as a whole. The contribution of total labor to the growth of value-added is composed of two factors, labor quality (9.88 per cent) and labor quantity (13.13 per cent).

The economy-wide contribution ratio of capital to growth of value-added is 70 per cent, that of labor is 23 per cent, and that of TFP is 7 per cent. In the value-added context the role of capital in production is therefore greater than labor, as shown in Table 5.6.

3.3   Sectoral Growth of TFP

In manufacturing, sectors such as electrical machinery, machinery, motor vehicles, rubber and instruments have shown relatively higher TFP growth rates during the entire period of 1984–2002, as shown in Figure 5.1 and Table 5.7. Among them, the electrical machinery sector, which is based on IT technology, has shown higher growth of productivity, but the labor-intensive sectors such as apparel, miscellaneous manufacturing, food, and fabricated metal have shown lower growth rates of total factor productivity.

On the other hand, the communications sector – which is strongly related to IT – recorded the highest growth rate (7.95 per cent) of TFP among services. But the sectors such as construction, public services, trade, gas utilities, other private services, transportation, and so on, have produced negative growth rates of TFP.

Therefore, it can be seen that the main sectors for productivity growth have been the IT-related sectors. The Korean economy has invested heavily in IT sectors since 1995 (Table 5.8), as analyzed in Ha and Pyo (2004).

3.4   Productivity Trend and Capital–Output Coefficient

A series of labor productivity measured by gross output per man-hour (GO/L) has been generated. During the entire period of 1984–2002, the growth rate of economy-wide labor productivity is estimated as 6.19 per cent; 8.71 per cent in manufacturing and 4.37 per cent in service (Table 5.9). As expected, the growth of labor productivity in manufacturing has been greater than that of the service sector. This may reflect product and process innovation in manufacturing. During the period 1988–2002, the decline of labor input has affected the growth of labor productivity in manufacturing. The trends in labor productivity are shown in Figure 5.2.

A series of capital–output coefficients measured by capital–gross output coefficients (K/GO) have also been generated, as shown in Table 5.10. The economy-wide capital–output coefficient has grown at an average rate

Table 5.6 Value-added growth accounting of TFP in whole industry

	Value-added	Capital input			Labor input			TFP
		Total capital	Quality of capital	Quantity of capital	Total labor	Quality of labor	Quantity of labor	
Average of Log Growth Rate (%)								
'84–'97	7.81	5.44	−0.01	5.45	2.01	0.82	1.19	0.36
'98–'02	4.12	2.99	−0.01	3.00	0.42	0.30	0.12	0.71
'84–'02	6.78	4.76	−0.01	4.77	1.56	0.67	0.89	0.46
Contribution Ratio to Output Growth (%)								
'84–'97	100.00	69.65	−0.13	69.78	25.74	10.50	15.24	4.61
'98–'02	100.00	72.57	−0.24	72.82	10.19	7.28	2.91	17.23
'84–'02	100.00	70.21	−0.15	70.35	23.01	9.88	13.13	6.78

Notes:
The growth rates of each input are weighted by its share of income.
Value-added is deflated by 1995 price.

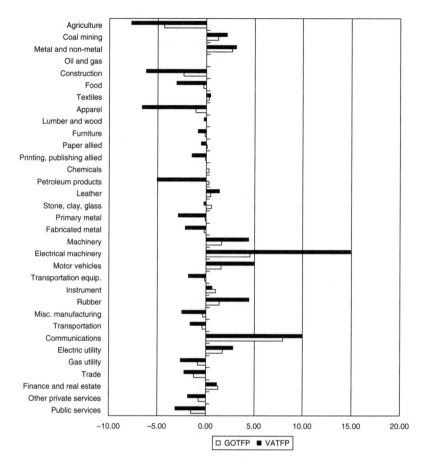

Notes:
GOTFP: TFP by gross output growth accounting.
VATFP: TFP by value-added growth accounting.

Figure 5.1 Sectoral growth of total factor productivity (average growth rate, %)

of 1.53 per cent. The economy-wide capital–labor ratio has grown at a rate of 7.72 per cent.

4. CONCLUSION

In the present chapter, a Korean database of gross output, GDP, and four input series during the period of 1984–2002 has been constructed in the

Table 5.7   Sectoral growth of TFP (gross output growth accounting:
1984–2002) (Average of Log Growth Rate: %)

Code	Industry	Gross output	Capital input	Labor input	Energy	Material	TFP
1	Agriculture	0.90	4.40	−0.07	0.14	0.74	−4.31
2	Coal mining	−7.28	−0.09	−5.66	−0.57	−2.17	1.21
3	Metal and non-metal	2.18	−0.95	−0.90	0.61	0.77	2.65
4	Oil and gas	0.00	0.00	0.00	0.00	0.00	0.00
5	Construction	4.63	2.00	1.12	0.15	3.69	−2.33
6	Food	2.42	0.48	0.11	0.04	2.06	−0.27
7	Textiles	2.69	0.46	−0.15	0.06	2.02	0.30
8	Apparel	−1.60	0.24	−0.26	0.01	−0.51	−1.08
9	Lumber and wood	1.22	0.51	−0.45	0.10	1.06	0.00
10	Furniture	8.09	1.45	0.56	0.24	5.97	−0.13
11	Paper and allied	6.03	1.48	−0.08	0.42	4.12	0.09
12	Printing, publishing, allied	6.87	1.00	0.75	0.09	5.14	−0.11
13	Chemicals	8.34	1.54	−0.06	1.34	5.25	0.27
14	Petroleum products	5.87	0.91	−0.10	3.89	0.89	0.28
15	Leather	1.46	0.08	−0.38	0.05	1.26	0.45
16	Stone, clay, glass	5.53	1.21	0.14	0.80	2.83	0.55
17	Primary metal	4.68	0.62	−0.04	0.88	3.30	−0.08
18	Fabricated metal	7.19	1.41	0.30	0.21	5.45	−0.18
19	Machinery	12.38	1.17	0.78	0.25	8.56	1.62
20	Electrical machinery	17.63	1.34	0.47	0.17	11.11	4.54
21	Motor vehicles	17.14	1.09	1.16	0.28	13.05	1.56
22	Transportation equip.	6.93	1.36	0.30	−0.06	5.48	−0.15
23	Instrument	11.80	1.13	0.74	0.20	8.71	1.02
24	Rubber	10.71	1.49	−0.31	0.38	7.79	1.36
25	Misc. manufacturing	1.65	0.77	−0.26	0.05	1.42	−0.33
26	Transportation	4.91	0.94	0.82	0.95	2.57	−0.37
27	Communications	19.43	5.31	2.09	0.25	3.83	7.95
28	Electric utilities	7.53	3.20	0.09	1.18	1.36	1.70
29	Gas utilities	15.66	3.38	1.06	10.40	1.66	−0.84
30	Trade	9.19	5.43	0.78	0.44	3.77	−1.23
31	Finance and real estate	9.97	3.80	1.51	0.38	3.00	1.28
32	Other private services	8.39	2.28	2.94	0.38	3.54	−0.75
33	Public services	3.14	0.39	2.46	0.18	1.61	−1.50
	Total	8.04	1.93	0.63	0.48	4.45	0.55

Note: Capital and labor are adjusted with quality, and weighted by each share of income.

Table 5.8   Investment in IT sector

Year	IT Investment (billion won)	Growth (%)
1995	15,125.7	–
1996	17,916.0	16.9
1997	19,122.0	6.5
1998	17,099.2	−11.2
1999	23,716.0	32.7
2000	32,190.9	30.6
2001	31,502.0	−2.2
2002	33,143.8	5.1
2003	31,551.8	−4.9
2004	31,391.9	−0.5

Note: Investment is real value in 2000 prices.

Source: Bank of Korea (http://ecos.bok.or.kr).

Table 5.9   The growth of labor productivity (Average Growth Rate: %)

	Period	Gross output	Labor input	Labor productivity
Whole Industry	'84–'97	8.58	2.44	6.14
	'98–'02	6.64	0.34	6.31
	'84–'02	8.04	1.85	6.19
Manufacturing	'84–'97	9.28	0.64	8.64
	'98–'02	8.15	−0.74	8.90
	'84–'02	8.97	0.26	8.71
Service	'84–'97	8.82	4.48	4.33
	'98–'02	5.50	1.02	4.48
	'84–'02	7.90	3.52	4.37

Note: Labor input is total working hours.

framework of the KLEM model. According to gross-output growth accounting, the Korean economy has recorded a significant growth of gross output at an average rate of 8.04 per cent during the period of 1984–2002. On the other hand, capital (K), labor (L), energy (E), and material input (M) have grown at a rate of 9.36 per cent, 3.15 per cent, 6.68 per cent, and 8.65 per cent respectively during the period. The average estimated shares of the four inputs were 0.20 (v_K), 0.20 (v_L), 0.08 (v_E), and 0.52 (v_M) respectively. As a consequence, total factor input and total factor productivity have increased at an average annual rate of 7.49 per cent and 0.55 per cent

Productivity in Asia

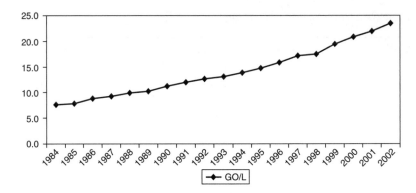

Note: GO=gross output, L=total working hours.

Figure 5.2   Labor productivity (GO/L) (1000 won/h)

Table 5.10   Trends in productivity and capital–output coefficients in Korea (1984–2002)

Year	Labor productivity GO/L (1000 won/h)	Capital–output coefficient K/GO	Capital–labor ratio K/L (1000 won/h)
1984	7.69	0.85	6.55
1985	7.87	0.89	6.99
1986	8.83	0.86	7.61
1987	9.27	0.83	7.73
1988	9.95	0.84	8.36
1989	10.30	0.89	9.22
1990	11.26	0.92	10.35
1991	12.04	0.96	11.59
1992	12.62	1.03	13.02
1993	13.15	1.08	14.26
1994	13.88	1.11	15.43
1995	14.79	1.12	16.59
1996	15.85	1.14	18.05
1997	17.09	1.16	19.75
1998	17.50	1.31	23.02
1999	19.42	1.23	23.85
2000	20.88	1.15	24.07
2001	21.93	1.15	25.21
2002	23.42	1.12	26.29
Average growth rate (%)	6.19	1.53	7.72

Notes:
Labor (L) is measured in terms of total working hours.
The growth rates are the average of logarithm growth rates.

Figure 5.3   Capital–output coefficient/capital–labor ratio

respectively. Therefore, the relative contribution of total factor productivity to gross output growth is estimated to be only 6.84 per cent, which is rather insignificant. It is concluded that the quality adjustment in labor input has played a role in estimating lower growth rate of total factor productivity. This study reconfirms Krugman's (1994) proposition and empirical findings by Young (1994) and Lau and Kim (1994). It is also noted that there was a discernable structural turning point after the 1997 economic crisis in Korea: both capital–gross output coefficient and capital–value-added coefficient started to fall after 1998 (Figure 5.3).

APPENDIX

Table 5A.1   Input–output tables for Korea (1970–2000)

a. Transaction tables at producers' prices (Number of Sector
Classifications)

Year	Basic	Small	Medium	Large
1970		153	56	
1973		153	56	
1975	392	164	60	
1978		164	60	
1980	396	162	64	19
1983	396	162	64	19
1985	402	161	65	20
1986		161	65	20
1987		161	65	20
1988		161	65	20
1990	405	163	75	26
1993		163	75	26
1995	402	168	77	28
1998		168	77	28
2000	404	168	77	28

b. Extended I/O tables with sector classification of the preceding
main I/O tables: Linked Input–Output Tables (Number of Sector
Classifications)

Year	Small	Medium	Large
1975–80–85	161	65	20
1980–85–90	161	75	

Source: The Bank of Korea Input–Output Tables (1970–2000) CD-ROM.

Table 5A.2   Reclassification of I/O tables into 33 sectors (basic classification)

33 Sectors	Classification in I/O Table (1983)	Classification in I/O Table (1985)
1. Agriculture	1–38	1–37
2. Coal mining	39	38–39
3. Metal and non-metal	40–54, 56–58	40–44, 46–51
4. Oil and gas	55	45
5. Construction	313–333	324–342
6. Food	59–98	52–91
7. Textiles	99–118, 121, 123–125	92–112, 117–122
8. Apparel	119–120, 122, 196	114–116, 123, 197
9. Lumber and wood	131–133, 135–138	129–131, 133–135
10. Furniture	134, 237, 243	132, 238, 244
11. Paper and allied	139–148	136–145
12. Printing, publishing and allied	149–151	146–148
13. Chemicals	152–172, 174–185	149–183
14. Petroleum products	186–194	186–195
15. Leather	126–130	124–128, 315
16. Stone, clay, glass	199–213	200–215
17. Primary metal	214–217, 228–232	216–218, 229–233
18. Fabricated machinery	218–227, 233–236, 238–242, 244–247	219–228, 234–237, 239–243, 245–248
19. Machinery	248–261	249–266
20. Electrical machinery	262–286	267–290
21. Motor vehicles	292–295	296–299
22. Transportation equip.	287–291, 296–299	291–295, 300–303
23. Instruments	300–303	304–307
24. Rubber and misc. plastic	173, 195, 197–198	184–185, 196, 198–199
25. Misc. manufacturing	304–312	308–314, 315
26. Transportation	344–356	347–360
27. Communications	357–359	361–363
28. Electric utilities	334–337	317–320
29. Gas and water utilities	338–340	321–323
30. Trade	341–343	343–346
31. Finance	360–366	364–370
32. Other private services	368–393	371–375, 378–399
33. Public services	367	376–377

Table 5A.2 (continued)

33 Sectors	Classification in I/O Table (1990)	Classification in I/O Table (1995/1998)
1. Agriculture	1–34	1–30
2. Coal mining	35–36	31–32
3. Metal and non-metal	39–50	35–45
4. Oil and gas	37–38	33–34
5. Construction	325–341	313–329
6. Food	51–93	46–88
7. Textiles	94–109, 113–115	89–104, 111–113
8. Apparel	110–112, 116, 122	105–108, 118
9. Lumber and wood	125–130	120–125
10. Furniture	131, 238, 240	296–298
11. Paper and allied	132–142	126–134
12. Printing, publishing and allied	143–145	135–138
13. Chemicals	146–176	150–173
14. Petroleum products	177–187	139–149
15. Leather	117–121, 123–124	109–110, 114–117, 119
16. Stone, clay, glass	194–209	180–195
17. Primary metal	210–212, 223–227	196–198, 209–213
18. Fabricated machinery	213–222, 228–237, 289, 241–245	199–208, 214–227
19. Machinery	246–264	228–246
20. Electrical machinery	265–293	247–275
21. Motor vehicles	298–302	282–288
22. Transportation equip.	303–311	289–295
23. Instruments	294–297	276–281
24. Rubber and misc. plastic	188–193	174–179
25. Misc. manufacturing	312–317	299–305
26. Transportation	346–358	334–346
27. Communications	359–360	347–349
28. Electric utilities	318–321	306–309
29. Gas and water utilities	322–324	310–312
30. Trade	342–345	330–333
31. Finance	361–368	352–359
32. Other private services	369–368, 378–402	350–351, 360–369, 372–399
33. Public services	376–377	370–371

Table 5A.2   (continued)

33 Sectors	Classification in I/O Table (2000)
1. Agriculture	1–30
2. Coal mining	31–32
3. Metal and non-metal	35–45
4. Oil and gas	33–34
5. Construction	312–328
6. Food	46–86
7. Textiles	87–102, 109–111
8. Apparel	103–106, 116
9. Lumber and wood	118–123
10. Furniture	295–297
11. Paper and allied	124–132
12. Printing, publishing and allied	133–136
13. Chemicals	148–171
14. Petroleum products	137–147
15. Leather	107–108, 112–115, 117,
16. Stone, clay, glass	178–193
17. Primary metal	194–196, 207–211
18. Fabricated machinery	197–206, 212–225
19. Machinery	226–245
20. Electrical machinery	246–274
21. Motor vehicles	281–287
22. Transportation equip.	288–294
23. Instruments	275–280
24. Rubber and misc. plastic	172–177
25. Misc. manufacturing	298–304
26. Transportation	333–345
27. Communications	346–349
28. Electric utilities	305–308
29. Gas and water utilities	309–311
30. Trade	329–332
31. Finance	352–360
32. Other private services	350–351, 361–371, 374–401
33. Public services	372–373

Table 5A.3   Reclassification of national accounts into 33 sectors

National Accounts	33 Sectors
1. Agriculture, Forestry and Fishing	1. Agriculture
2. Mining and Quarrying	2. Coal mining
	3. Metal and non-metal
	4. Oil and gas
3. Food, Beverage and Tobacco	6. Food
4. Textiles and Leather	7. Textiles
	8. Apparel
	15. Leather
5. Wood, Paper, Publishing and Printing	9. Lumber and wood
	11. Paper and allied
	12. Printing, publishing and allied
6. Petroleum, Coal, and Chemicals	13. Chemicals
	14. Petroleum products
	24. Rubber and misc. plastic
7. Non-Metallic Mineral Products except Petroleum and Coal	16. Stone, clay, glass
8. Metal, Fabricated Metal Products	17. Primary metal
	18. Fabricated machinery
9. Machinery and Equipment	19. Machinery
	20. Electrical machinery
	23. Instruments
10. Transport Equipment	21. Motor vehicles
	22. Transportation equip.
11. Furniture and Other Manufacturing Industries	10. Furniture
	25. Misc. manufacturing
12. Electricity, Gas and Water	28. Electric utilities
	29. Gas and water utilities
13. Construction	5. Construction
14. Wholesale and Retail Trade, Restaurants and Hotels	30. Trade
15. Transport, Storage and Communication	26. Transportation
	27. Communications
16. Finance, Insurance, Real Estate and Business Services	31. Finance
17. Community, Social and Personal Services	32. Other private services
18. Producers of Government Services	33. Public services

NOTE

1. The Kuroda and Nomura (1999) formula could not be used because investment data in National Income Accounts are classified either by asset type or by industry, but not by both.

REFERENCES

Bank of Korea (1984, 1994, 1999, 2004), National Accounts.
Bank of Korea (1970–2000), Input–Output Tables CD-ROM.
Bureau of Economic Analysis (BEA) (1993), 'Fixed reproducible tangible wealth in the United States, 1925–85', Washington, DC: US Government Printing Office.
Chinese Petroleum Corporation and Energy Yearbook (1988, 1995, 2002), Taiwan, Republic of China: Energy Commission, Ministry of Economic Affairs (MOEA).
Commodity Price Monthly (1981–1999), Taiwan, Republic of China: The Directorate General of Budget, Accounting and Statistics (DGBAS), Executive Yuan.
Energy Balance in Taiwan, ROC (2002), Taiwan, Republic of China: Bureau of Energy, Ministry of Economic Affairs (MOEA).
Financial Statistics Monthly (1981–1999), Taiwan, Republic of China: Department of Economic Research, Central Bank.
Forsgerau, M. and A. Sorenson (1999), 'Deflation and decomposition of Danish value-added growth using the KLEMS methodology', mimeograph, 7 December, Copenhagen: Centre for Economic and Business Research, Ministry of Trade and Industry.
Ha, Bong Chan and Hak K. Pyo (2004), 'The measurement of IT contribution by decomposed dynamic input–output tables in Korea (1980–2002)', *Seoul Journal of Economics*, **17**(4).
Hall, R.E. and D.W. Jorgenson (1967), 'Tax policy and investment behavior', *American Economic Review*, **57**(3), 391–414.
Import–Export Trade Monthly (1981–1999), Taiwan, Republic of China: The Statistics Office, Directorate General of Customs. Ministry of Finance (MOF).
Industry and Commercial Census (1996, 2001), Taiwan, Republic of China: The Directorate General of Budget, Accounting and Statistics (DGBAS), Executive Yuan.
Input–Output Tables (various years), Taiwan, Republic of China: The Directorate General of Budget, Accounting and Statistics (DGBAS), Executive Yuan [1981, 1984, 1986, 1989, 1991, 1996, and 1999].
Jorgenson, D.W. and Ralph Landau (1993), *Tax Reform and the Cost of Capital*, Washington, DC, The Brookings Institution.
Jorgenson, D.W. and K.Y. Yun (1991), *Tax Reform and the Cost of Capital*, Oxford: Oxford University Press.
Jorgenson, D.W., F.M. Gollop and B.M. Fraumeni (1987), *Productivity and US Economic Growth*, Cambridge, MA: Harvard University Press.
Kim, Kwang Suk and Sung Duk Hong (1997), *Accounting for Rapid Economic Growth in Korea, 1963–1995*, Korea Development Institute, Seoul: KDI Press.
Kim, K.S. and J.K. Park (1985), *Sources of Economic Growth in Korea, 1963–1982*, Seoul: KDI Press.

King, M. and Don Fullerton (1984), *The Taxation of Income from Capital*, Chicago: University of Chicago Press.

Krugman, Paul (1994), 'The myth of Asia's miracle', *Foreign Affairs*, **73**(6) November/December, 62–89.

Kuroda, M. (2001), 'The international comparison of the productivity among pan-Pacific countries', mimeo.

Kuroda, M. and K. Nomura (1999), 'Productivity comparison and international competitiveness', *Journal of Applied Input–Output Analysis*, **5**.

Kwon, J.K. and Kyhyang Yuhn (1990), *Analysis of Factor Substitution and Productivity Growth in Korean Manufacturing 1961–1981*, Korean Economic Development. Westport, CT: Greenwood Press.

Lau, Lawrence J. and Jong-Il Kim (1994), 'The sources of growth of East Asian newly industrialized countries', *Journal of Japanese and International Economies*, **8**, 235–71.

Monthly Bulletin of Earnings and Productivity Statistics (1981–1999), Taiwan, Republic of China: The Directorate General of Budget, Accounting and Statistics (DGBAS), Executive Yuan.

National Income Account (2002), Taiwan, Republic of China: The Directorate General of Budget, Accounting and Statistics (DGBAS), Executive Yuan.

National Income and Product Accounts (2002), Taiwan, Republic of China: The Directorate General of Budget, Accounting and Statistics (DGBAS), Executive Yuan.

National Wealth Census (1988), Taiwan, Republic of China: The Directorate General of Budget, Accounting and Statistics (DGBAS), Executive Yuan.

Pyo, Hak K. (1988), 'Estimates of capital stock and capital/output coefficients by industries: Korea, 1953–1986', *International Economic Journal*, Summer, **2**(3), 79–121.

Pyo, Hak K. (1992), 'A synthetic estimate of national wealth of Korea, 1953–1990', *KDI Working Paper No.9212*, Seoul: Korea Development Institute.

Pyo, Hak K. (1998), 'Estimates of fixed reproducible tangible assets in the Republic of Korea, 1953–1996', *KDI Working Paper No.9810*, Seoul: Korea Development Institute.

Pyo, Hak K. (2001), 'Economic growth in Korea (1911–1999): A long-term trend and perspective', *Seoul Journal of Economics*, Spring, **14**(1).

Pyo, Hak K. (2003), 'Estimates of capital stocks by industries and types of assets in Korea (1953–2000)', *Journal of Korean Economic Analysis*, Panel for Korean Economic Analysis and Korea Institute of Finance. Seoul.

Rhee, Keun-Hee (2001), *Total Factor Productivity Analysis in Korean Manufacturing*, Korea Productivity Center (in Korean).

Survey of Family Income and Expenditure (1981–1999), Taiwan, Republic of China: the Directorate General of Budget, Accounting and Statistics (DGBAS), Executive Yuan.

Timmer, M.P. (2000), 'Towards European productivity comparisons using the KLEMS approach – An overview of sources and methods, mimeo, Groningen Growth and Development Centre and The Conference Board.

Timmer, M.P. and B. van Ark (2000), *Capital Formation and Productivity Growth in South Korea and Taiwan: Realising the Catch-up Potential in a World of Diminishing Returns*, Groningen Growth and Development Centre, University of Groningen.

Won Yunhi and Jin Kwon Hyun (2000), 'Marginal effective tax rates in Korea: 1960–1998', *Working Paper 00-02*, Korea Institute of Public Finance.

Yearbook of the Ministry of Finance (2002), Taiwan, Republic of China: Department of Statistics, Ministry of Finance (MOF).

Young, Alwyn (1994), 'Lessons from the East Asian NICs: a contrarian view', *European Economic Review*, **38**(3–4), 964–73.

Yun and Kim (1997), 'Marginal effective tax rate of corporate investment in Korea', *Korean Journal of Public Economics*, **2**, November, (in Korean).

6. Industry-wide total factor productivity and output growth in Taiwan, 1981–1999

Chi-Yuan Liang*

1. INTRODUCTION

The argument based on the empirical results mainly of Young (1994b) and Krugman (1994), but also of Kim and Lau (1994), Lau (1994) and Young (1994a), maintains that the secret of the economic miracle in the four Newly Industrializing Economies (NIEs), that is, Singapore, Hong Kong, Korea and Taiwan, during the past three decades was 'input-driven growth'. In other words, it had little to do with total factor productivity (TFP) or technical change, and much to do with the rapid increase in factor inputs. Hence, the economic miracle could not be sustained owing to the law of diminishing returns. Hereafter, this will be referred to as the Krugman–Kim–Lau–Young hypothesis.

In response to the Krugman–Kim–Lau–Young hypothesis, Liang (1995) extended the research approach developed by Jorgenson and his associates – Christensen and Jorgenson (1970) and Gollop and Jorgenson (1980) – to consider the changes in the quality of inputs caused by industrial structural change, or the 'reallocation effect of inputs' as Liang (2001) called it, as another heterogeneous characteristic of inputs. In so doing, he measured Taiwan's TFP growth during different sub-periods between 1961 and 1993. He argued that Krugman's findings are, at least in Taiwan's case, valid only for a longer period, say, 1961–93, but are in fact invalid for 1982–93. *The Economist* (1997) similarly criticized Krugman's thesis and remained optimistic for East Asia's future development.

Comparing the TFP growth of the whole economy among 14 countries provided by Young (1994a), Liang (2002) concluded that Taiwan was one of the greatest in TFP growth (that is, 2.3 per cent per annum). He also found that the same conclusion can apply to Hong Kong (2.3 per cent) and Korea (1.7 per cent) as well, and hence Krugman's input-driven growth for the NIEs is unfounded. Liang and Mei (2005) found also that the Krugman–Kim–Lau–Young hypothesis was incorrect for the period 1978–99.

However, these aforementioned papers discuss only the relationship between value-added and factor inputs, such as labor and capital. In fact, intermediate input accounts for a greater portion of total cost than do capital and labor. The substitutability and complementarities between intermediate input and capital and between intermediate input and labor are so important that it is inappropriate to ignore them. In addition, since the oil price shocks, the relationship between energy input and other factor inputs has become a worldwide concern. Consequently, the value-added model should be replaced with a model in which the changes in total output can be explained by the changes in factor inputs, including capital, labor, energy and intermediate input, as well as changes in TFP or technical change.

Consequently, the objective of this chapter is to measure the growth of industry-wide output, input and productivity change and to analyze the causes of growth in output and total factor productivity of the Asian NIEs by employing Taiwan's data on 26 sectors during 1981–99 as an example. To verify the Krugman–Kim–Lau–Young hypothesis, we compare the industry-wide TFP growth of Taiwan with that of the United States and Japan. Finally, conclusions and implications are drawn from the findings. For this a translog production function – which is more general than the conventional Cobb-Douglas and constant elasticity of substitution (CES) production function – is employed.

2. METHODOLOGY AND DATA COMPILATION

2.1 Methodology

The methodology of this chapter follows Jorgenson and his associates as well as Liang's extensions.[1] First, consider an industry production function f, characterized by constant returns to scale (CRS):[2]

$$Q = f(K,L,E,M,T),$$ (6.1)

where Q is total output, K, L, E and M are capital, labor, energy and intermediate service inputs respectively, and T denotes time, which indexes technology level.

Define the rate of total factor productivity (TFP) change, say R_T, as the growth of output with respect to time, holding capital and labor constant:

$$R_T = \frac{\partial \ln Q}{\partial T}.$$

It is worth noting that the TFP change is sometimes used as synonymous with technical change. However, according to Kumbhakar and Lovell (2000), the TFP change is composed of three parts, that is, technical change, scale economies effect, and time-variant technical efficiency. If technical efficiency is time invariant and constant return to scale prevails, then the TFP growth is identical to technical change. Consequently, if constant return to scale does not hold empirically, the TFP growth might overstate the technical change in the case of increasing return to scale, while it might understate the technical change in the case of decreasing return to scale.

Under the assumption of a competitive product market, R_T can be expressed as the rate of output growth minus a weighted average of the rates of growth of capital, labor, energy and intermediate inputs, where the weights are given by corresponding value shares:

$$\frac{\partial \ln Q}{\partial T} = \frac{d \ln Q}{dT} - \frac{\partial \ln Q}{\partial \ln K}\frac{d \ln K}{dT} - \frac{\partial \ln Q}{\partial \ln L}\frac{d \ln L}{dT} - \frac{\partial \ln Q}{\partial \ln E}\frac{d \ln E}{dT} - \frac{\partial \ln Q}{\partial \ln M}\frac{d \ln M}{dT}$$

$$= \frac{d \ln Q}{dT} - S_K \frac{d \ln K}{dT} - S_L \frac{d \ln L}{dT} - S_E \frac{d \ln E}{dT} - S_M \frac{d \ln M}{dT}. \tag{6.2}$$

The above expression is referred to as the *Divisia index of TFP change*.

To handle practical data at discrete points in time, a specific form of production process called the *translog* function is used:

$$\begin{aligned}
\ln Q = {}& \alpha_0 + \alpha_T T + \alpha_K \ln K + \alpha_L \ln L + \alpha_E \ln E + \alpha_M \ln M \\
& + 1/2\beta_{KK}(\ln K)^2 + \beta_{KL}\ln K \cdot \ln L + \beta_{KE}\ln K \cdot \ln E + \beta_{KM}\ln K \cdot \ln M \\
& + \beta_{KT}\ln KT + 1/2\beta_{LL}(\ln L)^2 + \beta_{LE}\ln L \cdot \ln E + \beta_{KM}\ln K \cdot \ln M \\
& + \beta_{LT}\ln LT + 1/2\beta_{EE}(\ln E)^2 + \beta_{EM}\ln E \cdot \ln M + \beta_{ET}\ln ET \\
& + 1/2\beta_{EE}(\ln M)^2 + \beta_{LT}\ln MT + 1/2\beta_{TT}T^2, \tag{6.3}
\end{aligned}$$

which is characterized by CRS if, and only if, the parameters satisfy the following conditions:

$$\alpha_K + \alpha_L + \alpha_E + \alpha_M = 1 \tag{6.4}$$

$$\beta_{KK} + \beta_{KL} + \beta_{KE} + \beta_{KM} = 0 \tag{6.5}$$

$$\beta_{LK} + \beta_{LL} + \beta_{LE} + \beta_{LM} = 0 \tag{6.6}$$

$$\beta_{EK} + \beta_{EL} + \beta_{EE} + \beta_{EM} = 0 \qquad (6.7)$$

$$\beta_{MK} + \beta_{ML} + \beta_{ME} + \beta_{MM} = 0 \qquad (6.8)$$

$$\beta_{KT} + \beta_{LT} + \beta_{ET} + \beta_{MT} = 0. \qquad (6.9)$$

In addition, for a well-behaved function the production should be satisfied by the concavity constraint. That is, that the Hessian's matrix is negative semi-definite.[3] Differentiating equation (6.3) with respect to K, L, E, M and T, the value-share equations of capital, labor, energy and intermediate can be expressed as:

$$S_K = \alpha_K + \beta_{KK}\ln K + \beta_{KL}\ln L + \beta_{KE}\ln E + \beta_{KM}\ln M + \beta_{KT}T, \qquad (6.10)$$

$$S_L = \alpha_L + \beta_{LK}\ln K + \beta_{LL}\ln L + \beta_{LE}\ln E + \beta_{LM}\ln M + \beta_{LT}T, \qquad (6.11)$$

$$S_E = \alpha_E + \beta_{EK}\ln K + \beta_{EL}\ln L + \beta_{EE}\ln E + \beta_{EM}\ln M + \beta_{ET}T, \qquad (6.12)$$

$$S_M = \alpha_M + \beta_{MK}\ln K + \beta_{ML}\ln L + \beta_{ME}\ln E + \beta_{MM}\ln M + \beta_{MT}T. \qquad (6.13)$$

In addition, the rate of change in TFP can be shown as:

$$R_T = \alpha_T + \beta_{KT}\ln K + \beta_{LT}\ln L + \beta_{ET}\ln E + \beta_{MT}\ln M + \beta_{TT}T. \qquad (6.14)$$

For the data at any two discrete points in time, say T and $T-1$, the average rate of TFP change can be derived from growth accounting, that is, the difference between successive logarithms of output less a weighted average of the differences between successive logarithms of capital, labor, energy and intermediate inputs with weights given based on average value shares:

$$\overline{R_T} = \ln Q(T) - \ln Q(T-1) - \overline{s_K}[\ln K(T) - \ln K(T-1)]$$

$$- \overline{s_L}[\ln L(T) - \ln L(T-1)] - \overline{s_E}[\ln E(T) - \ln E(T-1)]$$

$$- \overline{s_M}[\ln M(T) - \ln M(T-1)] \qquad (6.15)$$

where

$$\overline{s_K} = 1/2[s_K(T) + s_K(T-1)] \qquad (6.16)$$

$$\overline{s_L} = 1/2[s_L(T) + s_L(T-1)] \qquad (6.17)$$

$$\overline{s_E} = 1/2[s_E(T) + s_E(T-1)] \qquad (6.18)$$

$$\overline{s_M} = 1/2[s_M(T) + s_M(T-1)] \qquad (6.19)$$

$$\overline{R_T} = 1/2[R_T(T) + R_T(T-1)]. \qquad (6.20)$$

The index of (6.15) is referred to as the *Tornqvist index of TFP* or the *translog index of TFP*.[4]

Similarly, for capital, labor, energy and intermediate inputs contributed by individual categories with different qualities, we can also employ translog functions to aggregate:

$$\ln K = \alpha_1 \ln K_1 + \alpha_2 \ln K_2 + ... + \alpha_m \ln K_m + 1/2\beta_{11}(\ln K_1)^2$$

$$+ \beta_{12} \ln K_1 \ln K_2 + ... + 1/2\beta_{kk}(\ln K_k)^2 \qquad (6.21)$$

$$\ln L = \alpha_1 \ln L_1 + \alpha_2 \ln L_2 + ... + \alpha_n \ln L_n + 1/2\beta_{11}(\ln L_1)^2$$

$$+ \beta_{12} \ln L_1 \cdot \ln L_2 + ... + 1/2\beta_{ll}(\ln L_l)^2 \qquad (6.22)$$

$$\ln E = \alpha_1 \ln E_1 + \alpha_2 \ln E_2 + ... + \alpha_n \ln E_n + 1/2\beta_{11}(\ln E_1)^2$$

$$+ \beta_{12} \ln E_1 \cdot \ln E_2 + ... + 1/2\beta_{ee}(\ln E_e)^2 \qquad (6.23)$$

$$\ln M = \alpha_1 \ln M_1 + \alpha_2 \ln M_2 + ... + \alpha_n \ln M_n + 1/2\beta_{11}(\ln M_1)^2$$

$$+ \beta_{12} \ln M_1 \cdot \ln M_2 + ... + 1/2\beta_{mm}(\ln M_m)^2. \qquad (6.24)$$

The difference between successive logarithms of aggregated capital, labor, energy and intermediate inputs can also be expressed as:

$$\ln K(T) - \ln K(T-1) = \sum_{i=1}^{k} \overline{s_{Ki}}[\ln K_i(T) - \ln K_i(T-1)];$$

$$(i = 1...k) \qquad (6.25)$$

$$\ln L(T) - \ln L(T-1) = \sum_{j=1}^{l} \overline{s_{Lj}}[\ln L_j(T) - \ln L_j(T-1)];$$

$$(j = 1...l) \qquad (6.26)$$

$$\ln E(T) - \ln E(T-1) = \sum_{k=1}^{e} \overline{s_{Ek}}[\ln E_k(T) - \ln E_k(T-1)];$$

$$(k = 1...e) \qquad (6.27)$$

$$\ln M(T) - \ln M(T-1) = \sum_{l=1}^{m} \overline{s_{Ml}}[\ln M_l(T) - \ln M_l(T-1)],$$

$$(l = 1...m) \qquad (6.28)$$

where

$$\overline{s_{Ki}} = 1/2[s_{Ki}(T) + s_{Ki}(T-1)] \qquad (6.29)$$

$$\overline{s_{Lj}} = 1/2[s_{Lj}(T) + s_{Lj}(T-1)] \qquad (6.30)$$

$$\overline{s_{Ek}} = 1/2[s_{Ek}(T) + s_{Ek}(T-1)] \qquad (6.31)$$

$$\overline{s_{Ml}} = 1/2[s_{Ml}(T) + s_{Ml}(T-1)]. \qquad (6.32)$$

2.2 Data Compilation

The observation period runs from 1981 to 1999. The economy is broken down into the following sectors: agriculture, mining, water, electricity and gas, construction, transportation and services, 19 manufacturing sectors (food and kindred products, textile mill products, apparel, lumber and wood, furniture and fixtures, paper and allied, printing, publishing and allied, chemicals, petroleum and coal products, leather, stone, clay and glass, primary metal, fabricated metal, non electrical machinery, electrical machinery, transport equipment and ordnance, instruments, rubber products and miscellaneous manufacturing), three service sectors (commerce, finance and insurance, personal services), and four energy sectors (coal, natural gas, oil refining, and electricity). It is noted that the government service sector is excluded from the whole economy, because the profit maximizing rule is not applicable to the government service sector. In addition, in the National Income Account, the output of the government service sector is identical with its labor compensation.

2.2.1 Capital input
The capital input is decomposed into four categories: (1) Construction (K_1), (2) other construction (K_2), (3) transportation equipment (K_3), and (4) machineries (K_4).

'Transportation equipment' means 'automobiles' in most of the sectors except refinery, electricity, steel, and petrochemical industries. Some big companies such as China Petroleum Corp, Taipower, China Steel, and Formosa Petrochemical company have their own ships. Also, Taiwan Sugar Company owns a small railroad system. However, owing to data limitations, we cannot separate the railway and ships from transportation equipment investment or stock.

Data on various types of capital stock are obtained from the *National Wealth Census*(1988), the *Industry and Commercial Census* (1996, 2001) and the Directorate General of Budget, Accounting and Statistics (DGBAS) of Executive Yuan. All types of capital are calculated by adding up corresponding net capital formation, which is the difference between gross capital formation and depreciation, starting from 1981. The gross capital formation during the period 1981–99 comes from the DGBAS; the types of depreciation are compiled by employing the constant rate depreciation method and the years of depreciation listed in the *National Wealth Census (1988)*. The time series capital stock during 1981–99 is then calculated by adding up the net capital formation starting from 1981. Finally, we adjust the time series data in relation to the capital stock by employing the *National Wealth Census (1988)*. The reason for adjusting the data is that the way of summing yearly capital formation up as capital stock is doubtful since the initial amount is unavailable. Thus, we use the stock value of various types derived from the National Wealth Census in 1988 as a base to adjust them.

The types of capital service price are compiled by using the following equation from Christensen and Jorgenson (1969, 1970):

$$P_{ki} = \frac{1 - \mu(T) \cdot Z_i(T)}{1 - \mu(T)} [P_{Ii}(T-1) \cdot (1 - \mu(T)) \cdot R_r(T)$$

$$+ \delta_i \cdot P_{Ii}(T) - (P_{Ii}(T) - P_{Ii}(T-1))]$$

$$+ P_{Ii}(T) \cdot \tau_i(T), \qquad (i = 1,2,3,4),$$

where

$\mu(T)$: The effective business income tax rate;
$Z_i(T)$: The present value of depreciation deducted for tax purposes on a dollar's investment in capital i;
$P_{Ii}(T)$: The price index of gross investment in relation to capital i;
δ_i: The depreciation rate in relation to capital i;
$t_i(T)$: The property tax rate for capital i;
$R_r(T)$: The rate of return for all types of capital.

The effective business income tax rate is the ratio of business income tax divided by the total profit of all sectors. The data on business income tax comes from the *Yearbook of the Ministry of Finance* (2002). The total profit of all sectors (excluding interest and rent) is taken from the *National Income Account* (2002).

By using the constant rate of depreciation method, the present value of deductions in relation to a dollar of investment goods, i, is calculated by means of the following equations:

$$\delta_i = 1 - \left(\frac{s_i}{c_i}\right)^{\frac{1}{N_i}} (given \; s_i = 0.1c_i)$$

$$Z_i(T) = \sum \left[\frac{(1 - \delta_i)^{N_i - 1} \cdot \delta_i}{(1 + r)^{N_i}} \right],$$

where

N: The time span of investment goods i,
δ_i: The constant rate of depreciation of capital i,
r: The one-year prime rate,
c_i: The cost of investment goods i,
S_i: The remaining value of investment goods i.

The data on N_i and r come from the *National Wealth Census (1988)* and *Financial Statistics Monthly* (1981–1999), respectively.

The deflator in relation to capital i for each sector is the quotient of the gross capital formation at current prices and the gross capital formation at constant 1986 prices. Both of these are provided by the Statistics Bureau of the DGBAS.

Based on the corresponding tax code, tax rates for property $(Z_i(T))$, construction (K_1), and miscellaneous construction (K_2) are assumed to be 3.0 per cent. No property tax is levied on machineries (K_4).

The property tax rate with regard to the transportation equipment (K_3) is calculated as:

$$K_3 = \frac{\text{The license revenue for mobile cars}}{\left[\begin{array}{c} K_3 \text{ at current prices} - \text{the value of the} \\ \text{transportation equipment of all residents} \end{array} \right]}$$

The internal rate of return $(Rr (T))$ is calculated by:

$$R_r(T) = \frac{PC - \sum_{i=1}^{6} \left[\frac{1 - \mu(T) \cdot Z_i(T)}{1 - \mu(T)} \cdot (\delta P_{Ii}(T) - P_{Ii}(T)) \right] \cdot K_i}{\sum_{i=1}^{6} (1 - \mu(T) \cdot Z_i(T)) \cdot P_{Ii}(T - 1) \cdot K_i(T)},$$

where PC denotes the property compensation, which is the sum of rent, interest and profit depreciation, and is equal to the summation of the products of K_i and P_k:

$$PC = \sum_{i=1}^{4} P_{Ki} \cdot K_i(T - 1)$$

Since the wage of unpaid workers, especially in agriculture, quarrying industries, and so on, tends to be counted as operational profit instead of labor compensation in the *National Income and Product Accounts* (2002), we use the value shares of capital and labor costs to output in the *Input–Output Tables* in various years instead. The wages of unpaid workers in family business are included in labor compensation in the I/O table. This is done not only for agricultural and quarrying sectors but also for the other sectors.

In addition, for an international comparison, we employ 1995 as a benchmark year. The capital stock (Ki) and property compensation for four categories by sector are presented in appendix Table 6A.1. For a comparable basis, the data on land and inventory are excluded.

2.2.2   Labor input

Seventy-two categories of labor for each industry are classified on the basis of:

a.   sex: male; female
b.   employment status: employed; self-employed and/or unpaid family worker
c.   age: 15–24; 25–34; 35–44; 45–54; 55–64; over 65
d.   education: junior high school graduate or less; senior or vocational high school graduate; college graduate and above.

Wages and labor inputs on the basis of 72 categories for each sector during 1981–99 are compiled from the magnetic tape of the *Survey of Family Income and Expenditure* (1981–1999). For consistency, the labor data comes from the Manpower Survey and the monthly wage of the 72 categories is adjusted by using the average monthly wage by sector from the *Monthly Bulletin of Earnings and Productivity Statistics* (1981–1999). The data on working hours by sector during 1981–99 also comes from the *Monthly Bulletin of Earnings and Productivity Statistics* (1981–1999).

Again, since the production of unpaid workers – especially in agriculture or quarrying industries and so on – tends to be omitted from the *National Income and Product Accounts* (2002), we employ the value shares of capital and labor costs to output using the *Input–Output Tables* in various years.

It is worth noting that Young (1994b) multiplies the sectoral compensation based on employee data reported in the national accounts by one plus his sectoral estimates of the ratio of implicit to explicit labor income to estimate the share of labor in total factor payments. However, in the case of Taiwan, his estimate of the share of labor compensation in total factor payments is quite large. For instance, the share of labor for the economy as a whole is fairly stable, ranging between 0.72 and 0.70 during 1966–90, which is much larger than the labor share reported in the 1991 input–output table, that is, 0.64. The input–output table of Taiwan has taken into account implicit labor income, such as that for unpaid family workers and self-employed income.

2.2.3   Energy input

Energy input consists of coal, oil products, natural gas and electricity. We calculated the translog index of energy. For this, we needed annual data on quantities and prices of types of energy by sector. Although input–output tables are useful, they are not provided for each year. Moreover, there are no annual data on input–output tables in constant prices. Consequently, we used other data sources instead. The quantities of energy consumed are available in *Energy Balance in Taiwan, ROC* (2002), issued by the Bureau of Energy, MOEA. The energy consumption data for the utility sector needs special treatment. Electricity consumption contains the electricity consumption on power generation, pumping storage and transmission loss. Cost shares of types of energy are calculated by using the energy consumption data mentioned above and the data on prices of types of energy. The price of coal products consists of three types of coal and coke, and comes from *Commodity Price Monthly* (1981–1999) and *Import–Export Trade Monthly* (1981–1999). The price of coal gas is imputed as 5/9 of the natural gas price. The price of electricity varies with its usage. For most of the price, resident use and commercial use is adopted. The data on prices of natural gas and oil products is obtained from the *Chinese Petroleum Corporation and Energy Yearbook* (1988, 1995, 2002).

2.2.4   Intermediate input

The intermediate inputs are split into 34 categories according to 160 input–output table classifications minus five energy sectors (coal, coal products, petroleum products, natural gas and electricity) plus import. For the concordance table between the 160 sectors in the I/O table and the 34 sectors in the ICPA project, please see Table 6A.2. The data on value shares of each intermediate input during 1981–99 is then obtained by interpolating the input–output table in 1981, 1986, 1989, 1991, 1996 and 1999.

   The value and value share of intermediate input as a whole comes from the *National Income Account* (2002). Since the data on intermediate input in the *National Income Account* (2002) includes energy input, we subtract the value of energy input from the value of intermediate input. The value of each detailed intermediate input (at current prices) is the product of multiplying value share of the intermediate input $\overline{s_{MI}}$ by the value of total intermediate input M_I. Finally, the value of each intermediate input with constant prices is produced by deflating the value of each intermediate input with a corresponding deflator. Although deflator data by 155 sectors during 1981–99 is available, a deflator by 30 sectors is available from DGBAS. Therefore, we employ the above 30 deflators to deflate the corresponding intermediate input by 34 classifications during 1981–99. As to the import intermediate input, it comes from *Import – Export Trade Monthly* (1981–1999), because no price index of the import intermediate input is available from the I/O tables in Taiwan.

3. EMPIRICAL RESULTS

It is useful to make a periodic comparison for understanding the trend in total factor productivity growth. Thus, we divide the whole observation period into three sub-periods, that is, 1981–99, 1981–90, and 1990–99, and calculate the annual average growth rate of the three sub-periods.

3.1 The Growth of Real Total Output

Comparing the real total output growth by sector during 1981–90 and 1990–99, we found that output growth decreased in all sectors except electrical machinery, electronics, primary metal, transportation and communication, and petroleum and coal products (see Table 6.1).

Not surprisingly, we found that electrical machinery registered the greatest growth among the 27 sectors during all three sub-periods of 1981–99. The other outstanding performers were non-electrical machinery, fabricated metal, finance, insurance and real estate (FIRE), and other private services during 1981–90, while during 1990–99 they were primary metal, other private services, transportation and trade. All of them are either heavy industries or service industries (see Table 6.1).

In contrast, mining and lumber and wood products were the poorest performers in total output growth during 1981–90 and 1990–99, respectively (see Table 6.1). The other laggards were (1) lumber and wood, (2) apparel, (3) textile mill products and (4) agriculture during 1981–90, while during 1990–99 the laggards were leather, apparel, miscellaneous manufacturing and mining. All of them are light industries except agriculture (see Table 6.1).

3.2 The Growth in Factor Inputs

3.2.1 The growth in capital input
Among the 27 sectors, the top performers, with a double-digit growth rate in capital input during 1981–99, were electrical machinery, other

Table 6.1   *The growth of real total output by industry (1981–1999) (%)*

Sector	1981–99	1981–90	1990–99
Agriculture	1.694	3.766	−0.377
Mining	−0.033	0.964	−1.031
Coal mining	−	−	−
Metal and non-metallic mining	−	−	−
Oil and gas extraction	−	−	−
Construction	5.634	6.465	4.804
Food and kindred products	2.693	5.549	−0.163
Textile mill products	3.196	3.761	2.630
Apparel	−1.860	2.278	−5.997
Lumber and wood	−4.112	1.198	−9.421
Furniture and fixtures	3.298	5.743	0.853
Paper and allied	3.529	5.379	1.680
Printing, publishing and allied	5.255	7.567	2.942
Chemicals	8.627	9.586	7.668
Petroleum and coal products	4.922	3.846	5.999
Leather	0.060	6.510	−6.390
Stone, clay and glass	4.989	6.562	3.417
Primary metal	9.200	8.282	10.118
Fabricated metal	8.529	11.807	5.250
Machinery, non-electrical	8.933	11.888	5.978
Electrical machinery	14.268	13.720	14.815
Motor vehicles	−	−	−
Transport equipment and ordnance	5.468	7.908	3.028
Instruments	5.185	9.836	0.535
Rubber products	5.880	9.685	2.074
Miscellaneous manufacturing	1.869	6.249	−2.511
Transportation	8.257	8.150	8.364
Communications	−	−	−
Electric utilities	7.688	7.903	7.472
Gas utilities	−	−	−
Trade	8.689	9.429	7.950
Finance, Insurance and Real Estate	9.346	11.518	7.174
Other private services	10.212	10.550	9.873
Public services	−	−	−

private services, finance, insurance and real estate, and instruments (see Table 6.2).

It is also worth noting that the ranking of the growth rate in capital input changed significantly between 1981–90 and 1990–99 (see Table 6.2). For instance, the annual growth rate of capital of electric utilities and

Table 6.2   The growth of capital input by industry (1981–1999) (%)

Sector	1981–99	1981–90	1990–99
Agriculture	2.402	3.691	1.113
Mining	−4.478	−4.716	−4.241
Coal mining	–	–	–
Metal and non-metallic mining	–	–	–
Oil and gas extraction	–	–	–
Construction	4.945	5.043	4.848
Food and kindred products	5.142	6.193	4.091
Textile mill products	6.140	5.220	7.060
Apparel	4.420	3.305	5.535
Lumber and wood	0.670	6.241	−4.900
Furniture and fixtures	2.559	3.473	1.645
Paper and allied	8.879	10.574	7.184
Printing, publishing and allied	6.431	9.558	3.303
Chemicals	9.174	8.578	9.770
Petroleum and coal products	4.258	7.462	1.054
Leather	6.563	10.209	2.918
Stone, clay and glass	4.699	2.458	6.941
Primary metal	6.438	0.086	12.789
Fabricated metal	9.627	13.047	6.207
Machinery, non-electrical	8.585	8.245	8.924
Electrical machinery	16.799	12.996	20.602
Motor vehicles	–	–	–
Transport equipment and ordnance	8.794	7.296	10.293
Instruments	10.008	13.437	6.579
Rubber products	7.313	6.140	8.487
Miscellaneous manufacturing	6.594	7.311	5.876
Transportation	6.195	5.094	7.295
Communications	–	–	–
Electric utilities	3.714	−0.863	8.292
Gas utilities	–	–	–
Trade	8.246	8.930	7.562
Finance, Insurance and Real Estate	10.544	11.834	9.254
Other private services	13.038	12.773	13.303
Public services	–	–	–

primary metal jumped from −0.863 per cent and 0.086 per cent during 1981–90, to 8.292 per cent and 12.789 per cent during 1990–99, respectively (see Table 6.2).

Compared with that during 1981–90, we found that the growth rate of capital input decreased in 14 out of 27 sectors during 1990–99.

Table 6.3 The growth of labor input (1981–1999) (%)

Sector	1981–99	1981–90	1990–99
Agriculture	−2.863	−2.047	−3.679
Mining	−6.590	−5.719	−7.460
Coal mining	−	−	−
Metal and non-metallic mining	−	−	−
Oil and gas extraction	−	−	−
Construction	2.309	1.919	2.699
Food and kindred products	0.500	0.698	0.303
Textile mill products	−1.622	−0.681	−2.563
Apparel	−2.108	−0.501	−3.716
Lumber and wood	−4.640	−2.320	−6.960
Furniture and fixtures	−2.585	−2.478	−2.691
Paper and allied	2.856	4.206	1.506
Printing, publishing and allied	3.366	5.343	1.388
Chemicals	1.594	4.343	−1.155
Petroleum and coal products	5.985	11.094	0.876
Leather	−3.292	−4.368	−2.215
Stone, clay and glass	−0.613	−3.197	1.970
Primary metal	2.521	2.992	2.050
Fabricated metal	4.280	5.099	3.461
Machinery, non-electrical	2.968	2.213	3.722
Electrical machinery	5.564	7.422	3.706
Motor vehicles	−	−	−
Transport equipment and ordnance	3.413	3.660	3.165
Instruments	3.360	3.603	3.118
Rubber products	2.183	4.213	0.154
Miscellaneous manufacturing	−0.655	4.339	−5.649
Transportation	1.048	1.720	0.376
Communications	−	−	−
Electric utilities	2.208	3.842	0.574
Gas utilities	−	−	−
Trade	3.270	3.769	2.771
Finance, Insurance and Real Estate	9.063	11.406	6.720
Other private services	4.450	4.962	3.938
Public services	−	−	−

3.2.2 The growth in labor input

Generally speaking, the industry-wide growth rates of labor input were smaller than those of total output and capital input during the whole observation period (1981–99). The top runners in labor growth during 1981–99 were finance, insurance, and real estate; petroleum and coal products; electrical machinery; other private services and fabricated metal (see Table 6.3).

Compared with 1981–90, the labor growth rate in 1990–99 decreased in all of the 27 sectors except the following four: construction, leather, stone, clay, and glass, and non-electrical machinery (see Table 6.3).

3.2.3   The growth in energy input

Among the 27 sectors, the top five in energy consumption growth were: (1) petroleum and coal products; (2) electrical machinery; (3) trade; (4) transportation; and (5) primary metal. All except transportation and primary metal recorded a double-digit growth rate during the whole observation period, 1981–99 (see Table 6.4).

In contrast, the following sectors had the lowest growth in energy consumption: (1) mining (-4.373 per cent); (2) miscellaneous manufacturing and instruments (-4.127 per cent); (3=) lumber and wood products (-0.184 per cent); (3=) furniture and fixtures (-0.184 per cent); (5) stone, clay and glass (0.936 per cent); and (6) agriculture (2.231 per cent) (see Table 6.4).

Compared with the energy consumption growth rate during 1981–90, 19 out of 27 sectors decreased during 1990–99 (see Table 6.4).

3.2.4   The growth in intermediate input

The top five in intermediate input growth were: (1) electrical machinery (13.72 per cent); (2) finance, insurance and real estate (13.48 per cent); (3) non-electrical machinery (10.17 per cent); (4) trade (9.06 per cent); and (5) transportation (8.98 per cent); during the whole observation period, 1981–99 (see Table 6.5).

Compared with 1981–90, the growth rates of the intermediate inputs in all 27 sectors were smaller during 1990–99, except the petroleum and coal products sectors (see Table 6.5). The intermediate input growth rate in petroleum and coal products jumped from -1.932 per cent during 1981–90, to 3.235 per cent during 1990–99 (see Table 6.5).

3.3   The Growth in Total Factor Productivity

The outperforming sectors in total factor productivity growth during the whole observation period, 1981–99, were: chemicals (3.387 per cent), mining (3.286 per cent), primary metal (2.751 per cent), electric utilities (2.484 per cent), other private services (2.409 per cent), and trade (2.342 per cent) (see Table 6.6).

The champion was mining, with an annual growth rate of 4.59 per cent during 1981–90, while it was primary metal (3.55 per cent) during 1990–99. The TFP growth performance in the high-tech industries, such as electrical machinery and transportation and communication, was not as good as

Table 6.4   The growth of energy input by industry (1981–1999) (%)

Sector	1981–99	1981–90	1990–99
Agriculture	2.231	5.549	−1.088
Mining	−4.373	−11.947	3.202
Coal mining	−	−	−
Metal and non-metallic mining	−	−	−
Oil and gas extraction	−	−	−
Construction	2.479	2.168	2.790
Food and kindred products	3.306	5.221	1.392
Textile mill products	4.252	4.721	3.783
Apparel	4.252	4.721	3.783
Lumber and wood	−0.184	1.641	−2.009
Furniture and fixtures	−0.184	1.641	−2.009
Paper and allied	3.634	5.343	1.925
Printing, publishing and allied	3.634	5.343	1.925
Chemicals	5.779	3.627	7.931
Petroleum and coal products	12.574	15.882	9.265
Leather	7.816	7.635	7.996
Stone, clay and glass	0.936	1.256	0.616
Primary metal	7.900	9.455	6.345
Fabricated metal	7.425	9.705	5.146
Machinery, non-electrical	5.147	9.007	1.286
Electrical machinery	12.162	11.243	13.080
Motor vehicles	−	−	−
Transport equipment and ordnance	6.746	9.011	4.480
Instruments	−4.127	−9.914	1.661
Rubber products	5.241	5.426	5.057
Miscellaneous manufacturing	−4.127	−9.914	1.661
Transportation	8.294	9.523	7.066
Communications	−	−	−
Electric utilities	7.482	6.688	8.275
Gas utilities	−	−	−
Trade	11.274	12.404	10.144
Finance, Insurance and Real Estate	6.742	11.515	1.969
Other private services	4.912	6.182	3.641
Public services	−	−	−

their input growth during 1981–90 (see Table 6.6). Electrical machinery grew a mere 1.24 per cent and 1.86 per cent per annum in TFP during 1981–90 and 1990–99, respectively. Conversely, transportation and communication grew with an annual growth rate of 1.13 per cent and 3.2 per cent during 1981–90 and 1990–99 respectively.

Productivity in Asia

Table 6.5   The growth of intermediate input by industry (1981–1999) (%)

Sector	1981–99	1981–90	1990–99
Agriculture	2.324	3.683	0.964
Mining	2.549	4.977	0.122
Coal mining	–	–	–
Metal and non-metallic mining	–	–	–
Oil and gas extraction	–	–	–
Construction	6.909	7.653	6.165
Food and kindred products	1.123	2.757	−0.511
Textile mill products	4.687	5.883	3.491
Apparel	0.337	2.972	−2.297
Lumber and wood	−5.785	−1.971	−9.600
Furniture and fixtures	2.870	8.153	−2.413
Paper and allied	3.012	5.770	0.255
Printing, publishing and allied	7.517	10.894	4.139
Chemicals	5.160	6.661	3.659
Petroleum and coal products	0.652	−1.932	3.235
Leather	1.717	9.257	−5.824
Stone, clay and glass	5.233	8.107	2.358
Primary metal	6.954	7.456	6.451
Fabricated metal	7.697	9.029	6.364
Machinery, non-electrical	10.168	11.560	8.776
Electrical machinery	13.723	13.795	13.652
Motor vehicles	–	–	–
Transport equipment and ordnance	6.967	9.368	4.565
Instruments	7.821	13.065	2.578
Rubber products	3.918	8.557	−0.722
Miscellaneous manufacturing	2.490	6.089	−1.108
Transportation	8.981	9.868	8.095
Communications	–	–	–
Electric utilities	7.845	12.784	2.906
Gas utilities	–	–	–
Trade	9.063	9.164	8.961
Finance, Insurance and Real Estate	13.479	18.991	7.968
Other private services	8.007	9.926	6.087
Public services	–	–	–

Transportation and communication, and electrical machinery ranked 15 and 14 respectively among 27 sectors during 1981–90. Conversely, they rank three and eight respectively during 1990–99 (see Table 6.6).

Compared with 1981–90, the TFP growth decreased in 17 out of 27 sectors during 1990–99 (see Table 6.6).

Table 6.6   Total factor productivity (1981–1999) (%)

Sector	1981–99	1981–90	1990–99
Agriculture	0.957	1.798	0.116
Mining	3.286	4.588	1.984
Coal mining	–	–	–
Metal and non-metallic mining	–	–	–
Oil and gas extraction	–	–	–
Construction	−0.187	−0.019	−0.356
Food and kindred products	1.453	2.969	−0.064
Textile mill products	−0.427	−0.803	−0.051
Apparel	−2.264	−0.147	−4.382
Lumber and wood	0.677	2.313	−0.958
Furniture and fixtures	1.380	0.294	2.466
Paper and allied	−0.137	−0.635	0.360
Printing, publishing and allied	−1.046	−1.711	−0.380
Chemicals	3.387	3.287	3.487
Petroleum and coal products	−5.100	−9.317	−0.883
Leather	−1.164	−0.240	−2.088
Stone, clay and glass	1.831	2.873	0.790
Primary metal	2.751	1.957	3.545
Fabricated metal	1.367	3.111	−0.376
Machinery, non-electrical	0.600	2.754	−1.553
Electrical machinery	1.551	1.240	1.862
Motor vehicles	–	–	–
Transport equipment and ordnance	−1.005	−0.291	−1.719
Instruments	−1.527	−0.649	−2.406
Rubber products	1.846	2.121	1.571
Miscellaneous manufacturing	0.006	0.964	−0.952
Transportation	2.166	1.128	3.204
Communications	–	–	–
Electric utilities	2.484	3.728	1.240
Gas utilities	–	–	–
Trade	2.342	2.573	2.110
Finance, Insurance and Real Estate	−0.508	−0.277	−0.739
Other private services	2.409	2.340	2.479
Public services	–	–	–

3.4   The Sources of Real Total Output Growth

From the above industry-wide input and output comparison during 1981–90 and 1990–99, we can conclude that the deceleration in inputs and TFP growth was the major cause for the deceleration of total output in most of the sectors during 1990–99. In this section we further analyze the sources of total output change by sector change during 1981–99. Table 6.7 presents the contribution of capital, labor, energy, intermediate inputs, and TFP to output growth by sector. From Table 6.7, we conclude the following:

3.4.1 Agriculture
Due to declines in the labor force, the role of agriculture in Taiwan's economic development is diminishing. The growth rate of agricultural outputs declined from 3.766 per cent per annum during 1981–90 to −0.377 per cent per annum during 1990–99. The labor input decreased with a pace of 2.05 per cent per annum during 1981–90. The labor decrease rate increased to −3.68 per cent per annum during 1990–99, making it the major contributing factor to the negative growth in total output. However, policies to encourage mechanical farming, R&D on new species and the promotion of value-added products are helpful in upgrading productivity, which grew 1.80 per cent per annum during 1981–90. The pace slowed down after 1990 (0.116 per cent in 1990–99). Meanwhile, contributions from capital and intermediate input kept expanding moderately in all periods, but still failed to cover the negative impact of the reduction in labor and TFP since 1990.

3.4.2 Manufacturing

Products of the necessities of life group According to DGBAS's classification, the products of the 'necessities of life' group include food, textile products, apparel and accessories, wood and bamboo products, furniture and fixtures and miscellaneous manufacturing products. This group is almost exclusively composed of products from light industries. Before the mid-1980s, it was the major source of the industrial sector's growth. However, after the great appreciation of the New Taiwan dollar against the US dollar and soaring labor costs, Taiwan mostly lost its international competitive edge. Coping with intense corporate environment changes, companies have been gradually relocating to other countries or have been using automated equipment, thereby replacing physical labor. Output growth in products of the necessities of life group has kept decreasing, even turning negative during 1990–99. The negative growth in labor services and TFP in most sectors in this group since 1987 could have been a contributory factor to this effect.

Chemistry group The chemistry group includes chemical materials, chemical products, petroleum and coal products, rubber products, plastic products, paper and paper products and printing. According to the *National Income and Product Accounts* (2002), the output of the chemistry group

Table 6.7 Contributions of inputs and TFP to sectoral output growth in Taiwan (%)

		1981–99		1981–90		1990–99	
		Growth Rate	Con. Rate	Growth Rate	Con. Rate	Growth Rate	Con. Rate
Agriculture							
	Q	1.694	100.00	3.766	100.00	−0.377	100.00
	K	2.402	26.77	3.691	18.90	1.113	−51.71
	L	−2.863	−51.45	−2.047	−16.88	−3.679	293.62
	E	2.231	5.36	5.549	5.68	−1.088	8.51
	M	2.324	62.85	3.683	44.55	0.964	−119.81
	T	0.957	56.48	1.798	47.75	0.116	−30.61
Mining							
	Q	−0.033	100.00	0.964	100.00	−1.031	100.00
	K	−4.478	3570.61	−4.716	−133.17	−4.241	106.73
	L	−6.590	5994.55	−5.719	−171.28	−7.460	228.09
	E	−4.373	2344.23	−11.947	−206.65	3.202	−41.43
	M	2.549	−1968.11	4.977	135.26	0.122	−0.98
	T	3.286	−9841.28	4.588	475.84	1.984	−192.41
Construction							
	Q	5.634	100.00	6.465	100.00	4.804	100.00
	K	4.945	7.66	5.043	8.12	4.848	7.04
	L	2.309	6.68	1.919	2.85	2.699	11.84
	E	2.479	0.64	2.168	0.59	2.790	0.70
	M	6.909	88.35	7.653	88.74	6.165	87.82
	T	−0.187	−3.33	−0.019	−0.30	−0.356	−7.40
Food and kindred products							
	Q	2.693	100.00	5.549	100.00	−0.163	100.00
	K	5.142	12.04	6.193	7.20	4.091	−153.35
	L	0.500	3.97	0.698	3.06	0.303	−27.10
	E	3.306	2.15	5.221	1.62	1.392	−15.94
	M	1.123	27.91	2.757	34.62	−0.511	257.21
	T	1.453	53.94	2.969	53.51	−0.064	39.18
Textile mill products							
	Q	3.196	100.00	3.761	100.00	2.630	100.00
	K	6.140	16.36	5.220	11.49	7.060	23.32
	L	−1.622	−9.68	−0.681	−3.53	−2.563	−18.47
	E	4.252	5.08	4.721	5.18	3.783	4.93
	M	4.687	101.61	5.883	108.22	3.491	92.14
	T	−0.427	−13.36	−0.803	−21.36	−0.051	−1.92
Apparel							
	Q	−1.860	100.00	2.278	100.00	−5.997	100.00
	K	4.420	−22.10	3.305	12.72	5.535	−8.88

Table 6.7 (continued)

		1981–99		1981–90		1990–99	
		Growth Rate	Con. Rate	Growth Rate	Con. Rate	Growth Rate	Con. Rate
	L	−2.108	21.30	−0.501	−4.51	−3.716	11.50
	E	4.252	−8.73	4.721	8.55	3.783	−2.16
	M	0.337	−12.24	2.972	89.69	−2.297	26.48
	T	−2.264	121.77	−0.147	−6.46	−4.382	73.06
Lumber and wood							
	Q	−4.112	100.00	1.198	100.00	−9.421	100.00
	K	0.670	4.96	6.241	56.55	−4.900	11.52
	L	−4.640	23.98	−2.320	−35.86	−6.960	16.37
	E	−0.184	−0.14	1.641	4.86	−2.009	0.50
	M	−5.785	87.68	−1.971	−118.56	−9.600	61.45
	T	0.677	−16.47	2.313	193.00	−0.958	10.17
Furniture and fixtures							
	Q	3.298	100.00	5.743	100.00	0.853	100.00
	K	2.559	12.63	3.473	6.87	1.645	51.40
	L	−2.585	−14.12	−2.478	−7.98	−2.691	−55.47
	E	−0.184	0.17	1.641	1.01	−2.009	−5.48
	M	2.870	59.47	8.153	94.98	−2.413	−179.75
	T	1.380	41.84	0.294	5.11	2.466	289.30
Paper and allied							
	Q	3.529	100.00	5.379	100.00	1.680	100.00
	K	8.879	27.65	10.574	23.26	7.184	41.74
	L	2.856	15.45	4.206	14.00	1.506	20.07
	E	3.634	6.13	5.343	5.97	1.925	6.64
	M	3.012	54.66	5.770	68.57	0.255	10.11
	T	−0.137	−3.90	−0.635	−11.81	0.360	21.45
Printing, publishing and allied							
	Q	5.255	100.00	7.567	100.00	2.942	100.00
	K	6.431	14.18	9.558	15.38	3.303	11.10
	L	3.366	12.02	5.343	12.60	1.388	10.53
	E	3.634	4.12	5.343	4.25	1.925	3.79
	M	7.517	89.58	10.894	90.38	4.139	87.50
	T	−1.046	−19.90	−1.711	−22.62	−0.380	−12.93
Chemicals							
	Q	8.627	100.00	9.586	100.00	7.668	100.00
	K	9.174	13.72	8.578	12.42	9.770	15.35
	L	1.594	1.76	4.343	4.56	−1.155	−1.75
	E	5.779	5.11	3.627	3.33	7.931	7.34
	M	5.160	40.16	6.661	45.41	3.659	33.59
	T	3.387	39.26	3.287	34.28	3.487	45.47

Table 6.7 (continued)

		1981–99		1981–90		1990–99	
		Growth Rate	Con. Rate	Growth Rate	Con. Rate	Growth Rate	Con. Rate
Petroleum and coal products							
	Q	4.922	100.00	3.846	100.00	5.999	100.00
	K	4.258	13.81	7.462	35.19	1.054	0.10
	L	5.985	22.01	11.094	56.28	0.876	0.05
	E	12.574	170.60	15.882	260.79	9.265	112.79
	M	0.652	−2.81	−1.932	−9.97	3.235	1.78
	T	−5.100	−103.61	−9.317	−242.29	−0.883	−14.71
Leather							
	Q	0.060	100.00	6.510	100.00	−6.390	100.00
	K	6.563	849.89	10.209	12.46	2.918	−3.35
	L	−3.292	−838.79	−4.368	−11.73	−2.215	3.89
	E	7.816	226.03	7.635	2.40	7.996	−1.82
	M	1.717	1792.27	9.257	100.56	−5.824	68.62
	T	−1.164	−1929.40	−0.240	−3.69	−2.088	32.67
Stone, clay and glass							
	Q	4.989	100.00	6.562	100.00	3.417	100.00
	K	4.699	14.06	2.458	5.82	6.941	29.88
	L	−0.613	−2.23	−3.197	−9.23	1.970	11.21
	E	0.936	1.38	1.256	1.25	0.616	1.65
	M	5.233	50.08	8.107	58.38	2.358	34.14
	T	1.831	36.71	2.873	43.78	0.790	23.13
Primary metal							
	Q	9.200	100.00	8.282	100.00	10.118	100.00
	K	6.438	7.63	0.086	1.04	12.789	13.02
	L	2.521	2.85	2.992	5.05	2.050	1.05
	E	7.900	6.22	9.455	9.29	6.345	3.71
	M	6.954	53.40	7.456	61.00	6.451	47.18
	T	2.751	29.90	1.957	23.63	3.545	35.03
Fabricated metal							
	Q	8.529	100.00	11.807	100.00	5.250	100.00
	K	9.627	11.02	13.047	11.78	6.207	9.28
	L	4.280	10.83	5.099	8.89	3.461	15.19
	E	7.425	3.20	9.705	3.32	5.146	2.92
	M	7.697	58.93	9.029	49.66	6.364	79.77
	T	1.367	16.03	3.111	26.35	−0.376	−7.17
Machinery, non-electrical							
	Q	8.933	100.00	11.888	100.00	5.978	100.00
	K	8.585	8.86	8.245	7.03	8.924	12.49
	L	2.968	7.19	2.213	3.91	3.722	13.69

Table 6.7 (continued)

	1981–99		1981–90		1990–99	
	Growth Rate	Con. Rate	Growth Rate	Con. Rate	Growth Rate	Con. Rate
E	5.147	1.68	9.007	2.24	1.286	0.58
M	10.168	75.55	11.560	63.65	8.776	99.22
T	0.600	6.72	2.754	23.16	−1.553	−25.99
Electrical machinery						
Q	14.268	100.00	13.720	100.00	14.815	100.00
K	16.799	10.70	12.996	7.18	20.602	13.96
L	5.564	6.41	7.422	9.93	3.706	3.15
E	12.162	1.10	11.243	1.20	13.080	1.01
M	13.723	70.92	13.795	72.65	13.652	69.31
T	1.551	10.87	1.240	9.04	1.862	12.57
Transport equipment and ordnance						
Q	5.468	100.00	7.908	100.00	3.028	100.00
K	8.794	12.54	7.296	6.66	10.293	27.91
L	3.413	11.15	3.660	9.28	3.165	16.03
E	6.746	1.94	9.011	2.01	4.480	1.76
M	6.967	92.75	9.368	85.73	4.565	111.08
T	−1.005	−18.38	−0.291	−3.68	−1.719	−56.79
Instruments						
Q	8.933	100.00	11.888	100.00	5.978	100.00
K	8.585	8.86	8.245	7.03	8.924	12.49
L	2.968	7.19	2.213	3.91	3.722	13.69
E	5.147	1.68	9.007	2.24	1.286	0.58
M	10.168	75.55	11.560	63.65	8.776	99.22
T	0.600	6.72	2.754	23.16	−1.553	−25.99
Rubber products						
Q	5.880	100.00	9.685	100.00	2.074	100.00
K	7.313	11.72	6.140	6.18	8.487	37.56
L	2.183	5.51	4.213	6.22	0.154	2.16
E	5.241	2.93	5.426	1.88	5.057	7.84
M	3.918	48.45	8.557	63.81	−0.722	−23.31
T	1.846	31.40	2.121	21.90	1.571	75.75
Miscellaneous manufacturing						
Q	1.869	100.00	6.249	100.00	−2.511	100.00
K	6.594	30.62	7.311	11.48	5.876	−17.00
L	−0.655	−8.48	4.339	14.96	−5.649	49.84
E	−4.127	−7.19	−9.914	−4.69	1.661	−0.96
M	2.490	84.72	6.089	62.81	−1.108	30.21
T	0.006	0.33	0.964	15.43	−0.952	37.91

Table 6.7 (continued)

		1981–99		1981–90		1990–99	
		Growth Rate	Con. Rate	Growth Rate	Con. Rate	Growth Rate	Con. Rate
Transportation							
	Q	8.257	100.00	8.150	100.00	8.364	100.00
	K	6.195	19.82	5.094	18.35	7.295	21.25
	L	1.048	2.45	1.720	3.27	0.376	1.65
	E	8.294	15.13	9.523	21.57	7.066	8.86
	M	8.981	36.37	9.868	42.98	8.095	29.93
	T	2.166	26.23	1.128	13.83	3.204	38.30
Electric utilities							
	Q	7.688	100.00	7.903	100.00	7.472	100.00
	K	3.714	13.84	−0.863	−4.89	8.292	33.66
	L	2.208	2.10	3.842	3.28	0.574	0.86
	E	7.482	33.36	6.688	27.71	8.275	39.34
	M	7.845	18.38	12.784	26.73	2.906	9.55
	T	2.484	32.31	3.728	47.17	1.240	16.60
Trade							
	Q	8.689	100.00	9.429	100.00	7.950	100.00
	K	8.246	22.52	8.930	25.10	7.562	19.46
	L	3.270	16.85	3.769	17.56	2.771	16.02
	E	11.274	3.46	12.404	3.89	10.144	2.96
	M	9.063	30.22	9.164	26.16	8.961	35.02
	T	2.342	26.95	2.573	27.29	2.110	26.54
Finance, Insurance and Real Estate							
	Q	9.346	100.00	11.518	100.00	7.174	100.00
	K	10.544	38.34	11.834	40.03	9.254	35.63
	L	9.063	34.17	11.406	33.34	6.720	35.50
	E	6.742	2.77	11.515	4.38	1.969	0.19
	M	13.479	30.15	18.991	24.65	7.968	38.98
	T	−0.508	−5.43	−0.277	−2.41	−0.739	−10.30
Other private services							
	Q	10.212	100.00	10.550	100.00	9.873	100.00
	K	13.038	31.23	12.773	22.40	13.303	40.68
	L	4.450	18.26	4.962	20.72	3.938	15.64
	E	4.912	1.23	6.182	1.94	3.641	0.47
	M	8.007	25.67	9.926	32.76	6.087	18.10
	T	2.409	23.60	2.340	22.18	2.479	25.11

Notes:
Q: real value added. K: capital input. L: labor input. E: energy input. M: material input. T: TFP.
Contribution Rate = (Moving Share $K_i \times$ Growth Rate K_i) / Growth Rate Q_i.

grew 12.4 per cent annually during 1982–86, yet after that, not unlike products of the necessities of life group, the appreciation of the New Taiwan dollar and soaring labor costs eroded its performance. Another serious problem for the chemistry group in Taiwan has been greater awareness of environmental issues. However, outstanding performers can still be found in this group. For instance, the output of chemical products and chemical materials outgrew the whole manufacturing sector during the whole observation period (1981–99). The chemical products sector registered one of the highest TFP growths in the manufacturing sector, that is, 3.39 per cent per annum during 1981–99. For the whole observation period 1981–99, intermediate input (40.16 per cent) and TFP (39.26 per cent) were the major contributors to the output growth in the chemical products sector.

Metal and machinery group   The metal and machinery group consists of primary metals, fabricated metal products, machinery, transportation equipment and precision instruments. Before the establishment of the China Steel Corporation in 1977, manufacturing in Taiwan mainly focused on products of 'the necessities of life' and the chemistry groups. The establishment of the China Steel Corporation motivated developments in the metal and machinery group. The metal and machinery group, consequently, experienced prosperous growth during the 1980s. For instance, the real total output of primary metals, fabricated metals, and machinery and precision instruments grew at a pace of over 8.5 per cent per annum during 1981–99. TFP grew strongly at more than 20 per cent per annum in most of the sub-sectors of this group, except transportation equipment and ordnance during 1981–90. However, after the 1990s, output growth dropped in all of the sub-sectors except primary metal, due to sluggish capital labor and material input. The whole group dropped significantly, due to the stagnation of the following three sub-sectors: fabricated metal products, transportation equipment and precision instruments. Also, it could be attributed to the slowing – even negative – growth of adjusted TFP in most of its subsectors except primary steel. The input growth of primary metal was outstanding, with a growth rate of 9.2 per cent per annum during 1981–99. TFP and intermediate input grew strongly with an annual growth rate of 3.54 per cent and 6.45 per cent respectively during 1990–99. TFP and intermediate input account for 82.2 per cent of output growth.

Electrical and electronic machinery group   Electrical and electronic machinery is Taiwan's leading industry at present. Prosperity in the field began as early as the 1980s, when the operations of the United Microelectronics Corp. and the Taiwan Semiconductor Manufacturing Company Ltd inspired the transformation of the electrical and electronic machinery group from simple OEM of consumer electric products, such as TVs and radios, to IC design production and other relevant industrial developments. Electrical and electronic machinery experienced double-digit growth (14.27 per cent) during 1981–99. The contribution from labor is negligible (1.10 per cent). TFP made a contribution approximately equal to capital services (10.87 per cent and 10.70 per cent respectively) in the whole observation period 1981–99. The rest of the contribution can be attributed to intermediate input (70.92 per cent) and energy (7.51 per cent).

3.4.3   Electricity, gas and water utilities

Most corporations in electricity, gas and water utilities are state-owned and hence enjoy the advantages of monopolies or oligopolies. Since the liberalization of these industries, they have attracted new private investments. This is especially the case with the electricity industry. Such developments allow for a new momentum for growth. The real total output of the whole sector increased 7.69 per cent per annum during the whole observation period. TFP (32.31 per cent) and energy input (33.26 per cent) are major contributors to this growth. TFP and energy input grew at a pace of 2.48 per cent and 7.48 per cent per annum during 1981–99. It is noted that the annual growth rate of capital input jumped from −0.86 per cent during 1981–90 to 8.29 per cent during 1990–99. It is also noted that the growth of labor input was negligible (0.86 per cent per annum).

Most electricity, gas and water utilities are large-size enterprises. Responding to liberalization policies, they began to streamline labor input and to upgrade efficiency. According to the Manpower Survey, the number of employees of electricity, gas and water utilities declined 4.2 per cent per annum during 1991–96, mostly attributed to electricity (−4.7 per cent) and water utilities (−9.1 per cent) downsizing. This explained the negative contribution of labor during the 1991–96 period. Although the gas sector hired 10.1 per cent more employees in 1996 than in 1991, its weight was so small that it did not affect the result.

In 1981–90, the TFP contributed 2.484 percentage points (or 32.31 per cent) to the output growth, then it gradually decreased. During the period 1990–99, TFP consistently contributed more than labor but less than capital. Energy was the largest contributor to the real output growth of this sector during the whole observation period, 1981–99. On the other hand, contributions from capital services revealed different patterns within the sample periods. During 1981–90, capital stock contributed −4.89 percentage points on average. During the period 1990–99, capital contributed 33.66 percentage points as new private power plants were established, which in turn depressed TFP's contribution.

3.4.4   Transportation and communication

Unlike most of the sectors, total output grew more quickly in the transportation and communication sector during 1990–99, compared with 1981–90. The growth rate of total output in the sector was 81.15 per cent per annum during 1981–90, while it was 8.36 per cent per annum during 1990–99. This could be attributed to the liberalization policy implemented in the wireless and cable sector. The liberalization policy induced investment and competition. Competition brought in efficiency and TFP growth. The TFP and capital grew, with an annual rate of 3.20 per cent and 7.30 per cent respectively during 1990–99, compared with 1.13 per cent and 5.09 per cent during 1981–90. Consequently, the contribution of TFP and capital to output growth jumped from 13.83 per cent and 18.35 per cent respectively during 1981–90 to 38.30 per cent and 21.25 per cent respectively during 1990–99.

3.4.5   Service sector

The service sector (excluding transportation and communication) includes trade (i.e., retail and wholesale), finance, insurance and real estate, and other private services. The total output grew with an annual rate of 8.69 per cent in trade, 9.35 per cent in finance, insurance and real estate, and 10.21 per cent in other private service sectors during the whole observation period, 1981–99. The output growth rate in the service sector was greater than most of the sectors mentioned above during 1981–99. Consequently, the share of the service sector (excluding transportation and communication but including the government services) in GDP increases from 44.3 per cent in 1981 to 61.3 per cent in 1999. The source of growth largely came from capital, intermediate input and labor. TFP also contributed significantly to the growth in trade and other private services. The contribution rate of TFP was 26.95 per cent in trade and 23.60 per cent in other private service sectors during 1981–99. However, it is noted that TFP growth was negative (-0.508 per cent) in the finance, insurance and real estate sector, and hence TFP did not have a positive contribution to its output growth. This could be attributed to over-protection during the period 1981–90, or over-banking during 1990–99.

3.5   International Comparison on TFP Growth

The results of Jorgenson et al. (2007), Jorgenson and Nomura (2005) and those of this study have been used in tabulating the industry-level comparison on total output TFP growth for the United States, Japan and Taiwan. Table 6.8 enables us to draw conclusions about the various subperiods.

Table 6.8 International comparison on TFP growth among US, Japan and Taiwan (1980–2000) (%)

Sector	1980–90		1990–95			1995–2000		
	Taiwan	US	Taiwan	US	Japan	Taiwan	US	Japan
Agriculture	1.798	3.15	0.001	0.88	1.56	0.259	1.71	-0.29
Coal mining	–	3.24	–	3.13	1.14	–	2.93	0.72
Metal and non-metallic mining	–	-0.33	–	-1.24	-4.08	–	-1.46	3.41
Oil and gas extraction	–	-1.93	–	1.95	–	–	0.89	–
Construction	-0.019	-0.48	0.639	-1.41	-2.13	-1.599	-1.59	-1.04
Food and kindred products	2.969	0.47	-0.436	0.71	-1.17	0.401	0.15	-0.29
Textile mill products	-0.803	1.06	0.054	1.64	2.3	-0.181	2.21	1.22
Apparel	-0.147	0.19	-7.119	0.21	-1.9	-0.96	1.94	-0.11
Lumber and wood	2.313	1.59	-3.98	-2.14	-0.88	2.819	0.09	0.9
Furniture and fixtures	0.294	-0.12	1.008	0.38	-2.18	4.289	2.07	-0.12
Paper and allied	-0.635	0.02	-0.764	-0.39	0.03	1.766	1.8	0.46
Printing, publishing and allied	-1.711	-0.57	-0.446	-0.84	-1.32	-0.298	0.51	-0.09
Chemicals	3.287	0.51	4.74	-0.02	0.2	1.92	0.5	-0.28
Petroleum refining	-9.317	1.96	-0.565	1.8	0.07	-1.28	-4.04	1.17
Leather	-0.24	-1.22	-5.249	-0.11	-1.82	1.863	3.39	-0.22
Stone, clay and glass	2.873	1.0	1.341	0.24	-0.63	0.102	0.94	0.19
Primary metal	1.957	0.36	2.808	0.5	-0.93	4.465	2.29	-0.48
Fabricated metal	3.111	-0.11	1.119	0.95	–	-2.246	1.52	–
Machinery, non-electrical	2.754	2.39	-1.303	4.01	-1.25	-1.866	5.85	0.06
Electrical machinery	1.24	2.29	3.764	5.89	–	-0.516	8.6	–
Motor vehicles	–	0.04	–	-0.45	-0.02	–	0.35	0.17
Other transport equipment	-0.291	-0.11	-0.27	0.05	-1.2	-3.531	0.9	0.21
Instruments	-0.649	1.03	-0.358	0.57	-1.11	-4.966	0.84	1.55

Table 6.8 (continued)

Sector	1980–90		1990–95			1995–2000		
	Taiwan	US	Taiwan	US	Japan	Taiwan	US	Japan
Rubber products	2.121	1.53	1.717	1.28	−1.64	1.389	1.39	0.22
Miscellaneous manufacturing	0.964	0.96	−0.95	0.13	−1.0	−0.955	0.08	0.48
Transportation	1.128	0.73	1.698	0.56	–	5.086	−0.36	–
Communications	–	−0.46	–	0.05	2.75	–	−0.26	3.58
Electric utilities	3.728	−0.58	2.821	1.09	−0.34	−0.736	2.29	−0.07
Gas utilities	–	−1.79	–	−2.15	1.39	–	0.29	1.57
Trade	2.573	0.78	1.491	0.33	0.04	2.884	0.67	−0.8
Finance, Insurance and Real Estate	−0.277	−0.16	−0.517	0.72	–	−1.016	−0.09	–
Other private services	2.34	−0.49	2.164	−0.44	1.38	2.872	−0.52	−0.12
Public services	–	0	–	0	0	–	0	0

Sources: US data from Jorgenson, Ho and Stiroh (2007); Japan data from Jorgenson and Nomura (2005); Taiwan data from this study.

174

3.5.1   1980–90

During the period 1980–90, Taiwan outperformed the United States in TFP growth in 16 out of 26 sectors.[5] Taiwan led the United States in construction, food and kindred products, lumber and wood, furniture and fixtures, chemicals, leather, stone, clay and glass, primary metal, fabricated metal, non-electrical machinery, rubber products, miscellaneous manufacturing, transportation, electric utilities, trade and other private services. The United States exceeded Taiwan in agriculture, textile mill products, apparel, paper and allied, printing, publishing and allied, petroleum refining, electrical machinery, other transport equipment, instruments, and finance, insurance and real estate.[6]

3.5.2   1990–95

During the period 1990–95, Taiwan exceeded the United States and Japan in TFP growth in 10 out of 22 sectors. In contrast, the United States and Japan led in 8 and 4 out of 22 sectors respectively. Taiwan outperformed the United States and Japan in construction, furniture and fixtures, printing, publishing and allied, chemicals, stone, clay and glass, primary metal, rubber products, electric utilities, trade, and other private services. The United States surpassed Taiwan and Japan in food and kindred products, apparel, petroleum refining, leather, non-electrical machinery, other transport equipment, instruments, and miscellaneous manufacturing. Japan led in agriculture, textile mill products, lumber and wood, and paper and allied.

3.5.3   1995–2000

During 1995–99, the United States outperformed Japan and Taiwan in TFP growth in 11 out of 22 sectors. Conversely, Taiwan and Japan excelled in 7 and 4 out of 22 sectors, respectively. Taiwan's performance in industry-wide TFP growth was worse than the United States but still better than Japan. The United States led in agriculture, textile mill products, apparel, paper and allied, printing, publishing and allied, leather, stone, clay and glass, non-electrical machinery, other transport equipment, rubber products and electric utilities. Taiwan led in food and kindred products, lumber and wood, furniture and fixtures, chemicals, primary metal, trade, and other private services. Japan led in construction, petroleum refining, instruments, and miscellaneous manufacturing.

The above findings imply that, based on the industry-wide international comparison among the United States, Japan and Taiwan, the hypothesis proposed by Krugman (1994), Kim and Lau (1994) and Young (1994a) – that the growth rate of TFP in the NIEs such as Taiwan is less than in the developed countries, such as Japan and the United States – is invalid during the period 1980–2000. As mentioned, based on an international comparison of TFP growth of the whole economy, Liang (2002) maintained that the Krugman–Kim–Lau–Young hypothesis was invalid during 1966–90. In addition, Liang and Mei (2005) found that the Krugman–Kim–Lau–Young hypothesis was also incorrect during 1978–99. Based on the industry-wide international comparison, this study reinforces the finding of Liang (2002) and Liang and Mei (2005).

4. CONCLUSIONS AND IMPLICATIONS

The objective of this chapter is to measure the growth of industry-wide output, input and productivity change and to analyze the causes of growth in output and total factor productivity of the Asian NIEs by employing Taiwan's data on 26 sectors during 1981–99 as an example. For verifying the Krugman–Kim–Lau–Young hypothesis, we compare the industry-wide TFP growth of Taiwan with that of the United States and Japan. Finally, conclusions and implications are drawn from the findings. The major findings of this chapter are as follows:

1. Comparing the real total output growth by sector during 1981–90 and 1990–99, we found that output growth decelerated in all sectors except electrical and electronics, primary metal, transportation and communication, and petroleum and coal products.
2. The deceleration of growth in inputs, such as capital, labor, energy, material, and TFP was the major cause for the deceleration of total output in most of the sectors during 1990–99, compared with that during 1981–90.
3. The outperforming sectors in TFP growth during 1981–90 were chemicals (3.387 per cent), mining (3.286 per cent), primary metal (2.75 per cent), electric utilities (2.484 per cent), other private services (2.41 per cent), and trade (2.342 per cent).
4. The growth of TFP was not as impressive as the inputs in the electrical and electronic machinery sector, with an annual growth rate of 1.24 per cent during 1981–90 and 1.86 per cent during 1990–99.
5. Material input is the biggest contributor to output growth in all sectors during 1981–99, except the following seven: mining, food and kindred products, apparel, petroleum and coal products, electrical utility, finance, insurance and real estate, and other private services.
6. Based on the industry-wide international comparison among the United States, Japan and Taiwan, the hypothesis proposed by

Krugman (1994), Kim and Lau (1994) and Young (1994a) – that the growth rate of TFP in the NIEs such as Taiwan is less than in the developed countries, such as Japan and the United States – is invalid during 1980–2000. This study reinforces the finding of Liang (2002) and Liang and Mei *(2005)*.

APPENDIX

Table 6A.1   Property compensation by sector (NT$ millions)

Sector	Construction	Other construction	Transportation equipment	Machineries
Agriculture	11,577.46	10,220.42	7,063.33	51,482.72
Mining	–	–	–	–
Coal mining	–	–	–	–
Metal and non-metallic mining	–	–	–	–
Oil and gas extraction	–	–	–	–
Construction	22,228.82	499.24	18,741.40	47,277.41
Food and kindred products	10,119.79	4,553.29	2,945.49	33,716.60
Textile mill products	6,915.03	751.89	772.19	20,816.92
Apparel	569.43	60.05	2,237.88	1,829.44
Lumber and wood	1,078.28	144.39	1,187.15	1,400.93
Furniture and fixtures	1,004.71	110.67	1,012.45	1,370.57
Paper and allied	756.81	129.33	359.60	7,511.16
Printing, publishing and allied	327.05	114.55	212.51	3,367.18
Chemicals	25,514.58	3,142.33	2,118.21	67,229.33
Petroleum and coal products	8,030.14	5,695.05	6,005.44	70,607.27
Leather	438.76	314.23	136.47	922.99
Stone, clay and glass	5,745.81	1,065.37	3,797.92	24,823.30

Table 6A.1   (continued)

Sector	Construction	Other construction	Transportation equipment	Machineries
Primary metal	4,054.64	802.95	2,133.87	53,695.05
Fabricated metal	4,924.11	393.89	3,668.03	15,879.17
Machinery, non-electrical	4,355.31	228.09	2,907.94	11,881.25
Electrical machinery	34,097.59	1,941.85	3,253.43	101,527.47
Motor vehicles	–	–	–	–
Transport equipment and ordnance	0.00	591.76	6,333.55	39,292.66
Instruments	–	–	–	–
Rubber products	4,575.31	452.31	2,191.37	25,330.33
Miscellaneous manufacturing	2,069.60	210.08	735.83	5,809.09
Transportation	6,661.20	29,169.92	105,408.28	38,747.59
Communications	6,661.20	29,169.92	105,408.28	38,747.59
Electric utilities	3,975.39	57,123.28	706.49	49,046.50
Gas utilities	–	–	–	–
Trade	167,383.72	8,765.69	63,944.76	80,389.21
Finance, Insurance and Real estate	584,192.65	14,182.89	58,224.43	331,220.15
Other private services	49,502.00	2,608.53	54,236.04	51,558.23
Public services	–	–	–	–

Table 6A.2   The concordance between 160 sectors in I/O table and 34 sectors in ICPA project

34 sectors in ICPA	160 sectors in I/O table of Taiwan[a]
01 Agriculture	001–012
02 Mining	013–017
03 Coal mining	013
04 Metal and non-metallic mining	–
05 Oil and gas extraction	–
06 Construction	117–120
07 Food and kindred products	018–033
08 Textile mill products	034–039
09 Apparel	040–042
10 Lumber and wood	046–048
11 Furniture and fixtures	049
12 Paper and allied	050–051
13 Printing, publishing and allied	052–053
14 Chemicals	054–065
15 Petroleum and coal products	066–067
16 Leather	043–045
17 Stone, clay and glass	071–075
18 Primary metal	076–079
19 Fabricated metal	080–085
20 Machinery, non-electrical	086–090
21 Electrical machinery	091–105
22 Motor vehicles	–
23 Transport equipment and ordnance	106–110
24 Instruments	111
25 Rubber products	068–070
26 Miscellaneous manufacturing	112–113
27 Transportation	125–133
28 Communications	–
29 Electric utilities	114–116
30 Gas utilities	–
31 Trade	121–123
32 Finance, Insurance and Real Estate	134–136
33 Other private services	137–160
34 Public services	–

Note: [a] please refer to table 6A.3.

Table 6A.3   160 sectors in I/O table of Taiwan

001 Paddy Rice	041 Knitted Garments
002 Other Common Crops	042 Fabric Products, Wearing
003 Sugarcane	Apparel and Accessories
004 Other Special Crops	043 Leather
005 Fruits	044 Leather Footwear
006 Vegetables	045 Other Leather Products
007 Other Horticultural Crops	046 Lumber
008 Hogs	047 Plywood
009 Other Livestock	048 Wood, Bamboo and Rattan
010 Agricultural Services	Products
011 Forestry	049 Non-Metallic Furniture
012 Fisheries	050 Pulp and Paper
013 Coal	051 Paper Products
014 Crude Oil, Natural Gas and	052 Newspapers, Books and
Geothermal Energy	Magazines
015 Metallic Minerals	053 Other Printed Matter and
016 Salt	Bookbinding
017 Other Non-Metallic Minerals	054 Basic Industrial Chemicals
018 Slaughtering and By-Products	055 Petrochemical Raw Materials
019 Edible Oil and Fat By-Products	056 Chemical Fertilizers
020 Flour	057 Synthetic Fibers
021 Rice	058 Other Artificial Fibers
022 Sugar	059 Plastics (Synthetic Resins)
023 Animal Feeds	060 Other Chemical Materials
024 Canned Foods	061 Coatings
025 Frozen Foods	062 Medicines
026 Monosodium Glutamate	063 Pesticides and Herbicides
027 Seasonings	064 Synthetic Detergents and
028 Dairy Products	Washing Preparations and
029 Sugar Confectionery and Bakery	Cosmetics
Products	065 Miscellaneous Chemical
030 Miscellaneous Food Products	Manufactures
031 Non-Alcoholic Beverages	066 Petroleum Refining Products
032 Alcoholic Beverages	067 Coal Products
033 Tobacco	068 Rubber and Rubber Products
034 Cotton and Cotton Fabrics	069 Plastic Footwear
035 Wool and Worsted Fabrics	070 Other Plastic Products
036 Artificial Fabrics	071 Ceramics
037 Knitted Fabrics	072 Glass and Glass Products
038 Other Fabrics and Fabric	073 Cement
Products	074 Cement Products
039 Printing, Dyeing and Finishing	075 Miscellaneous Non-Metallic
040 Tatted Garments	076 Pig Iron and Crude Steel

Table 6A.3   (continued)

077	Primary Iron and Steel Products	112	Education and Entertainment Articles
078	Aluminum	113	Other Manufactures
079	Miscellaneous Metals	114	Electricity
080	Metallic Products for Household Use	115	Gas
		116	City Water, Steam and Hot Water
081	Metallic Hand Tools	117	Residential Building Construction
082	Iron and Steel Products		
083	Aluminum Products	118	Non-residential Building Construction
084	Miscellaneous Metallic Products		
085	Surface Treating of Metal Products	119	Public Works
		120	Other Construction
086	General Industrial Machinery	121	Wholesale Trade
087	Metal Processing Machinery	122	Retail Trade
088	Industrial Machinery	123	International Trade
089	Other Machinery	124	Food and Beverage Services
090	Machinery Parts, Repair and Maintenance	125	Railway Transportation
		126	Other Land Transportation
091	Household Electrical Appliances	127	Water Transportation
092	Lighting Equipment	128	Air Transportation
093	Power Generation, Transmission and Distribution Machinery	129	Services Incidental to Transport
		130	Travel Agency Services
094	Wires and Cables	131	Warehousing
095	Other Electrical Materials	132	Postal Services
096	Computer Products	133	Telegram and Telephone
097	Computer Peripheral Equipment	134	Finance
098	Data Storage Media	135	Security and Future
099	Computer Components	136	Insurance
100	Video and Radio Electronic Products	137	House Services
		138	Hotel Services
101	Communication Apparatus	139	Real Estate Services
102	Electronic Tube	140	Legal and Accounting Services
103	Semi-conductors	141	Consulting Services
104	Optoelectronic Components and Materials	142	Data Processing and Information Services
105	Electronic Components and Parts	143	Advertising Services
106	Shipbuilding	144	Renting and Leasing Services
107	Motor Vehicles	145	Miscellaneous Services For Business
108	Motorcycles		
109	Bicycles	146	Public Administration Services
110	Other Transport Equipment	147	Environmental Sanitary Services
111	Precision Instruments and Apparatus	148	Educational Training Services
		149	Scientific Research and Services

Productivity in Asia

Table 6A.3   (continued)

150 Medical and Health Services	155 Recreational and Cultural Services
151 Social Welfare Services	156 Vehicles Services
152 Services of Civil Association	157 Other Repair Services
153 Other Social Services	158 Household Services
154 Radio, Television and Movies Services	159 Other Personal Services
	160 Undistributed

NOTES

*   The author would like to thank Ms Ting Lie, Mr Chih-Chun Liu, Ms Wan-Jou Liu, Ms Shiou-Wen Tsai and Mr Chih-Sheng Hsieh for their capable assistance in data compilation, programming, calculating and typing. The research grant from the National Science Council, Taiwan and METI of Japan is also gratefully acknowledged.
1. These studies include Christensen and Jorgenson (1970), Gollop and Jorgenson (1980), Jorgenson et al. (1986), Jorgenson and Liang (1995), Liang and Jorgenson (1998).
2. Although this chapter follows many of the TFP researchers by assuming CRS as reference technology, it is noted that this CRS assumption is still an issue under continual debate. (Please refer to Fare et al. (1994), Ray and Desli (1997), and Fare et al. (1997).)
3. Please refer to Gollop and Jorgenson (1980), Lau (1978), Liang (1983), Jorgenson and Liang (1985), and Liang (1987) for imposing the 'concavity' constraint in translog production (cost) function estimation.
4. The Tornqvist index, the discrete approximation for the Divisia index, was proven by Diewert (1976) to be exact to the homogeneous translog function and such proof, consequently, provides the translog from a theoretical foundation in productivity analyses.
5. Jorgenson and Nomura (2005) do not have data for Japan for the period 1980–90.
6. Jorgenson and Nomura (2005) do not present the TFP growth figures for 1980–90.

REFERENCES

Christensen, L.R. and D.W. Jorgenson (1969), 'The measurement of US real capital input, 1929–1967', *Review of Income and Wealth*, **15**(4), December, 293–320.
Christensen, L.R. and D.W. Jorgenson (1970), 'US real product and real factor inputs, 1929–67', *Review of Income and Wealth*, **16**(1), March, 19–50.
Diewert, W.E. (1976), 'Exact and superlative index numbers', *Journal of Econometrics*, **4**(2), May, 115–45.
Economist, The (1997), 'The Asian miracle: is it over?', 1 March, pp. 23–5.
Fare, R., S. Grosskopf and M. Norris (1997), 'Productivity growth, technical progress, and efficiency change in industrialized countries: Reply', *American Economic Review*, **87**(5), 1040–43.
Fare, R., S. Grosskopf, M. Norris and Z. Zhang (1994), 'Productivity growth, technical progress, and efficiency change in industrialized countries', *American Economic Review*, **84**(1), 66–83.

Gollop, F.M. and D.W. Jorgenson (1980), 'US productivity growth by industry, 1947–73', in J.W. Kendrick and B. Vaccara (eds), *New Developments in Productivity Measurement and Analysis*, Chicago: University of Chicago Press, pp. 17–136.

Jorgenson, D.W. and C.Y. Liang (1985), 'On the dynamic energy-economic model of Taiwan', *TROC Project Report of the Energy Research and Development Fund* No. 72X313BA, 180, Energy Committee, Ministry of Economic Affairs, Taipei, Taiwan, ROC, May 1985.

Jorgenson, D.W. and C.Y. Liang (1995), 'The industry-level output growth and total factor productivity changes in Taiwan, 1961–1993', Project report submitted to the Chiang Ching-Kuo Foundation for International Scholarly Exchange, Taipei, Taiwan, April 1996.

Jorgenson, D.W. and K. Nomura (2005), 'The industry origins of Japanese economic growth', *Journal of the Japanese and International Economies*, **19**(4), 482–542.

Jorgenson, D.W., Frank M. Gollop and Barbara M. Fraumeni (1986), 'Productivity and sectoral output growth in the United States', in John W. Kendrick (ed.), *Interindustry Differences in Productivity Growth*, Cambridge, MA: Ballinger.

Jorgenson, D.W., M.S. Ho and K.J. Stiroh (2007), 'The sources of growth of US industries', Chapter 3 of this volume.

Kim, J.I. and L.J. Lau (1994), 'The sources of economic growth in the East Asian newly industrialized countries', *Journal of Japanese and International Economics*, 8(3), 235–71.

Krugman, Paul (1994), 'The myth of Asia's miracle', *Foreign Affairs*, **73**(6) November/December, 62–89.

Kumbhakar, S.C. and C.A.K. Lovell (2000), *Stochastic Frontier Analysis*, Cambridge: Cambridge University Press.

Lau, Lawrence J. (1978), 'Testing and imposing monotonicity, convexity, and quasi-convexity constraints', in M. Fuss and D. McFadden (eds), *Production Economics: A Dual Approach to Theory and Applications*, Amsterdam: North-Holland, pp. 409–53.

Lau, Lawrence J. (1994), 'Sources of long-term economic growth: empirical evidence from developed and developing countries', mimeograph, May.

Liang, Chi-Yuan (1983), 'The dynamic energy economic model of Taiwan – A case study of the manufacturing sector', in T.S. Yu, K. Paul, C. Liu and C.B Lin (eds), *Essays on the Economic Development of Taiwan and Hong Kong*, Taipei: Academia Sinica, pp. 79–136.

Liang, Chi-Yuan (1987), 'A study on the energy-economic model of Taiwan', *Studies of Modern Economy Economies Series*, vol. 7, Taipei: Institute of Economics, Academia Sinica.

Liang, Chi-Yuan (1995), 'The productivity growth in the Asian NICs: A case study of the Republic of China', *APO Productivity Journal*, Winter edition, pp. 17–40.

Liang, Chi-Yuan (2001), 'An international comparison of total factor productivity changes, 1961–1993', Submitted to the International Conference on the Effect of Entering the WTO on the Chinese Economy. The Chinese University of Hong Kong.

Liang, Chi-Yuan (2002), 'An international comparison of total factor productivity changes, 1960–1993', *World Economy*, **25**(8), Blackwell Publishers Ltd. (SSCI).

Liang, Chi-Yuan and D.W. Jorgenson (1998), 'The productivity growth in Taiwan's manufacturing industry, 1961–93', in T.T. Fu, C.J. Huang and C.A. Knox Lovell (eds), *Economic Efficiency and Productivity Growth in the Asia-Pacific Region*, Cheltenham, UK and Lyme, USA: Edward Elgar, pp. 265–85.

Liang, C.Y. and J.Y. Mei (2005), 'Underpinnings of Taiwan's economic growth: 1978–99 productivity study', *Economic Modeling*, **22**, 347–87.

Ray, R.C. and E. Desli (1997), 'Productivity growth, technical progress, and efficiency change in industrialized countries: Comment', *American Economic Review*, **87**(5), 1033–39.

Young, A. (1994a), 'Lessons from the East Asian NICs: A contrarian view', *European Economic Review*, **38**, 964–73.

Young, A. (1994b), 'The tyranny of numbers: Confronting the statistical realities of the East Asian growth experience', NBER Working Paper No. 4680, *Quarterly Journal of Economics*, **110**(3), 641–80, 1995.

7. Purchasing power parities for international comparisons of output and productivity in Japan, South Korea, Taiwan and the United States

Marcel P. Timmer and Gerard Ypma*

1. INTRODUCTION

In this chapter, we report on the development of a database of output price relatives for 34 industries in four Asia-Pacific economies, namely the US, Japan, South Korea and Taiwan, for the year 1997. The output price relatives are used to make level comparisons of output and total factor productivity between this set of countries and China as part of the ICPA project (International Comparisons of Productivity in Asian economies) as discussed in Chapter 8 of this volume.

Comparisons of output and productivity levels across countries require the conversion of output and factor inputs expressed in their own national prices denominated in national currencies into values at common prices denominated in a common currency. In contrast to the case for final expenditure prices, there is no internationally co-ordinated survey for collecting information on industry-level output and input prices. Generally, there are two alternatives for deriving output price relatives and input price relatives: expenditure purchasing power parities (EPPPs) and unit value ratios (UVRs). Even though the aggregate GDP PPP from the ICP (International Comparisons Project) is particularly suited to make productivity comparisons at the aggregate level, at the industry-level detailed expenditure PPPs need to be adjusted to provide the correct output price concept as they are based on expenditures rather than output prices. Also they refer only to final expenditure items and do not cover intermediate products. In contrast, unit value ratios are based on producer output prices. They do not require adjustment and cover output of both intermediate and final demand products. They are available through work in the ICOP project (International

Comparisons of Output and Productivity) at the University of Groningen. However, contrary to ICP expenditure PPPs, UVRs are not based on detailed specification prices, but on unit values, which might be prone to quality biases. As argued in van Ark and Timmer (2008), for international comparisons of industry productivity levels, a combination of EPPPs and unit value ratios is needed to take advantage of the complementary strengths of both alternatives. This is also the approach taken in this study. In section 2, we outline the unit value ratio methodology. In section 3, we present the set of output price relatives and discuss the sources used for each industry on a country-by-country basis. In section 4, we provide an overview of the chapter and offer concluding remarks.

2. METHODOLOGIES FOR OUTPUT PRICE RELATIVES

For comparisons at the industry level, two alternatives have been explored to arrive at producer output and input price relatives: (1) by reallocating existing expenditure purchasing power parities (EPPP) to industry groups, and 'peeling' off transport, distribution and tax margins; or (2) by calculating unit value ratios based on producer output prices using the industry-of-origin approach. The former is used extensively in the work of Jorgenson and Kuroda (1995) and the latter has been developed and used in the ICOP project (International Comparisons of Output and Productivity) at the University of Groningen (Maddison and van Ark, 2002). Both approaches have their advantages and disadvantages. A full discussion including references can be found in van Ark and Timmer (2008), from which the text in this section is derived.

2.1 Adjusted Expenditure PPPs

The expenditure-based PPP comparisons are based on comparisons of prices of final products and services with a detailed product specification. To apply them to productivity comparisons by industry, the expenditure PPPs need to be reallocated from expenditure categories to industry groups. Some researchers simply use the aggregate EPPP for total GDP as a proxy for industry-level output price relatives (OPR). Others have attempted to refine these proxies by computing weighted averages of disaggregated EPPPs specific to certain industries. This is best done at the detailed basic heading level (of which there were 221 in the latest OECD PPP round for 1999).

The use of EPPPs as proxies for output price relatives has several potentially significant drawbacks. Firstly, a complete correspondence between the expenditure categories and industries is not possible since, by definition, prices of goods produced as intermediate input for other industries are not covered by EPPPs. To bridge the gap, some studies have included close substitutes for a given industry's intermediate deliveries based on its deliveries to final demand.

Secondly, EPPPs are based on a different price concept than output statistics. Expenditure prices reflect cross-country differences in wholesale and retail distribution margins and transportation costs while output prices should not. Expenditure prices also include indirect taxes and subsidies, which can vary across countries. Therefore, the use of expenditure PPPs as proxies requires an adjustment of expenditure prices to producer output prices. The adjusted component EPPP approach has been pioneered by Jorgenson and associates by 'peeling off' indirect taxes and transport and distribution margins from the expenditure prices (see, for example, Jorgenson et al., 1987):

$$E - PPP^{BA}_{adjusted} = \left[\frac{1 + T^A}{1 + T^B} \right] E - PPP^{BA} \tag{7.1}$$

Hence the PPP between country A and B for output in a particular industry is proxied by the adjusted EPPP, calculated as the component EPPP for this industry multiplied by the ratio of tax, transportation and distribution margins (T) in country A over those in country B. Input–output tables are often used to calculate indirect taxes as well as transport and distribution margins, but not many countries make this kind of data publicly available at a sufficiently detailed level.

Thirdly, expenditure PPPs are based on final consumption rather than domestic output prices. Hence, import prices are included, while export prices are excluded. We will use the adjusted EPPP approach for those sectors in which the disadvantages are not very serious, or for cases in which no better alternative is available. For example, as the import and export of construction, financial and personal services are still limited, the coverage of EPPPs is reasonable.

2.2   The Unit Value Ratio Approach

The alternative to making international comparisons of productivity levels is to apply the industry-of-origin approach, which has been specifically developed for making comparisons by industry rather than by expenditure category. In the industry-of-origin approach, industry-specific conversion factors are derived on the basis of relative product prices.[1] As a first step, unit values (*uv*) are derived by dividing ex-factory output values (*o*) by produced quantities (*q*) for each product *i* in each country:

$$uv_i = \frac{o_i}{q_i} \qquad (7.2)$$

The unit value can be considered an average price, calculated throughout the year for all producers and across a group of nearly similar products. Subsequently, in a bilateral comparison, broadly defined products with similar characteristics are matched. For each matched product, the ratio of the unit values in both countries is taken. This unit value ratio (UVR) is given by:

$$UVR_i^{BA} = \frac{uv_i^A}{uv_i^B} \qquad (7.3)$$

with *A* and *B* the countries being compared, and *B* being the base country. The product UVR indicates the relative producer price of the matched product in the two countries. Product UVRs are used to derive UVRs at more aggregated levels in a stepwise procedure. Within manufacturing, product UVRs are first aggregated to industries, then to branches and finally to aggregate manufacturing. The industry UVR (UVR$_j$) is given by the mean of the UVRs of the matched products. Product UVRs are weighted by their output value, as more important products should have a bigger weighting in the industry UVR:

$$UVR_j^{BA} = \sum_{i=1}^{I_j} w_{ij} UVR_{ij}^{BA} \qquad (7.4)$$

with $i=1,..,I_j$ the matched products in industry *j*; $w_{ij} = o_{ij}/o_j$ the output share of the *i*th commodity in industry *j*; and $o_j = \sum_{i=1}^{I_j} o_{ij}$ the total matched value of output in industry *j*. In bilateral comparisons, the weights of the base country (*B*) or the other country (*A*) can be used, which provide a Laspeyres and a Paasche-type UVR, respectively. As the quantity weights are consistent with those that are used to derive the unit values, the weights and unit value ratios are consistent. This is an important advantage over the use of specified prices for ICP (International Comparison Project). The geometric average of the Laspeyres and Paasche indices is used (Fisher) when a single currency conversion factor is required. The next aggregation steps are made by using the gross output of industries to obtain an industry-weighted mean of all industry UVRs in a branch, similarly to the aggregation from product to industry. Again, weights from base country B and the other country A can be used to arrive at a Laspeyres and Paasche index of the branch UVRs. The latter step is repeated for the final aggregation step from the branch level to the level of total manufacturing.

An important point of critique on the unit value ratio method is that the matched product groups are not representative at the product level or industry level, but biased towards relatively homogeneous, less sophisticated products. Values and quantities are usually readily available from national industry statistics, from which these measures are obtained. For example, in basic goods industries, such as pulp and paper, wood products, metallic and non-metallic mineral products, and in transport and communication, output coverage is usually quite large as there are relatively few product differences between countries. Product matching is more difficult in manufacturing industries that produce durable consumer goods and investment goods. Therefore, for industries such as non-electrical machinery, transport equipment and instruments, we used also information based on expenditure PPPs.

In contrast to other sectors of the economy, the trade sector is the only one in which we have systematically applied a double deflation procedure right from the beginning. Double deflation, that is separate UVRs or PPPs for the purchases and sales of the goods, is needed for this sector more than elsewhere because the purchase value makes up most of the total sales value in the trade sector. The approach suggested here resembles double deflation by deriving retail input and wholesale output prices on the basis of the trade margins. It mirrors the statistical practice of inter-temporal comparisons and is built upon the idea that margin prices can be measured through dividing the margin value by the quantity of trade services. The crucial assumption is that the quantity of trade services is proportional to the amount of goods sold (or purchased). The reader is referred to Timmer and Ypma (2005) for a full discussion.

3. RELATIVE INDUSTRY OUTPUT PRICE LEVELS IN JAPAN, SOUTH KOREA, TAIWAN AND THE UNITED STATES

This section describes the development of the set of industry-level output price relatives for the purpose of the ICPA project. Only major results and sources are discussed here, as full details are provided in Timmer and Ypma (2004). Table 7.1 provides the PPPs and relative prices for Japan, Korea and Taiwan for each ICPA industry. Relative prices are calculated by dividing the PPP by the exchange rate of the country.[2] Next, we discuss sources and results on an industry-by-industry basis.

Table 7.1   PPPs and relative prices of industry output in Japan, South Korea and Taiwan relative to the United States, 1997

ICPA Industry	Fisher PPPs			Relative prices		
	Japan	South Korea	Taiwan	Japan	South Korea	Taiwan
	Yen/ US$	Won/ US$	NT$/ US$	Jap/ US	Kor/ US	Tai/ US
1 Agriculture	749	3304	67.8	6.19	3.47	2.08
2 Coal mining	656	2180	139.8	5.42	2.29	4.28
3 Metal and non-metallic mining	132	1096	28.9	1.09	1.15	0.89
4 Oil and gas extraction	362	1322	80.7	2.99	1.39	2.47
5 Construction	218	799	16.2	1.80	0.84	0.50
6 Food and kindred products	292	1438	34.2	2.42	1.51	1.05
7 Textile mill products	150	930	24.4	1.24	0.98	0.75
8 Apparel	168	1399	25.0	1.39	1.47	0.77
9 Lumber and wood	261	998	26.0	2.16	1.05	0.80
10 Furniture and fixtures	234	561	23.6	1.94	0.59	0.72
11 Paper and allied	158	973	24.3	1.31	1.02	0.74
12 Printing, publishing and allied	158	973	24.3	1.31	1.02	0.74
13 Chemicals	167	947	23.1	1.38	1.00	0.71
14 Petroleum and coal products	265	962	23.1	2.19	1.01	0.71
15 Leather	213	927	19.6	1.76	0.98	0.60
16 Stone, clay and glass	126	679	21.0	1.05	0.71	0.64
17 Primary metal	129	985	24.8	1.07	1.04	0.76
18 Fabricated metal	176	788	25.9	1.46	0.83	0.79
19 Machinery, non-elect.	138	705	17.7	1.14	0.74	0.54
20 Electrical machinery	102	798	19.2	0.85	0.84	0.59
21 Motor vehicles	111	815	31.4	0.92	0.86	0.96
22 Transportation equipment	116	773	31.4	0.96	0.81	0.96
23 Instruments	162	1295	24.3	1.35	1.36	0.75
24 Rubber and misc. plastics	114	726	24.3	0.95	0.76	0.74
25 Misc. manufacturing	202	1361	23.6	1.67	1.43	0.72
26 Transportation	205	802	46.7	1.69	0.84	1.43

Table 7.1 (continued)

ICPA Industry	Fisher PPPs			Relative prices		
	Japan	South Korea	Taiwan	Japan	South Korea	Taiwan
	Yen/ US$	Won/ US$	NT$/ US$	Jap/ US	Kor/ US	Tai/ US
27 Communications	139	874	12.5	1.15	0.92	0.38
28 Electric utilities	236	967	31.9	1.95	1.02	0.98
29 Gas utilities	94	1000	59.1	0.78	1.05	1.81
30 Trade	186	1029	22.2	1.54	1.08	0.68
31 Finance, insurance and real estate	205	871	13.6	1.70	0.92	0.42
32 Other private services	316	685	21.6	2.61	0.72	0.66
33 Public services	167	553	41.1	1.38	0.58	1.26

3.1 Agriculture

For Japan and South Korea, PPPs on farm prices of agricultural products for 1995 are obtained from a study by the Groningen Growth and Development Centre, using agricultural producer (farm gate) prices for about 185 products from the Food and Agriculture Organization (van Ark et al., 2005). It is assumed that farm products' PPPs are also representative for forestry and fishing. Various binary and multilateral aggregation procedures have been used in this study. To stay in line with the methodology for the other industries in this study, we take the bilateral Fisher results. For Taiwan, no data are available in the *FAOSTAT Database 2003* and therefore this country was not included in the van Ark et al. study. The detailed product list from their study has been used here, too. In this way, Taiwan could be compared quite easily with both Japan and the United States. The *Agricultural Production Statistics Abstract 2003, Republic of China* (Council of Agriculture, 2003) delivered quantities and values for 41 matchable products. The *Statistical Yearbook of the Republic of China, 2002* (DGBAS, 2003c) provided data for three more matches. Results have been updated to 1997 with deflators from the *GGDC 60-Industry Database, October 2004* (GGDC, 2004).

Table 7.2 shows the ICOP PPPs for 1997 for all three countries. Relative prices (see Table 7.1) show that the farm gate prices in Japan and Korea especially are much higher than in the United States.

Table 7.2   ICOP PPPs in agriculture, 1997

		Laspeyres	Paasche	Fisher
Japan	Yen/US$	786.4	714.0	749.3
South Korea	Won/US$	3723.1	2931.3	3303.6
Taiwan	NT$/US$	97.51	47.09	67.8

3.2   Mining

For mining, we also used the ICOP method. For South Korea, quantity and value data on major mining products have been obtained from the *1997 Report on Mining and Manufacturing Survey* (Korea National Statistical Office, 1997). Japanese quantity and value data stem from the *1997 Mining Yearbook of Japan* (Research and Statistics Department Minister's Secretariat, 1998). For Taiwan, the *Annual Statistical Report of Mineral 2002* from the Bureau of Mines (2003) contains yearly value and quantity data for almost all mining products. These products have been matched with American product data from the *US 1997 Economic Census* (US Census Bureau, 2000). However, because mining is a very small sector in all three Asian countries, only a few matches could be made. To obtain a total for mining, the PPPs have been weighted with the value of the matched products. Table 7.3 shows the results of the comparisons for Japan, South Korea and Taiwan with the United States.

3.3   Construction

Table 7.4 shows the PPPs for the construction sector for the countries that are involved in the ICP project.[3] ICP PPPs (code 14.02.00.0) for several types of building (dwellings, non-residential buildings and civil engineering works) for 1999 were used for both Japan and South Korea. The expenditure-weighted PPP of these categories are used assuming that the national expenditure and production structures are the same. The PPPs are backdated to 1997 with deflators from the *OECD STAN Database 2003* (OECD, 2003a). Purchase and producer prices are the same in this industry as there are no transport or trade margins for their output.

For Taiwan, we use the ICOP UVR method. Data have been collected about the constructed square meters of residential buildings, commercial buildings, manufacturing buildings, schools and hospitals (Table 7.5). The *Statistical Yearbook of Interior 1997 The Republic of China* (Ministry of Interior of the Republic of China, 1998) contains both constructed floor area and construction expenditure by type of building in Taiwan, while the

Table 7.3   ICOP PPPs in mining, 1997

Japan		Laspeyres	Paasche	Fisher
Coal mining	Yen/US$	652.2	659.7	656.0
Metal and non-metallic mining	Yen/US$	133.0	130.4	131.7
Oil and gas extraction	Yen/US$	404.8	323.9	362.1
Total mining	Yen/US$	**408.9**	**197.2**	**284.0**
South Korea				
Coal mining	Won/US$	2180.2	2180.2	2180.2
Metal and non-metallic mining	Won/US$	1380.3	870.0	1095.8
Oil and gas extraction	Won/US$	1800.5	970.2	1321.7
Total mining	Won/US$	**1800.5**	**970.2**	**1321.7**
Taiwan				
Coal mining	NT$/US$	139.83	139.83	139.83
Metal and non-metallic mining	NT$/US$	27.10	30.88	28.93
Oil and gas extraction	NT$/US$	82.52	78.87	80.68
Total mining	NT$/US$	**90.64**	**54.53**	**70.30**

Table 7.4   PPPs for construction in Japan and South Korea, 1997

Construction		ICP PPPs			Backdated		
		1999 Laspeyres	1999 Paasche	1999 Fisher	1997 Laspeyres	1997 Paasche	1997 Fisher
Japan	Yen/US$	172.9	173.3	173.1	217.8	217.8	217.8
South Korea	Won/US$	732.1	675.0	703.0	799.1	799.1	799.1

Table 7.5   PPPs for construction in Taiwan, 1997

		Laspeyres	Paasche	Fisher
PPP unadjusted	NT$/US$	8.32	7.97	8.14
Quality adjustment		50%	50%	50%
PPP adjusted	**NT$/US$**	**16.64**	**15.94**	**16.28**

Statistical Abstract of the United States 1998 (US Census Bureau, various issues) contains data about the construction value and floor area of construction contracts in the United States. The results have been adjusted in the same way as Yotopoulos and Lin (1993) have done in their calculations

of a 1985 PPP for this sector. This means that an adjustment of 50% has
been applied to cope with the difference in quality of buildings.[4]

3.4 Manufacturing

For all three countries, the ICOP industry-of-origin procedure was fol-
lowed. Data for South Korea come from the *1997 Report on Mining and
Manufacturing Survey* (Korea NSO, 1997), for Japan from the *1997 Census
of Manufacturers, Report on Enterprises and Commodities* (Research and
Statistics Department, Economic and Industrial Policy Bureau, 1999), for
Taiwan from the *1996 Report on Industry, Commerce and Service Census*
(DGBAS, 1997) and the US data are from the *1997 Economic Census –
Manufacturing* (US Census Bureau, 2000) supplemented by additional
product information from the *Current Industrial Reports* (US Census
Bureau, 1999). For each country, unit values were matched with those for
the United States. Following the ICOP approach, the aggregation of
product UVRs to branch and industry PPPs has followed a step-wise procedure of weighting from product level, to 3/4-digit industry level to 2-digit
manufacturing branches (see Timmer et al., 2005). Industry output weights
for South Korean industry data are again taken from the *1997 Report on
Mining and Manufacturing Survey* (Korea NSO, 1997), Japanese industry
data are taken from *1997 Census of Manufacturers, Report on Enterprises
and Commodities* (Research and Statistics Department, Economic and
Industrial Policy Bureau, 1999), Taiwanese data stem from *1996 Report on
Industry, Commerce and Service Census* (DGBAS, 1997) and the US industry data from the *1997 Economic Census* (US Census Bureau, 2000).
Further details concerning the Japan–US comparison can be found in
Inklaar et al. (2003). For South Korea–US and Taiwan–US comparisons,
the reader is referred to Stuivenwold and Timmer (2003).

ICOP PPPs are conceptually the correct PPPs to use as they refer to producer prices of domestic output. However, in some industries the number
of matches which could be made was low, or there was a lack of product
detail which could lead to quality problems. As discussed in section 2, ICP
expenditure PPPs might provide an alternative measure of output PPPs in
some cases. ICP PPPs can be used for those industries in which final expenditures make up a large part of the output while the share of imports is low.

In practice, this means that ICP PPPs provide a useful addition to the
ICOP data in the following ICPA industries: furniture and fixtures, non-
electric machinery, transportation equipment, instruments and miscellaneous manufacturing. In some cases, ICP basic headings were added to
matches already being made with the ICOP method (such as in non-electric
machinery), while in other cases, the industry PPP was based on ICP data

only (like in miscellaneous manufacturing and transportation equipment). Below we give a detailed description of the ICP data used.

For Japan and South Korea, we have added matches in furniture and fixtures (ICP code 11.05.11.1). Extra matches in machinery, non-electric have only been added for Japan. ICP codes 14.01.18.1 (office and data-processing machines) and 11.09.13.1 (information processing equipment) are used in this industry. For transportation equipment in Japan and South Korea ICP codes 11.07.12.1 (motor cycles and bicycles), 14.01.32.1 (boats, steamers, tugs, floating platforms, rigs), 14.01.32.2 (aircraft, helicopters, hovercraft and other aeronautical equipment), 14.01.32.3 (locomotives, rail-cars, vans and wagons, other rail equipment), and 14.01.32.2 (other transport equipment) could be used. 14.01.19.1 (precision instruments), 11.06.13.2 (other therapeutic appliances and equipment), 14.01.22.1 (tele-communication equipment, measuring equipment), 11.06.13.1 (eye-glasses and contact lenses), 11.09.12.1 (photographic and cinematographic equipment and optical instruments), 14.01.19.2 (optical instruments and photographic equipment), 11.12.31.1 (jewellery, clocks and watches) fit the instruments industry and the matches of miscellaneous manufacturing exist of 11.12.31.1 (jewellery, clocks and watches), 11.09.21.1 (major durables for outdoor and indoor recreation), 11.09.31.1 (games, toys and hobbies), 11.09.32.1 (equipment for sport, camping and open-air recreation) and 11.09.54.1 (stationery and drawing materials). ICP PPPs have been matched with the value of shipment data from the manufacturing censuses of Japan, South Korea and the United States. A split of data into detailed categories has been conducted using nominal value-added data from ICP projects.

In all cases, the ICP PPPs have been adjusted for trade and transportation margins from the 1997 I/O table for the United States and the 1995 I/O table for Japan. For South Korea, we do not have margins from I/O tables; therefore, the Japanese margins have been used. Taiwan is not included in the ICP project and therefore no ICP PPPs could be used here.

Table 7.6 shows the results for Japan, Korea and Taiwan with the United States as the base country. No matches or ICP PPPs were available in printing and publishing; therefore, we used the UVR for the paper industry. For Taiwan, the UVR for total manufacturing is used for furniture and fixtures and other manufacturing, and the UVR for chemicals serves as an estimate for petroleum and coal products.

3.5 Transport

For Japan, South Korea and Taiwan, ICOP UVRs are calculated. These are essentially based on comparisons of passenger and ton-kilometers by transport mode for the movement services (in combination with output

Table 7.6 PPPs for manufacturing, 1997

ICPA Industry	ISIC rev 3	Japan			South Korea			Taiwan		
		Laspeyres Yen/US$	Paasche Yen/US$	Fisher Yen/US$	Laspeyres Won/US$	Paasche Won/US$	Fisher Won/US$	Laspeyres NT$/US$	Paasche NT$/US$	Fisher NT$/US$
6 Food and kindred products	15–16	306.4	279.8	292.8	1548.8	1336.8	1438.9	37.45	31.28	34.23
7 Textile mill products	17	163.0	138.6	150.3	963.8	898.0	930.3	26.48	22.51	24.41
8 Apparel	18	185.6	153.3	168.7	1330.9	1471.1	1399.2	25.66	24.40	25.02
9 Lumber and wood	20	353.2	193.2	261.2	977.2	1021.0	998.9	25.98	25.98	25.98
10 Furniture and fixtures	36	234.7	234.7	234.7	680.9	463.1	561.5	22.84	24.36	23.59
11 Paper and allied	21	174.4	144.9	158.9	979.0	968.4	973.7	24.75	23.86	24.30
12 Printing, publishing and allied	22	174.4	144.9	158.9	979.0	968.4	973.7	24.75	23.86	24.30
13 Chemicals	24	183.5	152.2	167.1	1242.2	722.6	947.4	24.48	21.77	23.09
14 Petroleum and coal products	23	312.5	225.1	265.2	1063.2	870.5	962.0	24.48	21.77	23.09
15 Leather	19	295.3	154.0	213.2	953.5	902.8	927.8	19.72	19.57	19.64
16 Stone, clay and glass	26	140.2	114.4	126.7	707.1	652.5	679.3	23.38	18.90	21.02
17 Primary metal	27	142.4	118.4	129.8	1178.8	823.9	985.5	26.97	22.77	24.78
18 Fabricated metal	28	212.4	147.2	176.8	891.6	697.9	788.8	25.88	25.88	25.88
19 Machinery, non-elect.	29	151.0	126.5	138.2	799.7	621.8	705.1	17.78	17.54	17.66
20 Electrical machinery	30–32	109.0	97.2	102.9	854.0	746.4	798.4	19.93	18.40	19.15

21	Motor vehicles	34	126.1	98.0	111.2	998.9	665.9	815.6	33.32	29.50	31.35
22	Transportation eq. and ordnance	35	*116.0*	*116.3*	*116.2*	*773.1*	*774.7*	*773.9*	*33.32*	*29.50*	*31.35*
23	Instruments	33	170.4	155.6	162.8	1357.0	1236.3	1295.2	24.33	24.33	24.33
24	Rubber and misc. plastics	25	123.8	106.1	114.6	744.6	708.5	726.3	25.08	23.51	24.28
25	Misc. manufacturing	37	*206.4*	*198.1*	*202.2*	*1440.3*	*1287.5*	*1361.7*	*22.84*	*24.36*	*23.59*

Note: For the figures in italics, no ICOP PPPs or ICP PPPs are available; therefore, PPPs for other industries serve as estimates. This is described in more detail in the text.

values for these modes) and comparisons of passengers and tons transported for auxiliary services. One exception is the unit value for ocean shipping, a transport mode for which no data about ton-kilometers is collected. In this case, the revenue is divided by the transported tons.

Statistical figures for Japan are based on quantity data from the *Monthly Statistics of Japan, October 2003* (Statistics Bureau Japan, 1999b) and the *Statistical Yearbook of Japan 2000* (Statistics Bureau Japan, 1999a). Revenue data was available in the *1995 Input–Output Table* (Statistics Bureau Japan, 2000a), which in 1997 was updated to the *1997 Input–Output Extension Table* (Statistics Bureau Japan, 2000b). Revenues in international air transport have been subdivided into passenger and freight with *Annual Reports of Japan Air Line (JAL)* (1998), *All Nippon Airways (ANA)* (1998) *and Japan Air System (JAS)* (1998) for 1998, which contains data for the book year March 1997–March 1998. For Japan, auxiliary services in railway transport are included in the movement. They have been removed by assuming that the share of transportation services is equal to the share in the United States. Passengers emplaned are estimated by the total amount of air passengers transported.

For South Korea, both quantity and revenue data come from the *Korea Statistical Yearbook 1999* (Korea NSO, 1999). Data from the *Korean Air 1997 Annual Report* (1997) have been used to make the distinction between revenues in passenger and freight. For the further subdivision into domestic and international, we make the assumption that the price of a domestic and international passenger-kilometer is the same. For freight, the same assumption for prices of domestic and international ton-kilometers has been made. Air passengers transported are used as a proxy for the total number of passengers emplaned.

The quantity data for Taiwan are derived from *Transportation Information 2003* (Institute of Transportation of the ROC, 2003b) and the *Monthly Bulletin of Statistics of Transport and Communications* (Institute of Transportation of the ROC, 2003a), *various issues*, while value data stem from *The Report on the 1996 Census of the Republic of China, vol. 7* (Census Bureau, 1998). The Census data are updated to 1997 with the trend in gross output from the detailed *National Accounts of the Republic of China* (DGBAS, 2003b). It was not possible to split air transport value data into domestic and international; therefore, it is assumed that the price of a domestic and international passenger kilometer is the same. The same assumption has been used for airfreight. Passengers emplaned are estimated by the total amount of air passengers transported.

Data for the United States have been derived from the *ATA Annual Report* (ATA, 1998) for air transport. In addition, the 'Waterborne databank' of the US Maritime Administration (2003) delivers quantities in water transport,

Table 7.7   PPPs for transportation, 1997

Japan		Laspeyres	Paasche	Fisher
Passenger transport	Yen/US$	175.6	138.3	155.8
Freight transport	Yen/US$	328.5	152.4	223.8
Transportation services	Yen/US$	220.7	159.8	187.8
Total transport	Yen/US$	**279.2**	**150.0**	**204.7**
South Korea				
Passenger transport	Won/US$	578.0	541.9	559.7
Freight transport	Won/US$	2083.8	454.3	972.9
Transportation services	Won/US$	474.3	214.8	319.1
Total transport	Won/US$	**1529.2**	**420.4**	**801.8**
Taiwan				
Passenger transport	NT$/US$	22.50	20.34	21.39
Freight transport	NT$/US$	80.58	55.05	66.60
Transportation services	NT$/US$	37.09	33.35	35.17
Total transport	NT$/US$	**61.50**	**35.51**	**46.73**

while the *Statistical Abstract of the United States 1999* (US Census Bureau), the *National Transportation Statistics 2002* (US Dept of Transportation, 2002) and the *1997 Economic Census* (US Census Bureau, 2000) have been used for other branches. The results are provided in Table 7.7.

3.6   Communication

For this sector, the same methodology as in transport has been used to calculate ICOP UVRs, with the distinction that the quantity measures are based on comparisons of phone calls or minutes, telephone subscribers and mail delivered (see van Ark et al., 1999 for a description). Dividing the revenues of postal activities and telephone services by the quantity measures described above results in unit values. To get a PPP for communication, UVRs are calculated and aggregated to an average with the revenues as weights.

Data on telecommunications for Japan, South Korea and the United States originate mostly from the *OECD Telecommunications Database* (2003b). For Japan, the *Monthly Statistics of Japan, October 2003* (Statistics Bureau Japan, 1999b) provides quantity data for the amount of mail handled and the number of subscribers on telephone services for a comparison with Taiwan. The *1995 I–O Table* in combination with the *1997*

Table 7.8   PPPs in communication, 1997

		Laspeyres	Paasche	Fisher
Japan	Yen/US$	173.4	110.9	138.7
South Korea	Won/US$	914.8	834.5	873.7
Taiwan	NT$/US$	13.67	11.46	12.51

I–O Extension Table (Statistics Bureau Japan, 2000a and b) delivers revenue data for postal and total telephone services. *The Statistical Yearbook of Korea 1999* (Korea NSO, 1999) provides both quantity and value figures for postal services. Taiwanese UVRs for communication in both Japan and the US comparisons are based on the number of telephone subscribers and the amount of mail handled. The *Monthly Statistics of Transportation and Communications August 2003* (Institute of Transportation of the ROC, 2003a) provides figures for both quantity measures. For values, *The Report on the 1996 Census of the Republic of China, vol. 7* (Census Bureau, 1998) gives the amount of information needed, but not for the correct year. Therefore, the 1996 value is updated to 1997 with the trend in communication from the *National Accounts of Taiwan* (DGBAS, 2003b). All other US data are derived from the *Statistical Abstract of the United States 2002* (US Census Bureau). The results are provided in Table 7.8.

3.7   Utilities

For this sector, the calculation of PPPs is based on a comparison of the industry revenues per gigawatt/hour (Gwh) electricity and per million cubic meters of gas. Data on the quantities of electricity and gas sold for Japan come from the *Japan Statistical Yearbook 2000* (Statistics Bureau Japan, 1999a), while revenue data stem from the *1995 I–O Table* in combination with the *1997 Extension Table* (Statistics Bureau Japan, 2000a and b). Because total gas supply was only measured in calories, the assumption has been made that the calories in a cubic meter of natural gas, for which metric information is available, are equal to the calories in other gas. South Korean utility data are all subtracted from the *Korea Energy Review Monthly, March 2003* (Korea Energy Economics Institute, 2003) while quantity data for the United States stem from the *Energy Information Administration*, and revenue data come from the *1997 US Economic Census* (US Census Bureau, 2000). Data on quantity and production for Taiwan both originate from the *Industrial Production Statistics Monthly*, (Department of Statistics, 1998).

Table 7.9 PPPs for electricity and gas, 1997

Japan		Laspeyres	Paasche	Fisher
Electricity	Yen/US$	235.7	235.7	235.7
Gas	Yen/US$	93.9	93.9	93.9
Total utilities	Yen/US$	**183.5**	**202.3**	**192.7**
South Korea				
Electricity	Won/US$	966.9	966.9	966.9
Gas	Won/US$	999.6	999.6	999.6
Total utilities	Won/US$	**978.9**	**971.4**	**975.1**
Taiwan				
Electricity	NT$/US$	31.94	31.94	31.94
Gas	NT$/US$	59.06	59.06	59.06
Total utilities	NT$/US$	**41.92**	**32.77**	**37.07**

Because there is only one match in each industry, the Laspeyres, Paasche and Fisher PPPs in Table 7.9 are all the same.

3.8   Wholesale and Retail Trade

For all countries, output PPPs are calculated separately for wholesale and retail trade, following the method outlined in Timmer and Ypma (2005). Essentially, retail sales have been deflated by the ICP expenditure PPPs for retail categories for 1999, which are adjusted for sales tax margins and backdated to 1997. A retail input PPP has been constructed by adjusting the ICP PPP used above for the differences in retail trade margins in both countries. The cost of goods sold can be deflated with this input PPP. Finally, the subtraction of the cost of goods sold from the sales leads to a 'double-deflated' gross margin, from which, in combination with the undeflated gross margin, the retail PPP can be derived. PPPs for wholesale trade are constructed in the same way, with the distinction that the cost of goods sold is the starting point in this case. Manufacturing UVRs from ICOP studies are used as a deflator for the cost of goods sold, while the adjusted UVRs with a mark-up for the wholesale margin are used for deflating wholesale sales. Again, the deflated and undeflated gross margins can be used for calculating a PPP. To get a PPP for the total trade sector, PPPs are weighted at a gross margin value of each retail category.

For Japan, the sales and cost of goods sold in wholesale and retail trade come from the *1999 Census of Commerce* (Research and Statistics Dept,

Economic and Industrial Policy Bureau, 2001). The *1995 I–O Table* (Statistics Bureau Japan, 2000a) contains both retail and wholesale margins on product level. For each specific trade category, the average margin of the products sold in this category has been used. Only for recovered materials were no products available. For this category, the margin for building materials has been used. The sales tax margins (5% for Japan in 1999) are from the *OECD Consumption Tax Trends* (OECD, 1999) and the deflators are taken from the *OECD STAN Database* (OECD, 2003a). 1999 ICP PPPs for consumer products have been backdated to 1997 and used for constructing retail PPPs, while UVRs from the 1997 manufacturing comparison have been used for deflating the cost of wholesale goods. The UVR for agricultural products comes from van Ark, Ypma and Rao (2005). For general merchandise, the UVR for total manufacturing has been used, while furniture, fixtures and house furnishing as well as recovered materials use the UVR of building materials. The UVR for chemicals has also been used for drugs and toiletries.

South Korean data stem from the *Korea Statistical Yearbook 1999* (Korea NSO, 1999) regarding sales and trade margins. Because no subdivision of motor vehicle trade in wholesale and retail trade was available, the ratio of the United States has been used. For deflators, the *OECD STAN Database* (OECD, 2003a) has been used and the sales taxes (10% in 1999) come from the *OECD Consumption Tax Trends* (OECD, 1999). The manufacturing UVRs are from the 1997 ICOP Comparison (see Stuivenwold and Timmer, 2003 for details) and the UVR for agricultural products comes from van Ark et al. (2005). For household goods not elsewhere classified and other wholesale, the UVR for total manufacturing has been used. The 1999 ICP PPPs for consumer products are used for the retail part.

For Taiwan, we take another approach for the retail sector. Because Taiwan is not included in the ICP project, expenditure PPPs are not available. We therefore use the wholesale output PPPs as retail input PPPs. Retail output PPPs were subsequently constructed by adjusting this input PPP for the trade margin differences. This was possible because wholesale and retail exist as almost the same branches in the Taiwanese census. For sales, cost of goods[5] and margins, *The Report on the 1996 Census of the Republic of China* (Census Bureau, 1998) has been used. Deflators come from the *National Accounts of the Republic of China* (DGBAS, 2003b) and the UVRs are from the *1997 Manufacturing Comparison* of the Stuivenwold and Timmer study. No UVRs were available for fuel products, photographic equipment, furniture and fixtures, jewellery and general merchandise. For the first two categories, the respective UVRs for chemicals as well as watches, spectacles and optical equipment have been used. Building materials are used for furniture and fixtures, while jewellery has the same

Table 7.10   ICOP PPPs in wholesale and retail trade, 1997

Japan		Laspeyres	Paasche	Fisher
Wholesale	Yen/US$	249.7	148.5	192.6
Retail	Yen/US$	202.6	175.6	188.6
Total	**Yen/US$**	**223.2**	**155.5**	**186.3**
South Korea				
Wholesale	Won/US$	1286.1	956.0	1108.9
Retail	Won/US$	1105.4	850.8	969.8
Total	**Won/US$**	**1180.0**	**896.5**	**1028.5**
Taiwan				
Wholesale	NT$/US$	27.26	18.04	22.18
Retail	NT$/US$	23.08	18.12	20.45
Total	**NT$/US$**	**27.26**	**18.04**	**22.18**

UVR as other wholesale, and for general merchandise the UVR for total manufacturing has been used. Two branches in retail do not exist as a wholesale branch: for used merchandise and other retail, therefore, the retail input PPP for general merchandising has been used.

Margins and sales data for the United States come from the *1997 US Economic Census* (US Census Bureau, 2000). Due to the great amount of detail in the census, it is possible to convert this data to the classifications used for the trade sector in Japan, South Korea and Taiwan. Sales tax rates differ per state; therefore, it is not possible to use a single tax rate. The sales tax rate we use now (5.33%) has been calculated as an average of all states, weighted with the GDP per state to prevent large influences of small states. Finally, deflators are from the *OECD STAN Database* (OECD, 2003a). Table 7.10 shows the results for the trade sector for the three Asian countries.

3.9   Finance, Insurance and Real Estate

For South Korea and Japan, ICP PPPs were used, adjusted for taxes, transport and distribution margins and backdated to 1997. For South Korea, no I/O table in purchaser prices is available and because the adjustments are very marginal (less than 1% for all countries), we use the Japanese *1995 Input–Output Table* (Statistics Bureau Japan, 2000a) for both Japan and South Korea, and deflators stem from the *GGDC 60-Industry Database* (GGDC, 2004). The *1997 BLS Input–Output Table* and the *GGDC 60-Industry Database* (GGDC, 2004) have been used for the United States.

Where possible, the separate industries within this sector are adjusted with their own margins and deflators. For both Japan and the United States, no separate margins were available for financial intermediation, insurance and financial services; therefore, they were adjusted with the margins of the whole financial sector. The finance, insurance and real estate PPP is based on five individual ICP PPPs, which are allocated to each of the three main finance industries. For Taiwan, no ICP PPP is available. Therefore, the 1985 PPPs for finance and actual and imputed rents from the Taiwan–Japan comparison of Yotopoulos and Lin have been updated to 1997, and converted to a comparison with the United States through using the Japan–United States estimate from above. The Yotopoulos–Lin comparison is based on a thorough ICP-like survey with detailed data from national statistical bureaux, which make the numbers more comparable with those for Japan and South Korea. Because the Yotopoulos and Lin figures are in consumer prices, an adjustment has been made for taxes, transport and trade margins. These margins come from the *1996 Input–Output Tables of Taiwan* (DGBAS, 1996), while deflators are from the *National Accounts of the Republic of China* (DGBAS, 2003b). The results are provided in Table 7.11.

3.10   Other Private Services

For Japan and South Korea, ICP PPPs for water supply (11.04.41.1), hotels and restaurants (11.11.11–21), business services (11.12.71.1), education (13.02), health and social work (13.03) and other community, social and personal services (13.04, 11.05.62) are adjusted for transportation and wholesale margins from the *1995 I–O Table* for Japan (Statistics Bureau Japan, 2000a).[6] For water supply, the margins and deflators for total utilities have been used. Aggregation to a total PPP for private services has been done with value added weights from the *GGDC 60-Industry Database* (GGDC, 2004).

For Taiwan, no ICP PPPs are available. Therefore, another strategy has been followed. Because compensation is the biggest part of value added in private services, it is reasonable to use the compensation per employee as a unit value in this sector. Another argument is that ICP expenditure PPPs for these services are mostly based on compensation per employee, too. For all industries included in this sector, compensation and employee data have been collected and a UVR is calculated. To get a figure for total private services, the UVRs are weighted with the value added in each sector for both the United States and Taiwan. Data for the United States are taken from the *GGDC 60-Industry Database* (GGDC, 2004). For Taiwan, *The Report on 1996 Census of the Republic of China* (Census Bureau, 1998) is used for most industries. The Taiwan *Statistical Data Book 2003* (Council for

Table 7.11 *PPPs in finance, insurance and real estate, 1997*

		ICP PPPs			Adjusted		
		1999 Laspeyres	1999 Paasche	1999 Fisher	1997 Laspeyres	1997 Paasche	1997 Fisher
Japan							
Financial intermediation	Yen/US$	135.6	135.6	135.6	162.1	162.1	162.1
Insurance	Yen/US$	197.0	197.0	197.0	237.7	237.7	237.7
Auxiliary services	Yen/US$	197.0	197.0	197.0	181.5	0.0	0.0
Real estate	Yen/US$	184.7	185.8	185.2	222.5	222.5	222.5
Total	**Yen/US$**				**205.3**	**205.0**	**205.2**
South Korea							
Financial intermediation	Won/US$	609.1	609.1	609.1	579.0	579.0	579.0
Insurance	Won/US$	884.8	884.8	884.8	848.9	848.9	848.9
Auxiliary services	Won/US$	884.8	884.8	884.8	671.0	671.0	671.0
Real estate	Won/US$	1034.1	1066.3	1050.1	1111.3	1111.3	1111.3
Total	**Won/US$**				**912.9**	**831.8**	**871.4**
Taiwan					Y & L, updated to 1997		
Total	**NT$/US$**				**13.59**	**13.59**	**13.59**

Planning and Development ROC, 2003) and the *1996 BLS I–O Table* (Bureau of Labor Statistics) have been used respectively for employees and compensation for the education sector. Value added comes from the *GGDC 60-Industry Database* (GGDC, 2004). To update the 1996 unit values to 1997, compensation per employee is adjusted with the change in monthly earnings from 1996 to 1997 with data from the *Earnings and Productivity Statistics Database* on the DGBAS website. The results are provided in Table 7.12.

3.11   Public Services

The PPP for public services in Japan and South Korea is based on ICP PPPs (13.01.11–13.01.15) in combination with expenditure values from the same source. Because the *Japanese 1997 I–O Table* (Statistics Bureau of Japan, 2000b) and *1996 BLS I–O Table* (Bureau of Labor Statistics) show that the tax, transport and trade margins in public services are equal to zero, the only adjustment is backdating the 1999 ICP PPPs to 1997 with data from the *GGDC 60-Industry Database* (GGDC, 2004).

For Taiwan, the same procedure as in the private services has been used. The only difference here is that in this sector, there is only a UVR for public administration. Compensation data for Taiwan comes from the *1996 I–O Table* (DGBAS, 1996), and the *Statistical Yearbook of the Republic of China 2003* (DGBAS, 2003c) gives data for the number of employees in 1996. Again, the 1996 unit values are updated to 1997 values with the change in monthly earnings from 1996 to 1997 in the *Earnings and Productivity Statistics Database* on the DGBAS website. The results are provided in Table 7.13.

4.   CONCLUDING REMARKS

This chapter describes the construction of an industry-level relative output price database for 33 industries in Japan, South Korea, Taiwan and the United States. We used a mix of adjusted expenditure PPPs and output PPPs as suggested by van Ark and Timmer (2008). For the agricultural, mining, manufacturing, utilities, transport and communication sectors, the ICOP UVR approach has been used to derive output PPPs. For the trade industry, a combination of ICP expenditure PPPs and ICOP UVRs has been used. (The number of matches and the coverage of matched data are provided in the Appendix.) The remaining industries have been estimated using an adjusted expenditure PPP. As discussed in section 3, a few problems still remain after constructing the dataset. The main problem is the

Table 7.12 PPPs in private services, 1997

		ICP PPPs			Adjusted for trade and transport margins and deflated to 1997		
		1999 Laspeyres	1999 Paasche	1999 Fisher	1997 Laspeyres	1997 Paasche	1997 Fisher
Japan							
Water supply	Yen/US$	43.4	43.4	43.4	43.7	43.7	43.7
Hotels and restaurants	Yen/US$	242.8	256.2	249.4	304.6	304.6	304.6
Business services	Yen/US$	537.7	537.7	537.7	663.5	663.5	663.5
Education	Yen/US$	112.0	101.4	106.6	138.8	138.8	138.8
Health and social work	Yen/US$	223.9	145.3	180.4	226.0	226.0	226.0
Other social services	Yen/US$	183.7	170.3	176.9	216.3	216.3	216.3
Total	**Yen/US$**				**386.1**	**259.2**	**316.3**
South Korea							
Water supply	Won/US$	201.5	201.5	201.5	166.1	166.1	166.1
Hotels and restaurants	Won/US$	1030.6	1041.3	1035.9	1107.8	1107.8	1107.8
Business services	Won/US$	794.9	794.9	794.9	833.1	833.1	833.1
Education	Won/US$	521.8	453.7	486.5	516.5	516.5	516.5
Health and social work	Won/US$	923.8	401.0	608.6	574.1	574.1	574.1
Other social services	Won/US$	560.8	700.1	626.6	689.1	689.1	689.1
Total	**Won/US$**				**696.9**	**672.8**	**684.7**
Taiwan							
Total	**NT$/US$**				**22.08**	**21.21**	**21.64**

Table 7.13   PPPs in public services, 1997

		ICP PPPs			Adjusted for trade and transport margins and deflated to 1997		
		1999 Laspeyres	1999 Paasche	1999 Fisher	1997 Laspeyres	1997 Paasche	1997 Fisher
Japan	Yen/US$	140.5	129.7	135.0	166.6	166.6	166.6
South Korea	Won/US$	638.2	497.3	563.3	553.1	553.1	553.1
Taiwan	NT$/US$				41.08	41.08	41.08

unavailability of expenditure PPPs for Taiwan. Without a full survey of relative expenditure prices analog to the ICP surveys, this problem cannot be remedied.

This set of relative prices can be used in various applications, such as comparisons of productivity levels and unit labour costs across countries, and it might also shed new light on issues of price convergence. It must be stressed that the relative prices presented here are gross output prices and can be used to compare gross output across countries. Comparisons of value added require the additional development of intermediate input PPPs (see van Ark and Timmer, 2008). Also, the PPPs are based on binary comparisons between each Asian country and the United States. As such, they are not transitive, that is, they do not generate internally consistent results for comparisons involving three or more countries. For a full set of transitive industry-level PPPs for a large set of OECD countries, including Japan, South Korea and Taiwan, the reader is referred to Timmer, Ypma and van Ark (2005).

APPENDIX

Table 7A.1 *Numbers of matches and coverage ratios by industry*

ICPA Industry	Number of matches			Coverage ratios					
				Japan–US		South Korea–US		Taiwan–US	
	Japan	South Korea	Taiwan	Japan	US	South Korea	US	Taiwan	US
1 Agriculture	52	46	44	0.96	0.88	0.97	0.85	0.89	0.83
2 Coal mining	3	1	1	1.00	0.58	0.76	0.55	1.00	0.55
3 Metal and non-metallic mining	14	7	6	0.70	0.20	0.76	0.21	0.39	0.11
4 Oil and gas extraction	2	0	2	1.00	0.98	n.a.	n.a.	1.00	0.98
5 Construction	n.a.	n.a.	n.a.	n.a.	n.a.	n.a.	n.a.	n.a.	n.a.
6 Food and kindred products	23	54	21	0.19	0.13	0.59	0.41	0.37	0.23
7 Textile mill products	15	11	7	0.38	0.34	0.11	0.24	0.39	0.18
8 Apparel	18	11	11	0.32	0.42	0.13	0.44	0.58	0.39
9 Lumber and wood	3	3	1	0.48	0.20	0.37	0.19	0.05	0.06
10 Furniture and fixtures	1	9	0	0.68	0.57	0.18	0.19	n.a.	n.a.
11 Paper and allied	9	5	6	0.29	0.27	0.43	0.30	0.32	0.20
12 Printing, publishing and allied	0	0	0	n.a.	n.a.	n.a.	n.a.	n.a.	n.a.
13 Chemicals	38	26	8	0.17	0.15	0.16	0.09	0.11	0.04
14 Petroleum and coal products	9	8	0	0.85	0.74	0.51	0.78	n.a.	n.a.
15 Leather	12	12	2	0.48	0.60	0.71	0.82	0.58	0.44
16 Stone, clay and glass	11	5	2	0.30	0.39	0.15	0.09	0.20	0.08
17 Primary metal	37	32	20	0.41	0.40	0.49	0.74	0.56	0.90
18 Fabricated metal	9	3	1	0.16	0.04	0.01	0.01	0.07	0.00
19 Machinery, non-elect.	24	15	2	0.27	0.20	0.11	0.03	0.03	0.01

Table 7A.1 (continued)

ICPA Industry	Number of matches			Coverage ratios					
				Japan–US		South Korea–US		Taiwan–US	
	Japan	South Korea	Taiwan	Japan	US	South Korea	US	Taiwan	US
20 Electrical machinery	12	11	13	0.16	0.68	0.16	0.08	0.21	0.06
21 Motor vehicles	6	6	5	0.46	0.55	0.49	0.23	0.48	0.26
22 Transportation equipment and ordnance	5	5	0	0.92	1.00	1.00	1.00	n.a.	n.a.
23 Instruments	7	7	1	1.00	1.00	1.00	1.00	0.05	0.00
24 Rubber and misc. plastics	4	4	2	0.07	0.06	0.14	0.07	0.02	0.06
25 Misc. manufacturing	5	4	0	0.45	0.48	0.31	0.43	n.a.	n.a.
26 Transportation	12	12	11	0.74	0.72	0.81	0.72	0.89	0.72
27 Communications	2	2	2	0.96	0.63	0.65	0.80	1.00	0.99
28 Electric utilities	1	1	1	1.00	1.00	1.00	1.00	1.00	1.00
29 Gas utilities	1	1	1	1.00	1.00	1.00	1.00	1.00	1.00
30 Trade	42	26	35	1.00	0.97	1.00	1.00	1.00	1.00
31 Finance, Insurance and real estate	n.a.	n.a.	n.a.	n.a.	n.a.	n.a.	n.a.	n.a.	n.a.
32 Other private services	n.a.	n.a.	n.a.	n.a.	n.a.	n.a.	n.a.	n.a.	n.a.
33 Public services	n.a.	n.a.	n.a.	n.a.	n.a.	n.a.	n.a.	n.a.	n.a.

Note: n.a. = not available as it is based on expenditure PPPs, or there are no matches at all.

ACKNOWLEDGEMENTS

Most data work was conducted during research visits by Gerard Ypma to RIETI in Tokyo, Seoul National University in Seoul and Academia Sinica in Taipei. We would like to thank in particular Prof. Dr Liang, Mr Toshiyuki Matsuura, Mr Kazu Motohashi, Prof. Pyo and Mr Takahashi for their hospitality, advice and excellent assistance.

NOTES

1. For a more elaborate discussion, see Timmer et al. (2005).
2. The exchange rates used for calculating relative prices are from the *IMF Financial Statistics, September 2003* (IMF, 2003) for Japan and Korea and from the *Taiwan Statistical Data Book 2003* for Taiwan (Council for Planning and Development Republic of China, 2003).
3. See OECD (2002), 'Purchasing power parities and real expenditures: 1999 benchmark year'.
4. We follow the procedure of Yotopoulos and Lin (1993). Their adjustment is based on the existence of stricter codes, more exacting standards of workmanship and so on in Japan and the United States compared to Taiwan. This assumption is debatable. In Appendix C of Yotopoulos and Lin, an example is used to illustrate how sensitive the calculation of the PPP for construction is to the 50% assumption. It shows that not using a quality adjustment will lead to a severe downward bias of the PPP.
5. Cost of goods itself was not given in the census but could be calculated by subtracting value added from revenues.
6. No I/O table in purchaser prices is available for South Korea; therefore, Japanese shares have been used. Because the adjustments are very small, this will not make much difference in final PPPs.

REFERENCES

Air Transport Association (1998), 'ATA Annual Report 1998'.
All Nippon Airways (1998), 'Annual Report 1998'.
Ark, B. van and M.P. Timmer (2008), 'Purchasing power parity adjustments for productivity level comparisons', Chapter 14 in D.S. Prasada Rao (ed.), *Purchasing Power Parities of Currencies*, Cheltenham, UK and Northampton, MA, USA, Edward Elgar, Forthcoming.
Ark, B. van, E. Monnikhof and N. Mulder (1999), 'Productivity in services: an international comparative perspective', *Canadian Journal of Economics*, **32** (2), 471–99.
Ark, B. van, G. Ypma and D.S. Prasada Rao (2005), 'Productivity levels in agriculture: A new ICOP dataset for 1997', GGDC Research Memorandum GD-84.
Bureau of Labor Statistics (BLS), 'BLS Input–Output tables', various issues.
Bureau of Mines of the Republic of China (2003), 'Annual Statistical Report of Mineral 2002'.

212   *Productivity in Asia*

Census Bureau (1998), 'The report on the 1996 Census of the Republic of China', Directorate General of Budget, Accounting and Statistics Executive Yuan (DGBAS).

Council of Agriculture (2003), 'Agricultural production statistics abstract 2003, Republic of China'.

Council for Planning and Development Republic of China (2003), 'Taiwan statistical data book 2003'.

Department of Statistics, Ministry of Economic Affairs (1998), 'Industrial production statistics monthly, Taiwan area, the Republic of China', March.

Directorate General of Budget, Accounting and Statistics Executive Yuan (DGBAS) (1996), '1996 Input–output table'.

Directorate General of Budget, Accounting and Statistics Executive Yuan (DGBAS) (1997), '1996 report on industry, commerce and service census'.

Directorate General of Budget, Accounting and Statistics Executive Yuan (DGBAS) (2003a), 'Earnings and productivity statistics database' http://eng.stat.gov.tw/1p.asp?CtNode=1613&CtUnit=763&BaseDSD=7.

Directorate General of Budget, Accounting and Statistics Executive Yuan (DGBAS) (2003b), 'National Accounts of the Republic of China (from Chinese website)'.

Directorate General of Budget, Accounting and Statistics Executive Yuan (DGBAS) (2003c), 'Statistical yearbook of the Republic of China 2002'.

Energy Information Administration, website, http://www.eia.doe.gov.

Food and Agriculture Organization of the United Nations (FAO) (2003), 'FAOSTAT database 2003'.

Groningen Growth and Development Centre (GGDC) (2004), '60-industry database, October 2004', http://www.ggdc.net/dseries/60-industry.html.

Inklaar, R., H. Wu and B. van Ark (2003), ' "Losing ground", Japanese labour productivity and unit labour cost in manufacturing in comparison to the US', GGDC Research Memorandum GD-63.

Institute of Transportation of the Republic of China (2003a), 'Monthly statistics of transportation and communications August 2003', The Ministry of Transportation and Communications.

Institute of Transportation of the Republic of China (2003b), 'Transportation information 2003', The Ministry of Transportation and Communications.

International Monetary Fund (2003), 'International financial statistics, September 2003'.

Japan Airlines (1998), 'Annual Report 1998'.

Japan Air System (1998), 'Annual Report 1998'.

Jorgenson, D.W. (1995), *Productivity, volume 2: International Comparisons of Economic Growth*, Cambridge, MA: The MIT Press.

Jorgenson, D.W. and M. Kuroda (1995), 'Productivity and international competitiveness in Japan and the United States, 1960–1985', Chapter 9 in D.W. Jorgenson, *International Comparisons of Economic Growth*, Cambridge, MA: The MIT Press.

Jorgenson, D.W., M. Kuroda and M. Nishimizu (1987), 'Japan–US industry-level productivity comparisons, 1960–1979', *Journal of the Japanese and International Economics*, 1, 1–30.

Korea Energy Economics Institute (2003), 'Korea energy review monthly', March.

Korea National Statistical Office (NSO) (1997),'1997 report on mining and manufacturing survey'.

Korea National Statistical Office (NSO) (1999), 'Korea statistical yearbook 1999'.

Korean Air (1997), 'Annual report 1997'.

Maddison, A. and B. van Ark (2002), 'The international comparison of real product and productivity', in A. Maddison, D.S. Prasada Rao and W.F. Shepherd (eds), *The Asian Economies in the Twentieth Century*, Cheltenham, UK and Northampton, MA, USA: Edward Elgar, pp. 5–26.

Ministry of Interior of the Republic of China (1998), 'Statistical yearbook of interior 1997, the Republic of China'.

Organisation for Economic Co-operation and Development (OECD) (1999), 'Consumption tax Trends'.

Organisation for Economic Co-operation and Development (OECD) (2002), 'Purchasing power parities and real expenditures: 1999 Benchmark Year'.

Organisation for Economic Co-operation and Development (OECD) (2003a), 'OECD STAN Database 2003'.

Organisation for Economic Co-operation and Development (OECD) (2003b), 'Telecommunications database 2003, release 01'.

Research and Statistics Department, Minister's Secretariat (1998), '1997 mining yearbook of Japan', Ministry of Economy, Trade and Industry (METI).

Research and Statistics Department, Economic and Industrial Policy Bureau (1999), '1997 Census of Manufacturers, report on Enterprises and Commodities', Ministry of Economy, Trade and Industry (METI).

Research and Statistics Department, Economic and Industrial Policy Bureau (2001), '1999 Census of Commerce', Ministry of Economy, Trade and Industry (METI).

Statistics Bureau of Japan (1999a), 'Japan statistical yearbook 2000', Ministry of Public Management, Home Affairs, Posts and Telecommunications.

Statistics Bureau of Japan (1999b), 'Monthly statistics of Japan, October 2003', Ministry of Public Management, Home Affairs, Posts and Telecommunications.

Statistics Bureau of Japan, Management and Coordination Agency (2000a), '1995 input–output tables for Japan', Ministry of Public Management, Home Affairs, Posts and Telecommunications.

Statistics Bureau of Japan, Management and Coordination Agency (2000b), '1997 extension input–output table', Ministry of Public Management, Home Affairs, Posts and Telecommunications.

Stuivenwold, E. and M.P. Timmer (2003), 'Manufacturing performance in Indonesia, South Korea and Taiwan before and after the crisis: An international perspective, 1980–2000', GGDC Research Memorandum GD-63.

Timmer, M.P. and G. Ypma (2004), 'Purchasing power parities for international comparisons of output and productivity in Japan, South Korea, Taiwan and the US', Final report for the ICPA Project.

Timmer, M.P. and G. Ypma (2005), 'Productivity levels in distributive trades: A new ICOP dataset for 1997', GGDC Research Memorandum GD-83.

Timmer, M.P., G. Ypma and B. van Ark (2005), 'PPP paper total economy', GGDC Research Memorandum GD-82.

US Census Bureau (2000), '1997 economic census', Washington, DC.

US Census Bureau, Department of Commerce (1999), 'Current industrial reports 1997', Washington, DC.

US Census Bureau, (various issues), 'Statistical abstract of the United States'.

US Department of Transportation, Bureau of Transportation Statistics (2002), 'National transportation statistics 2002', BTS02-08, Washington, DC: US Government Printing Office.
US Maritime Administration (2003), 'Waterborne databank'.
Yotopoulos, P.A. and J.Y. Lin (1993), 'Purchasing power parities for Taiwan: the basic data for 1985 and international comparisons', Center for Economic Policy Research, Stanford University.

8. Assessing Japan's industrial competitiveness by international productivity level: comparison with China, Korea, Taiwan and the United States[1]

Kazuyuki Motohashi

INTRODUCTION

Economic growth in Japan dropped off sharply in the 1990s. This is thought to be in large part a cyclic phenomenon reflecting the collapse of the bubble economy in the late 1980s. But slow growth continued, with an average annual growth of 1.4% through the 1990s, prompting comment that structural factors may also have been involved. Moreover, certain industries appear to be losing competitiveness. Japan's electronics industry, for example, boasted overwhelming export competitiveness in the 1980s, but manufacturers in South Korea, Taiwan and elsewhere in East Asia have been catching up, with the result that Japanese manufacturers now face serious competition, especially in the area of semiconductors and other information devices (Motohashi, 2003). And, thanks to China's continued vigorous courting of foreign investment, foreign-invested enterprises are pouring in and helping China to gain ground on the developed nations in the IT sector. China already commands top share worldwide in the production of many consumer electronic items, where Japan's export competitiveness has plummeted.

This chapter provides Japan's total factor productivity (TFP) levels relative to China, Korea, Taiwan and the United States in order to assess Japan's industrial competitiveness compared to these countries. Higher relative productivity suggests superior production technology, which implies that the industry in question can supply international markets with more attractive goods and services. In addition, changes in relative TFP level show the dynamics of international competitiveness. These statistics can directly address the question of whether, and to what extent, other Asian countries are catching up with Japan. In addition, benchmarking with the United States provides us with further information on the relative position of Asian countries in the world economy.

Productivity performance of Asian economies has been investigated in some studies such as Young (1995) and Collins and Bosworth (1996). In addition, Young (2003) has conducted a careful study on TFP growth in China, by taking into account possible biases associated with its official statistics. However, all of these studies are on productivity growth at macro economy, or fairly aggregated industry levels. In addition, productivity level comparisons cannot be found[2] The Research Institute of Economy, Trade and Industry (RIETI) has started the ICPA (International Comparison of Productivity among Asian Countries) project in order to fill in this missing information. This study shows the preliminary results of this project, focusing on productivity level comparison by industry.

The structure of this chapter is as follows: the next section provides the theoretical model to estimate industry productivity levels. This project is based on the KLEM framework, that is, industry-level data on capital (K), labor (L), energy (E) and material (M). Relative TFP is derived from relative prices of industry output as well as these inputs. A section on data and issues regarding relative prices follows. Then, the results of TFP level estimation by industry and discussion on the results are provided. This chapter concludes with a summary of findings and agenda for future research.

1. THEORY OF TFP LEVEL ESTIMATION

The methodology is based on the growth accounting framework, with internationally comparable measurements of the service flow of labor, capital and other intermediate inputs, gross output, and productivity at economy-wide and industry levels. The analytical framework on international comparison of TFP growth and level is provided in Kuroda et al. (1996), and empirical works of this framework include Jorgenson and Kuroda (1990), Kuroda and Nomura (1999), Jorgenson et al. (2002) and Keio University (1996). This framework must be consistently related to national accounts statistics and the input–output tables of each country.

This framework starts with the following production function for industry 'j' with multiple inputs, such as K, L, E and M.

$$Y^j = f^j(K^j, L^j, E^j, M^j, TFP(c)) \qquad (8.1)$$

Y is gross output, and $TFP(c)$ is TFP level of country 'c'. Taking the derivative of log of equation (8.1) in terms of 'c' gives the following equation:

$$d\log Y/dc = \sum_{X \in K,L,E,M} (\partial \log Y/\partial c)(d\log X/dc) + \partial \log TFP/\partial c \quad (8.2)$$

Therefore, relative TFP across countries can be defined as follows:

$$\partial \log TFP/\partial c = d\log Y/dc - \sum_{X \in K,L,E,M} (\partial \log Y/\partial c)(d\log X/dc) \quad (8.3)$$

Under the condition of constant rate of return, the value of output (Y^*Py) is equal to the sum of value of inputs ($K^*Pk + L^*Pl + E^*Pe + M^*Pm$). In this case, relative TFP in equation (8.3) can be written as price information of output and inputs as follows:

$$\partial \log TFP/\partial c = \sum_{PX \in PK,PL,PE,PM} (\partial \log P_Y/\partial c)(d\log P_X/dc) - d\log P_Y/dc \quad (8.4)$$

Under the condition of perfect competition at output and factor input markets, equation (8.4) can be modified as follows:

$$\partial \log TFP/\partial c = \sum_{PX \in PK,PL,PE,PM} s_x(d\log P_X/dc) - d\log P_Y/dc \quad (8.5)$$

where s_x is the value share of factor input X. Finally, a discrete type approximation of (8.4), relative TFP of the United States to Japan, in this case is as follows:

$$\log TFP_{US/JP} = \sum_{X \in K,L,E,M} \overline{S}_X(\log P_{X,US} - \log P_{X,JP}) - (\log P_{Y,US} - \log P_{Y,JP})$$

$$(8.6)$$

where $\overline{S}_X = 1/2^*(S_{X,JP} + S_{X,US})$

In Equation (8.6), there are a couple of issues which should be noted. First, relative prices for output and input are derived as in the following equation:

$$P_{Y(orX),US/JP} = P_{Y(orX),US} \cdot e_{JP/US}/P_{Y(orX),JP} \quad (8.7)$$

where $e_{JP/US}$ is the exchange rate of Japanese yen per US dollar at the time of comparison. For example, if the price of one box of tobacco is US$1.2 in the US and 100 yen in Japan, and the exchange rate is 100 yen/dollar, the relative price of this tobacco in the US compared to Japan is calculated as 1.2 (1.2*100/100). In this case, this tobacco is 20% more expensive in the US than in Japan.

Second, it is important to control the quality of output and inputs in order to come up with relative prices. In the case of the relative price of tobacco, it is important to find the same products in both countries. In addition, relative input prices should be controlled for cross-country quality differences. In order to make such comparisons fair, detailed input data by type were prepared for this project. For example, labor data is cross-classified by sex, educational attainment and age group. Detailed information on the data used in this chapter is provided in the following section.

2. DATA ISSUES FOR RELATIVE OUTPUT AND INPUT PRICES

In this study, the relative TFP of China, Korea, Taiwan and the US as compared to Japan is calculated by using equation (8.6). Industrial classification in this study is provided in Table 8A.1 of the Appendix. There are 33 sectors, but the data for all 33 sectors is not always available for some countries. For example, the data for sector 4 (oil and gas extraction) is not available in Japan, because the industrial activity of this sector is so small. As was described in the previous section, labor and capital input data is cross-classified by type as well as by industry, as shown in Table 8A.2 and Table 8A.3 of the Appendix. As for labor data, there are 18 types (two types of sex, three types of age category and three types of educational attainment). As for capital data, there are three types, that is, structure, equipment and vehicles. In this study, only depreciable assets are taken into account for capital inputs, and the data for land and inventory is not available for some countries. The data used for this study comes from the KLEM datasets of five countries in the ICPA project, and the detailed information for each dataset can be found in Ren and Sun (2007) for China, Pyo et al. (2005) for Korea, Kuroda et al. (2005) for Japan, Liang (2005) for Taiwan, and Jorgenson Ho and Stiroh (2007) for the US.

2.1 Output Price

There are two types of methodology used to come up with relative output prices across countries. One is called unit value ratios (UVRs) and the other one is called expenditure base PPPs (EPPPs). The unit value ratio is calculated by the ratio of unit value of one country to that of another. For example, the manufacturing censuses in many countries usually provide values and quantities of sales by very detailed product category. It is possible to come up with the value per unit (unit value) from these statistics, and if one can match this value to that of the same category in another country, the ratio of unit value can be calculated. A group at GGDC (Groningen Growth and Development Center) at Groningen University has published numerous studies on UVRs among various countries.

The EPPPs approach is based on official statistics of PPP (Purchasing Power Parity) on the expenditure side. The OECD regularly conducts PPP surveys for its member countries, and publishes the results. In order to come up with producer-level relative prices to be used for productivity analysis, the original data on the expenditure side has to be modified. For example, the distribution margin has to be 'peeled off' from expenditure prices. In addition, adjustments associated with international trade have to be done, because the original data may include a substantial number of imported product prices. However, once proper adjustment has been done, EPPPs can be used as relative producer prices to be used for productivity analysis. Jorgenson and Kuroda (1990) and Kuroda and Nomura (1999) are some examples using this methodology.

There are merits and demerits to both approaches. For example, UVRs are strong for manufacturing products, because manufacturing censuses provide information on unit value by detailed product category in many countries. Comparing unit value of the same product across two countries gives the relative producer price of such a product. However, such information is available only for goods, and not for services. On the other hand, EPPPs can be derived for services as well, but such data is available only for final demand products. There is no data for intermediate input goods and business services in PPP surveys.[3]

In this RIETI ICPA project, the relative output prices of Korea, Taiwan and the US are estimated by a team at GGDC, Groningen University, described in detail in Chapter 7. As for the price comparison with China, we use the data between China and the US in Zheng and Ren (2004). Basically, their studies rely on UVR methodology, as EPPPs cannot be applied to China and Taiwan, because OECD-PPP data, – the data source of the EPPP approach – is not available for non-OECD countries. In addition, OECD-PPPs for Korea are available only in 1999, since Korea only joined the OECD recently. Therefore, the UVR approach is a practical choice for this study. The relative output data from these studies is summarized in Table 8.1. In this study, the benchmark year of productivity level comparison is 1995, while 1997's data is used in many sectors. We use the 1997 data as it is, and assume that relative price changes from 1995 to 1997 across countries are not so large as compared to cross-country differences.

It should be noted that producer prices derived from the UVR approach are at commodity level. In order to estimate industry-level productivity, we need the data by industry. Conversion from commodity to industry data can be conducted by using a V-table (make matrix) of input–output tables.

Table 8.1 Relative output price (original data)

	Year	Yen/US$ GGDC	Won/US$ GGDC	NT$/US$ GGDC	RMB/US$ Ren
1 Agriculture	1995	653	2880	59.1	7.16
2 Coal mining	1997	656	2180	139.8	4.34
3 Metal and non-metallic mining	1997	132	1096	28.9	1.88
4 Oil and gas extraction	1997	362	1322	80.7	8.05
5 Construction	1997	218	799	15.9	3.68
6 Food and kindred products	1997	293	1439	34.2	4.09
7 Textile mill products	1997	150	930	24.4	4.67
8 Apparel	1997	169	1399	25.0	4.14
9 Lumber and wood	1997	261	999	26.0	5.79
10 Furniture and fixtures	1997	154	653	23.6	5.79
11 Paper and allied	1997	159	974	24.3	4.56
12 Printing, publishing and allied	1997	159	974	24.3	4.56
13 Chemicals	1997	167	947	23.1	6.13
14 Petroleum and coal products	1997	265	962	23.1	6.13
15 Leather	1997	213	928	19.6	1.94
16 Stone, clay, glass	1997	127	679	21.0	4.53
17 Primary metal	1997	130	986	24.8	5.10
18 Fabricated metal	1997	177	789	25.9	5.10
19 Machinery, non-elect.	1997	153	705	17.7	5.59
20 Electrical machinery	1997	103	798	19.2	3.67
21 Motor vehicles	1997	111	816	31.4	5.59
22 Transportation equipment and ordnance	1997	156	816	31.4	5.59
23 Instruments	1997	103	836	24.3	3.67
24 Rubber and misc. plastics	1997	115	726	24.3	2.37
25 Misc. manufacturing	1997	154	882	23.6	4.93
26 Transportation	1997	205	802	46.7	3.32
27 Communications	1997	139	874	12.5	4.34
28 Electrical utilities	1997	236	967	31.9	4.35
29 Gas utilities	1997	94	1000	59.1	1.43
30 Trade	1997	186	1029	22.2	1.08
31 Finance, Insurance and Real Estate	1997	205	871	13.6	4.32
32 Other private services	1997	316	685	21.6	0.73
33 Public services	1997	167	553	41.1	1.03

Notes:
GGDC data: 1997 data except Agriculture in 1995.
Ren data: 1995.

Presumably however, such an adjustment does not make a big difference at the fairly aggregated level of 33 sectors.[4] Therefore, we have not conducted V-table adjustments in this study. In addition, an appropriate concept of output price for productivity analysis is basic price, which is derived after indirect tax and subsidy adjustment to producer price. Such adjustment has not been conducted either in this study. Relative output prices used in this study are presented in Table 8.2.

2.2 Relative Intermediate Input Prices

Relative input prices in equation (8.6) consist of prices for capital (*PK*), labor (*PL*), energy (*PE*) and material (*PM*). In this section, *PE* and *PM* (intermediate input prices) are discussed. Intermediate input prices can be derived by using information from the U-table (use matrix). First, we assume that relative output price at commodity level in Table 8.2 can be used as an input price for the corresponding sector. Then, the relative input price (*PE* and *PM*) of the US to Japan can be estimated as follows:

$$P^i_{E(or M),US/JP} = \sum_{j \in E(or M)} 1/2 * (s^{US}_{i,j} + s^{JP}_{i,j}) \cdot P^j_{Y,US/JP} \qquad (8.8)$$

where $s_{i,j}$ is share of '*j*' commodity to total energy (or material) input of '*i*' industry in each country, and P^j_Y is relative output price of '*j*' commodity. Among the 33 sectors in Table 8A.1 of the Appendix, the energy sectors include sector 2 (coal mining), sector 4 (oil and gas extraction), sector 14 (petroleum and coal products), sector 28 (electric utilities) and sector 29 (gas utilities). The other sectors are classified as material inputs. In all countries except Taiwan, U-tables for 1995 are available. For Taiwan, a 1996 X-table (commodity × commodity) is used, because an I/O table with detailed industrial classification is not available for 1995.

An appropriate concept of input price for productivity analysis is purchase price, instead of producer price. In this study, adjustment for relative differences of distribution margin across countries is not conducted. In addition, the prices for domestic input and imported input are not separately treated by using so-called competitive type input–output tables. Energy and material prices for the four countries relative to Japan are presented in Table 8.3 and Table 8.4.

2.3 Relative Labor Prices

Relative labor prices are derived from the 1995 data of per hour wage and labor compensation cross-classified by labor type, described in Table 8A.2

Table 8.2   Relative output price (JP=1.00)

	China	Korea	Taiwan	US
1 Agriculture	0.12	0.54	0.32	0.14
2 Coal mining	0.10	0.42	0.79	0.18
3 Metal and non-metallic mining	0.21	1.06	0.82	0.92
4 Oil and gas extraction	0.32	0.46	0.83	0.33
5 Construction	0.24	0.47	0.27	0.56
6 Food and kindred products	0.20	0.62	0.43	0.41
7 Textile mill products	0.45	0.79	0.60	0.81
8 Apparel	0.36	1.06	0.55	0.72
9 Lumber and wood	0.32	0.49	0.37	0.46
10 Furniture and fixtures	0.55	0.54	0.57	0.79
11 Paper and allied	0.42	0.78	0.56	0.76
12 Printing, publishing and allied	0.42	0.78	0.56	0.76
13 Chemicals	0.53	0.72	0.51	0.72
14 Petroleum and coal products	0.34	0.46	0.32	0.46
15 Leather	0.13	0.56	0.34	0.57
16 Stone, clay, glass	0.52	0.68	0.61	0.95
17 Primary metal	0.57	0.97	0.71	0.93
18 Fabricated metal	0.42	0.57	0.54	0.68
19 Machinery, non-elect.	0.53	0.58	0.43	0.79
20 Electrical machinery	0.52	0.99	0.69	1.18
21 Motor vehicles	0.73	0.93	1.04	1.09
22 Transportation equipment and ordnance	0.52	0.67	0.74	0.78
23 Instruments	0.52	1.04	0.88	1.18
24 Rubber and misc. plastics	0.30	0.80	0.78	1.05
25 Misc. manufacturing	0.46	0.73	0.57	0.79
26 Transportation	0.24	0.50	0.85	0.59
27 Communications	0.45	0.80	0.33	0.87
28 Electrical utilities	0.27	0.52	0.50	0.51
29 Gas utilities	0.22	1.35	2.32	1.28
30 Trade	0.08	0.70	0.44	0.65
31 Finance, Insurance and Real Estate	0.30	0.54	0.25	0.59
32 Other private services	0.03	0.28	0.25	0.38
33 Public services	0.09	0.42	0.91	0.72

of the Appendix. In order to control the quality of labor inputs, Divisia aggregate indices for relative labor input price in equation (8.8) is estimated as follows:

$$\log(P_{L,US/JP}) = \sum_{s,e,a} \bar{v}_{s,e,a}\ln(P_{L,US/JP}^{s,e,a}) \qquad (8.9)$$

Table 8.3   Relative energy price (JP=1.00)

	China	Korea	Taiwan	US
1 Agriculture	0.31	0.50	0.40	0.51
2 Coal mining	0.25	0.52	0.50	0.39
3 Metal and non-metallic mining	0.30	0.50	0.38	0.53
4 Oil and gas extraction	–	–	–	–
5 Construction	0.32	0.52	0.41	0.49
6 Food and kindred products	0.26	0.63	0.62	0.67
7 Textile mill products	0.26	0.63	0.58	0.60
8 Apparel	0.27	0.56	0.51	0.60
9 Lumber and wood	0.27	0.54	0.49	0.55
10 Furniture and fixtures	0.28	0.57	0.51	0.58
11 Paper and allied	0.26	0.55	0.54	0.60
12 Printing, publishing and allied	0.27	0.57	0.55	0.60
13 Chemicals	0.28	0.52	0.49	0.56
14 Petroleum and coal products	0.27	0.46	0.62	0.41
15 Leather	0.27	0.56	0.47	0.59
16 Stone, clay, glass	0.26	0.52	0.62	0.60
17 Primary metal	0.28	0.51	0.47	0.55
18 Fabricated metal	0.27	0.56	0.53	0.62
19 Machinery, non-elect.	0.27	0.56	0.53	0.60
20 Electrical machinery	0.27	0.59	0.50	0.58
21 Motor vehicles	0.27	0.56	0.51	0.59
22 Transportation equipment and ordnance	0.28	0.55	0.52	0.58
23 Instruments	0.27	0.63	0.55	0.59
24 Rubber and misc. plastics	0.27	0.55	0.51	0.58
25 Misc. manufacturing	0.27	0.58	0.46	0.58
26 Transportation	0.32	0.49	0.40	0.49
27 Communications	0.28	0.57	0.58	0.61
28 Electrical utilities	0.23	0.58	0.52	0.49
29 Gas utilities	0.23	0.78	1.02	0.74
30 Trade	0.30	0.53	0.47	0.55
31 Finance, Insurance and Real Estate	0.26	0.64	0.63	0.61
32 Other private services	0.28	0.66	0.77	0.65
33 Public services	0.28	0.59	0.51	–

where $\bar{v}_{s,e,a} = (v_{s,e,a,JP} + v_{s,e,a,US})/2$ and $v_{s,e,a}$ is the share of labor compensation of each category (sex=‘s’, education=‘e’ and age=‘a’).
The results are presented in Table 8.5.

Table 8.4　Relative material price (JP=1.00)

	China	Korea	Taiwan	US
1 Agriculture	0.23	0.59	0.41	0.42
2 Coal mining	0.30	0.49	0.39	0.61
3 Metal and non-metallic mining	0.32	0.54	0.56	0.71
4 Oil and gas extraction	–	–	–	–
5 Construction	0.37	0.62	0.53	0.68
6 Food and kindred products	0.18	0.57	0.39	0.40
7 Textile mill products	0.37	0.69	0.50	0.68
8 Apparel	0.36	0.69	0.51	0.70
9 Lumber and wood	0.26	0.54	0.39	0.45
10 Furniture and fixtures	0.35	0.61	0.45	0.68
11 Paper and allied	0.33	0.70	0.50	0.68
12 Printing, publishing and allied	0.35	0.66	0.50	0.68
13 Chemicals	0.37	0.64	0.48	0.65
14 Petroleum and coal products	0.28	0.72	0.61	0.72
15 Leather	0.22	0.61	0.42	0.61
16 Stone, clay, glass	0.34	0.70	0.57	0.74
17 Primary metal	0.44	0.88	0.63	0.82
18 Fabricated metal	0.44	0.77	0.58	0.78
19 Machinery, non-elect.	0.46	0.68	0.53	0.81
20 Electrical machinery	0.43	0.81	0.59	0.90
21 Motor vehicles	0.54	0.82	0.79	0.90
22 Transportation equipment and ordnance	0.47	0.70	0.61	0.79
23 Instruments	0.41	0.73	0.62	0.86
24 Rubber and misc. plastics	0.36	0.66	0.50	0.68
25 Misc. manufacturing	0.37	0.67	0.52	0.72
26 Transportation	0.32	0.52	0.53	0.59
27 Communications	0.29	0.51	0.36	0.61
28 Electrical utilities	0.27	0.56	0.41	0.60
29 Gas utilities	0.27	0.58	0.44	0.60
30 Trade	0.26	0.53	0.35	0.57
31 Finance, Insurance and Real Estate	0.27	0.48	0.29	0.55
32 Other private services	0.28	0.55	0.41	0.59
33 Public services	0.26	0.53	0.49	–

2.3　Relative Capital Price

Relative capital prices are derived by the same methodology as labor prices. There are three categories of capital products, as described in Table 8A.3 of the Appendix. Divisia aggregation is conducted by using relative rental

Table 8.5   *Relative labor price (JP=1.00)*

	China	Korea	Taiwan	US
1 Agriculture	0.01	0.47	0.45	0.71
2 Coal mining	0.02	0.18	0.26	0.60
3 Metal and non-metallic mining	0.04	0.34	–	1.00
4 Oil and gas extraction	0.07	–	–	0.97
5 Construction	0.08	0.36	0.39	0.84
6 Food and kindred products	0.04	0.26	0.35	0.87
7 Textile mill products	0.03	0.31	0.36	0.93
8 Apparel	0.04	0.32	0.36	0.82
9 Lumber and wood	0.02	0.30	0.30	0.80
10 Furniture and fixtures	0.02	0.22	0.27	0.68
11 Paper and allied	0.04	0.22	0.29	0.80
12 Printing, publishing and allied	0.02	0.19	0.28	0.65
13 Chemicals	0.02	0.13	0.14	0.58
14 Petroleum and coal products	0.06	0.32	0.42	1.06
15 Leather	0.09	0.33	0.38	0.95
16 Stone, clay, glass	0.04	0.25	0.31	0.83
17 Primary metal	0.06	0.22	0.29	0.83
18 Fabricated metal	0.04	0.25	0.30	0.86
19 Machinery, non-elect.	0.02	0.23	0.28	0.82
20 Electrical machinery	0.04	0.22	0.31	0.82
21 Motor vehicles	0.03	0.18	–	0.97
22 Transportation equipment and ordnance	0.01	0.20	0.25	0.66
23 Instruments	0.01	0.23	–	0.97
24 Rubber and misc. plastics	0.04	0.25	0.29	0.76
25 Misc. manufacturing	0.04	0.27	0.35	0.84
26 Transportation	0.02	0.14	0.23	0.47
27 Communications	0.03	0.19	–	0.61
28 Electrical utilities	0.02	0.17	0.36	0.79
29 Gas utilities	0.04	0.31	–	1.11
30 Trade	0.02	0.18	0.24	0.46
31 Finance, Insurance and Real Estate	0.08	0.25	0.52	1.00
32 Other private services	0.02	0.20	0.28	0.53
33 Public services	–	–	–	–

prices and an average share of each capital product over countries compared, as follows:

$$\log(P_{K,US/JP}) = \sum_i \bar{v}_i \ln(P^i_{K,US/JP}) \qquad (8.10)$$

where $\bar{v}_i = (v_{i,JP} + v_{i,US})/2$ and v_i is the share of capital compensation of each category (capital type = 'i'). In this equation, relative rental service price (PK) can be broken down into the following two parts:

$$P^i_{K,US/JP} = \frac{annualization\_factor_{US}}{annualization\_factor_{JP}} \cdot P^i_{I,US/JP} \qquad (8.11)$$

The annualization factor is the conversion factor of investment asset price to capital service price. The following is a typical capital service price formula, which consists of two parts, corresponding to each part of equation (8.11). The annualization factor depends on the tax structure of each country, and is estimated in each country.[5]

$$P_k = \left(\frac{1-zu}{1-u} \cdot (r(1-\pi) + \delta - \pi) + \tau \right) \cdot P_I \qquad (8.12)$$

As for the relative investment asset prices (P_I) by type of asset, the relative output prices of sectors are used as follows:

- Structure: Relative output price of (5) Construction.
- Machinery: Weighted average of (19) Machinery, (20) Electrical machinery and (23) Precision machinery.
- Vehicles: Weighted average of (21) Motor vehicles and (22) Transportion equipment.

Capital service prices of the four countries relative to Japan are calculated by using all of this data, and the results are presented in Table 8.6. In the original datasets, some very large relative capital prices can be found, particularly in China's apparel, furniture and fixtures, and leather sectors. Such large numbers come from a high annualization factor in China, and more specifically, the rate of return (r) in this factor is very large. Unreasonably high rates of return in some Chinese industries may come from underestimates of capital stock for these sectors.[6] The sectors with very high rates of return are dominated by small firms, which are not covered by investment surveys (Sun and Ren, 2005). Since the annualization factor depends on the ratio of small numbers (the rate of return, depreciation rate and inflation rate), small biases within one country may lead to an unreasonable figure at the end. Therefore, we have introduced a boundary of annualization factors, between 2 or 0.5 in this study. If it becomes more than 2, the corrected figure is set to 2, and if it becomes less than 0.5, 0.5 is used for the relative TFP calculation.

Table 8.6   *Relative capital price (JP=1.00)*

	China	Korea	Taiwan	US
1 Agriculture	0.65	1.22	0.80	0.97
2 Coal mining	0.84	1.10	–	1.57
3 Metal and non-metallic mining	0.75	1.12	–	0.67
4 Oil and gas extraction	–	–	–	–
5 Construction	0.71	1.06	1.21	1.62
6 Food and kindred products	0.81	1.16	0.87	1.56
7 Textile mill products	0.87	0.93	0.62	1.02
8 Apparel	0.81	1.29	0.70	1.53
9 Lumber and wood	0.83	1.40	1.14	1.71
10 Furniture and fixtures	0.75	1.32	0.97	1.40
11 Paper and allied	0.73	1.04	0.24	1.30
12 Printing, publishing and allied	0.94	1.56	0.58	1.85
13 Chemicals	0.66	1.11	0.87	1.59
14 Petroleum and coal products	0.85	0.71	0.91	0.56
15 Leather	1.10	1.28	0.61	1.67
16 Stone, clay, glass	0.84	1.44	1.03	1.53
17 Primary metal	0.78	0.50	0.64	0.83
18 Fabricated metal	0.79	1.37	0.66	1.67
19 Machinery, non-elect.	0.79	1.03	0.60	1.39
20 Electrical machinery	0.85	1.61	0.94	1.98
21 Motor vehicles	0.84	1.19	–	1.93
22 Transportation equipment and ordnance	0.83	0.55	0.61	1.31
23 Instruments	0.82	1.60	–	1.75
24 Rubber and misc. plastics	0.90	1.37	0.85	1.16
25 Misc. manufacturing	0.85	1.47	0.78	1.78
26 Transportation	0.78	1.40	1.06	1.36
27 Communications	0.74	1.19	–	1.32
28 Electrical utilities	0.40	0.80	0.48	0.78
29 Gas utilities	0.25	0.31	–	0.50
30 Trade	0.76	1.36	1.11	1.73
31 Finance, Insurance and Real Estate	0.60	0.93	0.77	1.28
32 Other private services	0.73	1.26	1.24	1.77
33 Public services	–	–	–	–

3.   RELATIVE TFP LEVELS

Based on all output and input prices described in the previous section, the relative TFP levels of China, Korea, Taiwan and the US to Japan are calculated by using equation (8.6). The results are presented in Table 8.7.

Table 8.7   Relative total factor productivity (JP=1.00)

	China	Korea	Taiwan	US
1 Agriculture	0.62	1.39	1.50	4.24
2 Coal mining	1.34	1.02	–	3.86
3 Metal and non-metallic mining	1.20	0.61	–	0.82
4 Oil and gas extraction	–	–	–	–
5 Construction	1.10	1.20	2.00	1.42
6 Food and kindred products	0.88	0.87	0.99	1.36
7 Textile mill products	0.50	0.72	0.77	0.94
8 Apparel	0.65	0.55	0.89	1.06
9 Lumber and wood	0.55	1.04	1.14	1.27
10 Furniture and fixtures	0.37	0.91	0.78	0.89
11 Paper and allied	0.61	0.79	0.78	1.02
12 Printing, publishing and allied	0.42	0.61	0.81	0.96
13 Chemicals	0.51	0.79	0.94	1.08
14 Petroleum and coal products	0.91	1.25	2.04	1.23
15 Leather	1.46	0.96	1.24	1.31
16 Stone, clay, glass	0.43	0.85	0.87	0.87
17 Primary metal	0.63	0.70	0.81	0.86
18 Fabricated metal	0.63	1.11	0.96	1.28
19 Machinery, non-elect.	0.51	0.96	1.14	1.08
20 Electrical machinery	0.59	0.72	0.79	0.85
21 Motor vehicles	0.51	0.70	–	0.88
22 Transportation equipment and ordnance	0.48	0.76	0.71	0.99
23 Instruments	0.37	0.55	–	0.80
24 Rubber and misc. plastics	0.83	0.71	0.58	0.70
25 Misc. manufacturing	0.55	0.80	0.87	1.05
26 Transportation	0.54	0.73	0.52	1.00
27 Communications	0.50	0.64	–	0.90
28 Electrical utilities	0.85	1.13	0.90	1.37
29 Gas utilities	0.79	0.35	–	0.53
30 Trade	1.45	0.64	0.88	0.91
31 Finance, Insurance and Real Estate	1.07	1.07	2.34	1.60
32 Other private services	4.29	1.47	1.71	1.72
33 Public services	–	–	–	–

Before getting into the details at industry level, Table 8.8 and Table 8.9 summarize the results of relative prices and TFP at aggregated levels. In Table 8.8, industry-level results are aggregated to macro economy level, and Table 8.9 shows aggregated figures for manufacturing. In the process of coming up with these tables, TFP estimates for the construction sector

Table 8.8   Economy-wide relative prices and TFP

	China	Korea	Taiwan	US
Output price	0.29	0.68	0.47	0.68
Capital price	0.69	1.07	0.81	1.29
Labor price	0.02	0.21	0.30	0.68
Energy price	0.27	0.53	0.50	0.53
Material price	0.30	0.57	0.37	0.60
TFP	0.64	0.77	0.91	1.07

Table 8.9   Manufacturing relative prices and TFP

	China	Korea	Taiwan	US
Output price	0.44	0.75	0.56	0.78
Capital price	0.80	1.15	0.77	1.47
Labor price	0.03	0.23	0.30	0.80
Energy price	0.27	0.52	0.53	0.51
Material price	0.36	0.72	0.54	0.70
TFP	0.59	0.81	0.90	1.00

(sector 5) and other private services (sector 32) are deleted from the samples, because possible errors in these two sectors with large value added share may bias aggregated TFP significantly. In the construction sector, the unit price of buildings is used for relative output price. However, relative land price is not controlled in this study. As shown in Table 8.2, the relative price of Japan is much higher than those of the other countries, which reflects higher land prices in Japan. Without controlling for land price, Japanese relative TFP will be biased downward significantly. In addition, private services consist of heterogeneous activities, and these are difficult sectors to come up with UVRs for.

In general, prices in Japan are higher than those of the other countries, except capital service price. This is due to the fact that the Japanese yen was relatively expensive as compared to other currencies at the benchmark year of 1995. In contrast, the capital service price of Japan is lower, because sluggish economic activities in the 1990s lowered the rate of return from investment. At a macro economy level, the TFP levels of China, Korea and Taiwan are 36%, 23% and 9% lower than that of Japan, respectively. On the other hand, the US TFP level is 7% higher than that of Japan. In Table 8.9, the aggregated relative TFPs are calculated for the manufacturing sector.

Here, Japan's manufacturing industry's position becomes better relative to China, and it is the same as that of the US. On the other hand, Korea's relative position improves, which reflects the fact that manufacturing productivity is relatively higher in Korea.

It is interesting to look at the results for China. Relative labor input price in China is very low, at around 2% or 3% of the Japanese level. However, relative capital price is relatively higher, due to the high rate of return on assets, while output price is very low. In the end, the TFP of China relative to Japan is not so low, at around 64% or 59%. This may be due to the results of economic reforms in China toward a market-based system, and its catching up with developed economies by attracting substantial amounts of foreign direct investment.

There are a couple of data issues to keep in mind in order to interpret the results in Tables 8.8 and 8.9 correctly. The first is the possible impact of exchange rate volatility on productivity estimates. Due to a relatively expensive Japanese yen in 1995, Japanese prices look high in general. The average US dollar exchange rate in 1995 was 94 yen per dollar, as compared to around 110 yen in 2005. Japanese prices will therefore obviously also look high when compared to other currencies pegged to the US dollar. Although such fluctuations of exchange rate affect relative prices, relative TFP is not subject to bias. As is shown in equation (8.6), changes in exchange rate in output and input prices will be cancelled out.

Second, the figures in these tables are those of bilateral comparisons with Japan, instead of multilateral comparison. In Table 8.8, the relative position of Korean TFP is lower than that of Taiwan, when they are compared to that of Japan. However, this does not always imply that Taiwanese TFP is higher than Korean TFP. In the bilateral comparison scheme presented in section 2, transitivity of index numbers (A-C can be derived from A-B and B-C) cannot be held. In order to make comparison between Taiwan and Korea, it is necessary to compare these two countries directly, instead of comparing the indices to Japan. Or, it is possible to come up with a multilateral comparative index. However, a downside of a multilateral index is losing bilateral productivity information, because the common denominators get smaller. Kuroda et al. (1996) provide a more detailed discussion on multilateral comparative indices.

Figures 8.1 and 8.2 present the industry-level relative TFPs of the four countries, showing (as a percentage) how much higher or lower their productivity level is than Japan's (Figure 8.1 for manufacturing sectors and Figure 8.2 for non-manufacturing sectors). In general, TFP levels of manufacturing industries in Japan are higher than the other countries. Exceptions include food production, lumber and wood, petroleum and leather. TFPs in the US and Korea are higher than that of Japan in fabricated metals, and

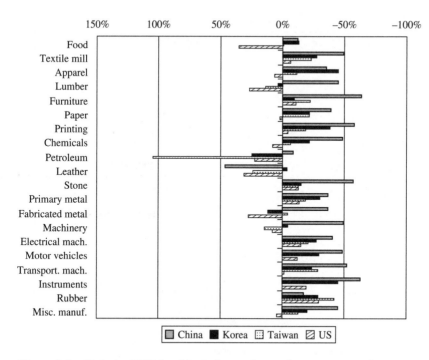

Figure 8.1   Relative TFP level by industry (manufacturing sector)

Japan's productivity in machinery is almost on a par with that of the US, Korea and Taiwan. On the other hand, Japan keeps a top position for primary metals, electrical machinery, motor vehicles, and instruments.

Japan's TFPs in non-manufacturing sectors are not so low. In general, low productivity levels are found in agriculture, construction, FIRE (financial services and real estate) and other services. On the other hand, Japanese productivity is higher in transportation, communication, and gas utility. However, it should be noted that productivity-level data in service industries may have more biases as compared to manufacturing industries, since output price is harder to measure and it is difficult to control for service quality. In addition, TFP levels in the construction sector and FIRE (real estate part) may have a downward bias, because the relatively high land price in Japan is not controlled here.

Cross-section information in Tables 8.8 and 8.9 can be extended to time series information, based on TFP growth statistics in each country, provided by ICPA project participants. Figures 8.3 and 8.4 show changes in the relative TFP positions of the five countries for their whole economies and manufacturing sectors, respectively.

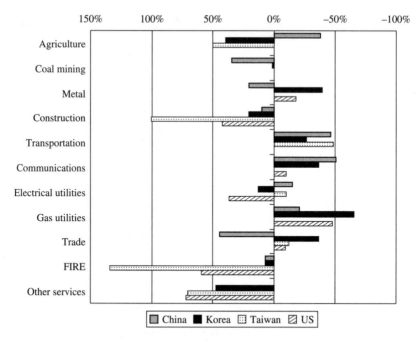

Figure 8.2   Relative TFP level by industry (non-manufacturing sector)

Within a period of about 20 years, it is difficult to see the long term trends of TFP for each country. However, China, Taiwan and Korea look like catching up with Japan, while the difference between Japan and the United States is increasing. This is due to the fact that Japan's TFP growth rate became slower in the 1990s. However, the productivity differences between Japan and other Asian countries are still great, and it will take a substantial amount of time for them to catch up with Japan's levels.

4.   CONCLUSION

In this chapter, Japan's productivity levels relative to China, Korea, Taiwan and the US are estimated to assess Japan's industrial competitiveness. Under RIETI's ICPA project, a comparable KLEM dataset has been constructed in these five countries. Relative output and input price data is matched with this KLEM data, and the relative TFP levels of 33 industries are estimated. This 1995 cross-sectional information is extended by using each country's TFP growth estimates, in order to see the dynamics of Japan's position among these other Asian countries, and the US.

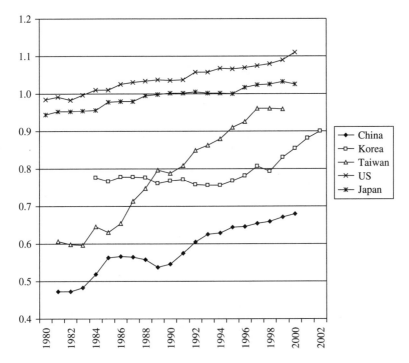

Figure 8.3   Changes in relative TFP positions for whole economy (Japan, 1995 = 1)

It is found that the TFP growth rate in Japan slowed down after the burst of the economic bubble, and China, Korea and Taiwan are catching up with Japan, particularly so in the 1990s. In addition, the US's productivity level is higher than that of Japan, and this gap has widened since the 1990s. These findings suggest that Japan is losing competitiveness in East Asia as well as in the world as a whole.

However, it is also found that the productivity differences between Japan and the three other Asian countries are still large. From 1981 to 2000, the TFP growth rate of China is about 0.8%, while that of Japan is 0.2%. The productivity gap between these two countries is 23.5% in 2000. By this simple trend estimate then, it will take 45 years for China to catch up with Japan.

Once such macro-level findings are broken down into industry-level observations, Japan is relatively strong in the manufacturing sectors, particularly electrical machinery, motor vehicles and instruments. However, it is also true that Japanese industries have caught up with Korea and Taiwan

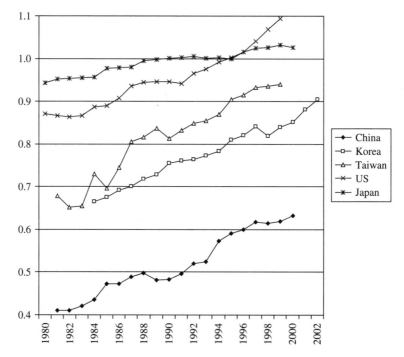

*Figure 8.4   Changes in relative TFP positions for manufacturing
            (Japan, 1995 = 1)*

in fabricated metals and general machinery. In this chapter, a great heterogeneity in productivity performance across industries can be found.
Therefore, Asian countries catching up to Japan is not a simple story of
macro-level trends. It is important to analyze changes of productivity level
in detail by industry.

In order to come up with robust conclusions from industry-level productivity performance, more effort for international comparability is
needed. The industrial classifications in the ICPA project are still broad.
Even though relative output prices are derived from detailed commodity-
level UVRs, further efforts in controlling for quality differences have to be
made. In addition it is important to keep in mind that there is a substantial
difference in data methodology among statistical offices between countries.
It is found that differences in the methodology of the IT price index
between Japan and the US make a significant change in growth accounting
results (Jorgenson and Motohashi, 2005). RIETI's ICPA project is a first
attempt to analyze industry-level productivity performance in Asian countries and the US. This is a great step to shed new light on structural changes

and the dynamics of Asian economies, but this is an initial step which needs further development.

APPENDIX: SECTOR CLASSIFICATION FOR ICPA PROJECT

Table 8A.1   Classification of industry

1	Agriculture
2	Coal mining
3	Metal and non-metallic mining
4	Oil and gas extraction
5	Construction
6	Food and kindred products
7	Textile mill products
8	Apparel
9	Lumber and wood
10	Furniture and fixtures
11	Paper and allied
12	Printing, publishing and allied
13	Chemicals
14	Petroleum and coal products
15	Leather
16	Stone, clay, glass
17	Primary metal
18	Fabricated metal
19	Machinery, non-elect.
20	Electrical machinery
21	Motor vehicles
22	Transportation equipment & ordnance
23	Instruments
24	Rubber and misc. plastics
25	Misc. manufacturing
26	Transportation
27	Communications
28	Electric utilities
29	Gas utilities
30	Trade
31	Finance, Insurance and Real Estate
32	Other private services(*)
33	Public services(*)

Note: * The definition of 33 is government administration only and the rest of services should be put into 32.

Table 8A.2   Labor input (cross classified as follows)

Industry	
	33 sectors in Table 8A.1

sex	
1	1. male
2	2. female

Age(*)	
1	16–34
2	35–54
3	55+

Education	
1	Junior high school or less
2	High school
3	College/University

Note: * A little modification can be made depending on data availability.

Table 8A.3   Capital input (cross classified as follows)

Industry	
	33 sectors in Table 8A.1

asset type(*)	
1	structure
2	equipment
3	vehicles

Note: * Land and inventory should be estimated as well, if possible.

NOTES

1. All original data in this chapter comes from numerous participants to this project, namely, Ruoen Ren and Ximing Yue for China, Masahiro Kuroda, Koji Nomura and Kasushige Shimpo for Japan, Hak Pyo for Korea, Chi-yuan Laing for Taiwan and Dale Jorgenson and Mun Ho for the US. Relative output price data among these countries is provided by Bart van Ark, Ruoen Ren, Marcel Timmer and Gerard Ypma. The author would like to thank all these participants, as well as RIETI for their financial support. The author would also like to thank Asako Okamura for her excellent research assistance.

2. One exception is van Ark and Timmer (2003). However, this study is for relative labor productivity comparison, instead of total factor productivity.
3. More detailed discussions on comparing these two methodologies can be found in OECD (1996) and van Ark and Timmer (2002).
4. Sensitivity analysis of V-table adjustment has been conducted by using the relative price of Korea to Japan and V-table in Japan. It was found that the degree of change was 4% at most, and within 1% for most sectors.
5. In the ICPA project, each participating country has conducted TFP growth estimates separately. In this process, an annualization factor is calculated, and used for this study. For details of datasets used for this factor, please refer to each corresponding paper.
6. The rate of return by industry is derived from the value of rental services in I/O tables and the value of capital stock. Underestimates of capital stock lead to overestimates of rental price (rental service over capital stock), which may push up the rate of return significantly.

REFERENCES

Ark, van B. and M. Timmer (2002), 'Measuring productivity levels: A reader', OECD Working Party on Industrial Statistics, Paris: OECD.

Ark, van B. and M. Timmer (2003), 'Asia's productivity performance and potential: The contribution of sectors and structural change', GGDC, University of Groningen, www.eco.rug.nl/~ark/pdf/Asia%20paper 4. pdf.

Collins, S.M. and B.P. Bosworth (1996), 'Economic growth in East Asia: Accumulation versus assimilation', *Brookings Papers on Economic Activities* No. 2, pp. 135–91.

Jorgenson, D.W. and M. Kuroda (1990), 'Productivity and international competitiveness in Japan and the United States, 1960–1985', in C.R. Hulten (ed.), *Productivity Growth in Japan and the United States, Studies in Income and Wealth*, vol. 53, Chicago: University of Chicago Press, pp. 29–55.

Jorgenson, D.W. and K. Motohashi (2005), 'Information technology and the Japanese economy', *Journal of Japanese and International Economics*, **19**(4), 460–81.

Jorgenson, D.W., K. Stiroh and M. Ho (2002), 'Growth of US industries and investments in information technology and higher education', presented at the *Conference on Research in Income and Wealth*, Washington, DC, April.

Jorgenson, D.W., M.S. Ho and K.J. Stiroh (2007), 'The sources of growth of US industries', Chapter 3 of this volume.

Keio University (1996), 'KEO database', Keio University Observatory Monograph series No. 8 (in Japanese).

Kuroda, M. and K. Nomura (1999), 'Productivity comparison and international competitiveness', *Journal of Applied Input Output Analysis*, **5**, 1–37.

Kuroda, M., K. Motohashi and K. Shimpo (1996), 'Issues on the international comparison of productivity: Theory and measurement', in OECD, *Industry Productivity: International Comparison and Measurement Issues*, Paris: OECD, pp. 49–95.

Kuroda, M., K. Shimpo and H. Kawai (2005), 'Interindustry effects of productivity growth in Japan, 1960–2000', *Journal of Japanese and International Economics*, **19**(4), 568–85.

Liang, C. (2005), 'Industry-wide total factor productivity and the output growth in Taiwan, 1981–1999', mimeo.

Motohashi, K. (2003), 'Japan's long-term recession in 1990s: Fall of industrial competitiveness', Hitotsubashi University, Institute of Innovation Research Working Paper No. 04-08.

OECD (1996), *Industry Productivity: International Comparison and Measurement Issues*, Paris: OECD.

Pyo, H., K. Rhee and B. Ha (2005), 'Growth accounting and productivity analysis by 33 Industrial Sectors in Korea, 1984–2002', mimeo.

Ren, R. and L. Sun (2007), 'Total factor productivity growth in Chinese industries, 1981–2000', Chapter 4 of this volume.

Sun, L. and R. Ren (2005), 'Estimates of capital input index by industries: The People's Republic of China', mimeo.

Young, A. (1995), 'The tyranny of numbers: Confronting the statistical realities of the East Asian growth experiences', *Quarterly Journal of Economics*, **110**, 641–80.

Young, A. (2003), 'Gold into base metals: productivity growth in the People's Republic of China during the reform period', *Journal of Political Economy*, **111**(6), 1220–61.

Zheng, H. and R. Ren (2004), 'A new benchmark comparison between China and US by ICOP approach', School of Economics and Management, BeiHang University, March.

Index